The People
of the
Covenant

*A Study of Israel
from Moses to the Monarchy*

Murray Lee Newman, Jr.

London
The Carey Kingsgate Press Limited

THE CAREY KINGSGATE PRESS LIMITED
6 Southampton Row
London, W.C.1

First British Edition 1965
© CAREY KINGSGATE PRESS

PRINTED IN GREAT BRITAIN BY OFFSET LITHOGRAPHY BY
BILLING AND SONS LTD., GUILDFORD AND LONDON

To
Janice

Foreword

THIS BOOK ORIGINATED IN A DISSERTATION FOR A TH.D. DEGREE RECEIVED in 1960 from the Union Theological Seminary in New York City. The title of the dissertation was: "The Sinai Covenant Traditions in the Cult of Israel." It attempted to trace the history of the two early covenant traditions in Exod. 19-24; 33-34 from their emergence in the Mosaic period until each reached its final form as part of its respective epic. A consideration of general historical questions was inevitably involved in this kind of study, but that was not its primary concern. The present work shifts the focus slightly from the history of the covenant traditions to the history of the people as reflected in their understanding of the nature of the covenant. These two traditions, however, provide the perspective from which this history is viewed. Moreover, a consideration of the emergence and development of the two traditions will be an integral part of the treatment.

Much of importance has necessarily been omitted or treated inadequately in this book. It does not pretend to be a work of the scope of the two histories of Israel recently published by John Bright and Martin Noth, even for the period it covers. Those masterful studies are presupposed, and the reader is urged to consult them for more detailed

7

discussions of Israel's history from Moses to the emergence of the monarchy.

One major omission which seemed necessary, if somewhat regrettable, was a literary analysis of Exod. 19-24; 32-34. This work was done in the writer's dissertation, which is available in microfilm. It seemed wise, however, not to include such technical material in a book of this nature, even though the entire study is based on it. A consultation of the standard commentaries on Exodus of course will reveal that the writer was guided by them in the literary analysis and took no significantly new positions.

The writer particularly regrets the fact that Walter Beyerlin's study, *Herkunft und Geschichte der ältesten Sinaitraditionen*,[1] appeared too late to be used as fully as desirable. It is a creative and scholarly treatment of the origin and history of the oldest Sinai traditions. Since Beyerlin's work was published in 1961, it was of course not used at all in the dissertation. It has contributed some to the present work, but not nearly as much as the writer would have liked. On many points Beyerlin and the writer are in full agreement, and a number of the same conclusions have been reached independently. For instance, the results of Beyerlin's literary analysis of the early Sinai traditions do not differ greatly from the conclusions of the writer, although at one or two points the differences are not insignificant.[2] The crucial difference is that Beyerlin views the early Sinai traditions as having emerged from *one* cultic stream which flowed through Israel's history, while the writer contends that *two* such streams were involved. Beyerlin's sees the one stream emerging clearly at Kadesh-barnea, then he finds it flowing at *northern* cult sites (especially Shechem and Shiloh) during the period of the twelve-tribe amphictyony, and finally coming to Jerusalem in the time of David. Both J and E covenant traditions derived from this one cultic stream in his view. On the other hand, I regard the E *covenant tradition* as having come from a stream that moved from Kadesh to Shechem, to Shiloh, and, after the division of the Kingdom, to Bethel. The *J covenant tradition,* however, came from

---

[1] Tübingen: J. C. B. Mohr, 1961.

[2] For example, Beyerlin assigns both Exod. 24:1-2, 9-11 and 24:3-8 to the Elohist (p. 32). Following a number of commentaries, I assign the former of the Jahwist and only the latter to the Elohist. Also Beyerlin views Exod. 33:7-11 as belonging to the Elohist (p. 32). I firmly believe that this is a Jahwist tradition. The significance of the divergences will be clear to one who reads the present volume.

a stream that flowed from Kadesh to Hebron, and then to Jerusalem. Another significant and closely related difference has to do with the ark of the covenant and the tent of meeting. Beyerlin holds that these two shrines of the Hebrew people were together from the Mosaic period, the ark being housed in the tent. Although the writer regards them both as Mosaic, he believes that after the thirteenth century conquest the ark was at Shechem and Shiloh, associated with the E covenant tradition, before being taken to Jerusalem; the tent, though, was at Hebron, associated with the J covenant tradition, before David brought it to Jerusalem.

The differences between the two studies are sufficiently marked as to persuade the writer that the present book should be published, even though Beyerlin's excellent work on the same theme has already appeared in German and, hopefully, will be translated into English soon. One must of course always reckon with the possibility that future studies of the same topic will result in conclusions quite different from either those of Beyerlin or the writer. In the meantime, perhaps the present volume will make some contribution to the study of the Old Testament and stimulate discussion of the life and faith of ancient Israel.

To cite the names of all those who have contributed to the publication of this book would be impossible. I would, however, like to mention my teachers at the Union Theological Seminary in New York City, James Muilenburg and Samuel Terrien, who stimulated my original interest in the field of Old Testament and guided me through graduate study.

I am indebted to the Board of Trustees of the Protestant Episcopal Theological Seminary of Virginia and its Dean, Jesse M. Trotter, for making possible a leave from my teaching duties in order to accept a grant from the American Association of Theological Schools for study in Heidelberg, Germany, where a substantial start was made on this book.

I am also grateful to the Virginia Seminary students of the classes of 1958, 59, 60, 61, 62, who elected senior Hebrew and read with me various Old Testament passages connected with the theme of this study.

In addition, I would like to express my gratitude to the several students who helped me in reading proofs, and particularly Robert S. Ripley.

Finally, I owe a special word of thanks to Bernhard W. Anderson, Dean of the Theological School of Drew University, who has read various drafts of this book as it was in progress and has made many valuable suggestions.

Contents

11

Prologue

IN THE YEAR 922 B.C. REHOBOAM, SON OF SOLOMON, WENT TO THE ancient cult site of Shechem for a momentous conclave. His father was dead and Rehoboam was pressing to gain acceptance as Solomon's successor. There was evidently no problem in Judah. David had belonged to the house of Judah and Rehoboam was David's grandson. It was a different matter, however, with the northern Hebrew tribes. If he was to be king of the whole Davidic kingdom, he had to deal with them. For this reason it was necessary for him to make the journey to the northern city of Shechem.

When he arrived, the elders of Israel were ready with their terms: "Your father made our yoke heavy. Now lighten the hard service of your father and his heavy yoke upon us, and we will serve you" (I Kings 12:4). This was more than a request for the alleviation of oppressive burdens; it was a clear declaration that they would recognize him as their king only if he would recognize that his sovereignty over them would have definite limitations. Three days later, after having consulted both with his older counselors and those of his own generation, he returned to Shechem with his reply. His words crackled as he spewed them forth: "My father made your yoke heavy, but I will add to your yoke; my father chastised you with whips, but I will chastise you with scorpions" (I Kings 12:14). He intended to be king over the North as well as the South and he would accept no limitations upon his sovereignty. If this was his attitude, the men of Israel grimly determined, then Rehoboam would not be their sovereign at all. The cry of rebellion went up:

> What portion have we in David?
> We have no inheritance in the son of Jesse.
> To your tents, O Israel!
> Look now to your own house, David.
>
> I KINGS 12:16

So Israel departed to their tents and the kingdom of David was rent asunder. Never again were its two parts to be reunited.

There were doubtless many reasons for the division of the kingdom. The immediate one was the oppressive policies of Solomon and the refusal of Rehoboam to change them. The issues, however, were much deeper and more complex than that. David himself had found it necessary to put down at least two revolts in which the northern tribes were involved. So, before Solomon's reign ever began, differences clearly existed between the Hebrews in northern Palestine and those in the South. For one thing, the two groups obviously differed in geographical orientation. There were also economic, social, and political factors which separated them. It is quite possible that ancient racial differences divided those in the North from those in the South. But perhaps the most basic difference of all was theological.

According to I Kings 11–12 a key figure in connection with the division of the kingdom was a prophet, Ahijah of Shiloh. His presence in these events strongly suggests the possibility that religion played a decisive role in the dispute. Indeed it seems likely that between the two groups there existed a fundamental difference in their understanding of what it meant to be the covenant people of Yahweh, their God. It was not a dispute between worshipers of Yahweh and worshipers of some other god; it was rather a difference within Yahwism

14

itself. They evidently diverged radically in regard to the nature of the covenant.

One group, the people from the North, seem to have believed that the covenant of Yahweh was directly and fully with all his people. Such a view is reflected in the covenant tradition found in Exod. 19: 3-6:

3 And Moses went up to God, and Yahweh called him out of the mountain, saying, "Thus you shall say to the house of Jacob, and tell the people of Israel: 4 You have seen what I did to the Egyptians, and how I bore you on eagles' wings and brought you to myself. 5 Now therefore, if you will obey my voice and keep my covenant, you shall be my own possession among all peoples; for all the earth is mine, 6 and you shall be to me a kingdom of priests and a holy nation. These are the words which you shall speak to the children of Israel."

Although prophets, priests, and kings might arise to serve various purposes in history, such functionaries could never claim permanent status or authority over God's people. According to this view the covenant was clearly with all God's people.

Another view of the nature of the covenant obtained in Judah, however. There it was believed that God had made a covenant with the royal house of David which gave his sons who ruled on his throne permanent authority over God's people. In Jerusalem there was a tradition concerning David:

Yea, does not my house stand so with God?
  For he has made with me an *everlasting covenant*,
  ordered in all things and secure.
For will he not cause to prosper
  all my help and desire?

II SAM. 23:5

This position, however, was rooted in a much older tradition that God had made his covenant at Mt. Sinai, not directly with the people, but first with Moses and only through him with the people:

And Yahweh said to Moses, "Write these words; in accordance with these words I have made a covenant with you and with Israel."

EXOD. 34:27

It is probable, then, that the theological controversy which resulted in the division of the Davidic kingdom had roots which extended back earlier than Solomon or even the monarchy. In the premonarchical period when the idea of a kingship for the Hebrew people first emerged, essentially the same theological division expressed itself. A particularly successful military leader in Israel during this time was a member of the northern tribe of Manasseh named Gideon. He heroically delivered his people from an invasion by some Midianites. As a consequence, some of his people expressed the desire to make him their king: "Rule over us, you and your son and your grandson also" (Judg. 8:22). Gideon's reply reflects a view of the nature of the covenant people that was undoubtedly the dominant one in his time: "I will not rule over you, and my son will not rule over you; Yahweh will rule over you" (Judg. 8:23). Yahweh will not exercise his sovereignty through a king, but directly and immediately over all his people.

Even before the conquest of Palestine differences concerning the nature of the covenant can be detected. Numbers 16 preserves the tradition of a controversy in the wilderness over the authority of Moses and Aaron. Soon after the events of the Exodus from Egypt and the covenant at Sinai a group of Israelites are said to have assembled themselves against Moses and Aaron to protest:

You have gone too far! For all the congregation are holy, every one of them, and Yahweh is among them; why then do you exalt yourselves above the assembly of Yahweh?

NUM. 16:3

To understand the basic theological differences which resulted in the division of the North and the South in the tenth century B.C. and separated them subsequently, therefore, it is necessary to begin this study with an analysis of the age and faith of Moses.

Chapter One

Mosaic
Religion

THE AGE OF MOSES WAS DETERMINATIVE FOR THE FAITH AND LIFE OF ancient Israel. The crucial events of that period are preserved in the book of Exodus. According to the traditions in Exodus, a group of Hebrew people experienced a miraculous release from Egyptian slavery after years of oppression. They attributed their escape to the power of God, whom they knew as Yahweh. Shortly after their Exodus from Egypt these Hebrews became self-conscious worshipers of Yahweh by entering into a covenant with him at a sacred mountain in the wilderness east of Egypt. Their human leader through these events was the man named Moses. Moses had been born in Egypt, but after reaching adulthood he had been forced to flee the country. He had gone to the land of Midian in the wilderness east of Egypt. At a mountain in the wilderness Moses was called by Yahweh to return to Egypt and lead the Hebrews to their freedom. This he did. Subsequently he led them back to the mountain of his call where he was instrumental in making the covenant.

This is the general picture which is found in the book of Exodus.

17

It is to be recognized, of course, that the book in its present form is a compilation of several sources which come from different ages and various groups in ancient Israel. Of the three primary sources comprising the book of Exodus, the Jahwist (J) is some three centuries removed from the Mosaic age,[1] having been composed around 950 B.C. Although the second source, the Elohist (E), is frequently dated 750 B.C., it is not at all unlikely that this strand was composed around 900 B.C., soon after the division of the Davidic-Solomonic kingdom. This would mean that it originated some 350 years after Moses. And the Priestly Writing (P) was probably written between 500 and 450 B.C., and thus is separated from the Mosaic period by nine hundred years. A recognition of the great time span between the original events and the composition of the documents preserving the memory of those events—ranging from some three hundred years to nine hundred years —should preclude hasty historical conclusions. These are by no means eye-witness reports concerning Moses and his times. They cannot be accepted uncritically as sources for the history of the Hebrew people during the Mosaic period.

On the other hand, the reliability of these documents as historical sources should not be underrated. When J and E are dated in the tenth century, this means they attained approximately their present form at that time. Many of the traditions which the author of each document used were much older, some indeed close to the events they describe. While P in most respects is not as valuable historically as J and E, some of the material it has preserved too is quite early and reliable. One important result of modern biblical archaeology has been to increase respect for the general reliability of the Old Testament historical traditions. While most biblical scholars of former years were extremely skeptical concerning the historicity of most of the material in the Pentateuch and much in the Former Prophets,[2] the situation today is quite different. Archaeological findings have substantiated and illumined the story of Israel at many points. This is true of the traditions in Exodus as well as the early material in Numbers and Deuteronomy which preserves the memory of the Mosaic age.

[1] The event of the exodus probably occurred close to 1280 B.C.
[2] Particularly in Joshua and Judges.

Archaeology leads the student of the Old Testament to approach its historical books with great respect, but this does not mean that all the traditions are to be accepted immediately as providing unbiased history at every point. Each tradition must be analyzed separately to determine its historical value. If there is archaeological material important for its interpretation, this of course is to be considered. It is also necessary, however, to determine the nature of the particular tradition under consideration, its literary form, what occasioned it, how it may have been used in the life of the people before it became a part of the larger document. This is an especially important task in the book of Exodus. For example, it is likely that the J and E traditions of the covenant at Sinai in Exod. 19–24; 33–34 were used in the cult in connection with covenant renewal ceremonies for a long period before each was incorporated into its respective document.[3] Even though these traditions do preserve the memory of the actual covenant at Sinai, their use in the cult suggests the possibility that in their present form they contain certain elements not a part of the original event but absorbed from later cultic practice. This possibility should be kept in mind in coming to historical conclusions on the basis of the traditions. Or again, it is quite possible that much of the material in Exodus 1–15 was originally used in the celebration of the Passover.[4] So in interpreting these passages it should be kept in mind that they probably have elements taken from the cult in addition to reflecting the experiences of the Hebrews in Egypt and their release from bondage.

The recognition that the basic traditions in the book of Exodus

[3] Sigmund Mowinckel seems to have been the first scholar to have identified this material as cultic in character: *Le Décalogue* (Paris: Libraire Félix Alcan, 1927), pp. 114-29. Subsequently Gerhard von Rad dealt with these traditions in more detail and with more perception: *Das formgeschictliche Problem des Hexateuch, Beiträge zur Wissenschaft vom Altenund Neuen Testament*, 4. Folge Heft 26 (Stuttgart: W. Kohlhammer, 1938), pp. 18-36. Reprinted in *Gesammelte Studien zum Alten Testament* (München: Chr. Kaiser, 1958), pp. 28-48. A very important recent treatment is Walter Beyerlin's *Herkunft und Geschichte der ältesten Sinaitraditionen* (Tübingen: J. C. B. Mohr, 1961).

[4] This position has been worked out by Johannes Pedersen, "Passafest und Passalegende," *Zeitschrift für die alttestamentliche Wissenschaft*, 52 (1934), pp. 161-75 and *Israel* (London: Oxford University Press and Copenhagen: Povl Branner, 1940), III-IV, 384-415, 728-37; cf. Sigmund Mowinckel, "Die vermeintliche 'Passalegende' Ex. 1–15," *Studia Theologica*, 1951, V, 66-88.

were used in the cult raises certain historical questions. If the traditions in Exodus 19–24; 33–34 received their present form in cultic usage and thus for a long period were transmitted apart from any of the traditions in Exodus 1–15, it is noteworthy that there are a number of Old Testament passages that recount the mighty acts of Jahweh in the early period of Israel's history which omit the covenant event. This is true of the old credo in Deut. 26:5b-9: [5]

5b A wandering Aramean was my father; and he went down to Egypt and sojourned there, few in number; and there he became a nation, great, mighty, and populous. 6 And the Egyptians treated us harshly, and afflicted us, and laid upon us hard bondage. 7 Then we cried to Yahweh the God of our fathers, and Yahweh heard our voice, and saw our affliction, our toil, and our oppression; 8 and Yahweh brought us out of Egypt with a mighty hand and an outstretched arm, with great terror, with signs and wonders; 9 and he brought us into this place and gave us this land, a land flowing with milk and honey.

The exodus, the wilderness wanderings, and the conquest appear here, but not the covenant. Does this lead one to the conclusion, as Martin Noth believes, that the events of the exodus from Egypt and the covenant at Sinai were originally experienced by two different groups of Hebrew people?[6] This is a possible conclusion, but not the only one. Even though it is recognized that the exodus traditions and the Sinai covenant traditions for a long period were transmitted separately as they were used in Israel's worship, it is also possible that both events were experienced in succession by the *same* group of Hebrew people.

The fact that the name *"Moses"* is firmly imbedded in both the tradition concerning the event of the exodus and that concerning the event of the covenant in the book of Exodus suggests that the two

[5] It is true of also Exod. 15:1-18; Deut. 6:20-24; Josh. 24:2b-13; I Sam. 12:8, *et al.*

[6] Noth, *The History of Israel* (New York: Harper & Brothers and London: A. & C. Black, 2nd ed., rev. Eng. tr., 1960), pp. 110-38. Noth's historical conclusions are based on von Rad's work (*op. cit.*) as well as *his own study, Überlieferungsgeschichte des Pentateuch* (Stuttgart: W. Kohlhammer, 1948).

events originally belonged together. There was presumably only one Moses, and it is unlikely that Moses was the leader of two different groups of people. Moreover, just as the early tradition in Exod. 15:21 praises *Yahweh* as the God responsible for the exodus, so also it is *Yahweh* with whom the covenant is made in the Sinai traditions (Exod. 20:1-2, etc.).[7] The fact that both key names, Yahweh and Moses, appear in both traditions in Exodus is good evidence that the two events were experienced in succession by the same group of people.

Furthermore, the omission of the event of the covenant in the ancient recitals of Yahweh's mighty acts, as in Deut. 26:5b-9, probably resulted from the view that the covenant was not a mighty act of Yahweh in the same way as the other events. It was rather Israel's response to Yahweh's action in the event of the exodus and the articulation of its meaning for her life. It simply did not belong in such a credo. This would have been the reason for its omission, not because it was experienced by a different group of people from that which was involved in the exodus.

That the covenant event was the next natural step after the exodus is clear. The covenant illuminated the significance of the exodus. Without the covenant the meaning of the exodus for the people would not have been understood and possibly would have been lost. The Sinai covenant tradition itself makes it clear that the two events belonged together:

And God spoke all these words, saying, "I am Yahweh your God, who brought you out of the land of Egypt, out of the house of bondage." Exod. 20:1-2; cf. Exod. 19:3-6.

It was precisely because the Hebrews were delivered by Yahweh from Egyptian bondage that the covenant was established. The exodus event was the foundation of the covenant event. A recent archaeological study has served to confirm this position.[8] It has been shown that

---

[7] Noth seems to be somewhat inconsistent in this respect. While he associates the worship of Yahweh originally with Sinai and thus the Sinai covenant tradition (*History*, p. 133), he also seems to accept that Yahweh from the first was viewed as the author of the exodus event (*Ibid.*, p. 115).

[8] George E. Mendenhall, *Law and Covenant in Israel and the Ancient Near East* (Pittsburgh, Pennsylvania: The Biblical Colloquium, 1955).

the covenant form found in Exodus 20 reveals many points of affinity with the suzerainty treaty of the ancient Hittite empire by which the Great King of the Hittites regulated his relations with his vassals. The parallels between the two are so many that it seems quite likely that the Hebrews used this kind of covenant form to express their relation to their God Yahweh. The Hittite treaty begins with a preamble which identifies the king, giving his name, genealogy, titles, and attributes. Then comes a historical prologue which stresses the help that the king has rendered to his vassal in the past, after which the vassal's obligations to his overlord are enumerated. This is precisely the pattern that is found in Exod. 20:1-17, where Yahweh identifies himself ("I am Yahweh your God" vs. 2a), recalls the help that he has rendered to the people in the past ("who brought you out of the land of Egypt, out of the house of bondage" vs. 2b), and then enumerates their obligations to him (i.e., the Ten Commandments vss. 3-17). Since the original covenant of the Hebrews with Yahweh was evidently patterned on a form like that of the Hittite suzerainty treaty, that covenant must have been based on the event of the exodus when it was initially established. The exodus event and the covenant event belonged together.

The Hebrews in Egypt

The event of the exodus probably occurred in the first half of the thirteenth century B.C. This was a century during which members of the Nineteenth Dynasty ruled Egypt. Ramses I was the founder of this important dynasty, but after a brief reign he was succeeded by his son Sethos I (1309-1290 B.C.). Sethos I began the job of rebuilding the Egyptian empire which had deteriorated greatly during the preceding century. This task was continued under Sethos' son, Ramses II (1290-1224 B.C.). Ramses inaugurated his rule by moving his troops out of Egypt into Palestine and Syria, grimly determined to restore the former glory that his nation had known. He soon came into conflict with the powerful Hittite kingdom, however, and bitter warfare broke out between the two peoples. It continued for over ten years with no

decisive result and was finally brought to an end by a treaty of peace. The peace which then reigned enabled Ramses to embark on numerous building projects. For labor in connection with these building activities he made extensive use of Semitic slaves. Two of the cities which it is known that Ramses built were Pithom and Ramses. These are the same sites mentioned in Exod. 1:11 as store cities which the Hebrews were forced to build for Pharaoh. Thus it was evidently from bondage under Ramses II that the Hebrews escaped in the exodus event.

The date when these Hebrews entered Egypt and which tribes they represented are very difficult questions. The traditions in Genesis which indicate that Joseph was the first of Jacob's sons to go to Egypt and the one who played the dominant role there suggest that the Joseph tribes probably were there. And since Moses is said to have been of Levitical ancestry (Exod. 2:1), it is not unlikely that some Levites were in Egypt too. It is possible that ancestors of one or two other Hebrew tribes were also in Egypt, but that all twelve tribes were ever there is improbable. The date of the descent of Joseph into the land of Egypt might have been during the Hyksos occupation of Egypt (ca. 1720-1570 B.C.), since they, like the Hebrews, were Semites and presumably would have been favorably inclined toward the entrance of these newcomers. The appearance of the "new king who did not know Joseph" (Exod. 1:8) might be a reference to the emergence of the Eighteenth Egyptian Dynasty (1570 B.C.) which was responsible for the expulsion of the Hyksos. Although the subsequent climate would not have been as favorable as formerly for the entrance of wandering Hebrews, there were undoubtedly times when others did find their way into Egypt, perhaps during the tolerant reign of Akhenaton (Amenophis IV, 1370-53 B.C.).

It is not impossible that the Joseph tribes first entered Egypt during his rule. If this was the case, the "new king" might refer to the Nineteenth Dynasty half a century after Akhenaton. In any event, by the beginning of the thirteenth century B.C. members of the tribes of Joseph and Levi were presumably in Egypt and they had been reduced to bitter servitude. It was at this juncture of human history, in the fulness of ancient time, that Moses emerged.

Moses

Moses was the decisive human personality in the period when the Hebrews emerged as a distinct people with a unique faith. Any attempt to reduce the authentic traditions concerning Moses to the one which preserves the memory of his tomb seems somewhat extreme.[9] It is no doubt true that subsequent generations tended to glorify Moses and often read back into his age and ascribed to him laws, cultic practices, and theological positions which could only have developed much later. But that he was the leader of the Hebrews as they escaped from Egypt and when the covenant was made at Sinai, as all three documents in the book of Exodus affirm, is entirely credible. There must have been one gifted individual who interpreted the meaning of the exodus event to his fellows as an act of God and then led them to establish a covenant with God at the holy mountain. That gifted individual was Moses.

Moses was a Hebrew with an Egyptian name, as in Thut-*mose*. His name suggests the authenticity of the traditions in Exodus 2 that place him in an Egyptian environment. He was evidently a man who was deeply touched by the suffering of his enslaved people (Exod. 2:11-15a), a concern which he carried with him when he fled Egypt. His flight brought him to the land of Midian (Exod. 2:15b-22). Midian was located to the east of the Gulf of Aqaba and thus across the Sinaitic wilderness from Egypt. In Midian Moses came into association with a priest named Jethro,[10] whose daughter he is said to have married.

During this sojourn outside Egypt the decisive event of Moses' life took place. It is reflected in Exod. 3:1-4:17. In the area of Sinai[11] Moses experienced a charismatic encounter with the personal presence of the Holy. The tradition speaks of a theophany at a burning bush with both visual and audible phenomena that convinced Moses of the

[9] This is the tendency of Noth, who observes: "In view of his [Moses'] obviously Egyptian name one might look for his original role within the framework of the deliverance from Egypt, possibly as the messenger of God who announces the imminent action of God (cf. Exod. iii, 16-17a), But perhaps the most concrete fact of all is the tradition of the tomb of Moses which was situated in a very definite spot." *History*, p. 136, n. 2.

[10] This is the name used by E (Exod. 3:1); J calls him Reuel (Exod. 2:18).

[11] It is assumed that Horeb and Sinai for all practical purposes are identical. The writer further sees no insuperable obstacles in accepting the traditional location of Sinai at Jebel Musa, although a site in Midian itself is not impossible. A location in the general vicinity of Kadesh-barnea could be mentioned as a third possibility.

immediate presence of God. The experience was charismatic. It seems to have been perceived as a new spiritual breakthrough into the life of Moses and evidently was not directly dependent upon traditional religious or cultic forms. It was quite unexpected and the initiative was entirely from God. The result of the encounter was a deep sense of obligation and responsibility both to God and to the enslaved people. Moses' conviction of a divine call and commission is preserved in these words which God speaks to him:

9 Now, behold, the cry of the people of Israel has come to me, and I have seen the oppression with which the Egyptians oppress them. 10 Come, I will send you to Pharaoh that you may bring forth my people, the sons of Israel, out of Egypt. Exod. 3:9-10

The tradition also associates with Moses' charismatic experience the introduction of the divine name Yahweh: [12]

13 Then Moses said to God, "If I come to the people of Israel and say to them, 'The God of your fathers has sent me to you,' and they ask me, 'What is his name?' what shall I say to them?" 14 God said to Moses, "I shall be present as I shall be present." [13]
And he said, "Say this to the people of Israel, 'I shall be present has sent me to you.'" 15 God also said to Moses, "Say this to the people of Israel, 'Yahweh, the God of your fathers, the God of Abraham, the God of Isaac, and the God of Jacob, has sent me to you': this is my name for ever, and thus I am to be remembered throughout all generations."

If the name "Yahweh" did first become known to Moses at this time, it is quite possible, as many believe, that this name originated with the Kenites, a clan of the Midianites, to which Jethro belonged.[14] Moses

[12] It is the view of E that the name Yahweh was first revealed to the Hebrews in the time of Moses. P shares the same view (Exod. 6:2-3), but J thinks of God as having been worshiped by this name from the time of the early man Enosh (Gen. 4:26).

[13] Following Martin Buber's translation rather than the RSV at this point. *Moses* (Oxford: East & West Library, 1946), p. 52. Whatever the original meaning of the name Yahweh may have been, in the light of the Hebrew text of 3:12, E seems to be interpreting it to mean: "He who will be present."

[14] This is known as the Kenite (or Midianite) hypothesis of the origin of Yahweh worship. This view was first popularized by Karl Budde, *The Religion of Israel to the*

would thus have learned the name from his father-in-law, the priest of Midian. The crucial passage in support of this hypothesis is Exod. 18:12 where, after Yahweh has demonstrated his great power by delivering the Hebrews from the hand of the Egyptians, it is *Jethro,* not Moses, who makes the sacrifices: "And Jethro, Moses' father-in-law, offered a burnt offering and sacrifices to God; and Aaron came with all the elders of Israel to eat bread with Moses' father-in-law before God." If Jethro was a priest who offered sacrifices to Yahweh, presumably he was a priest of Yahweh. And if Moses first learned the name of Yahweh in this period, he probably learned it from Jethro.

The acceptance of this hypothesis leads one to the conclusion that Moses may have sought to combine a charismatic understanding of God's manifestation of himself with more traditional and priestly forms from Kenite Yahwism.[15] One might say that from its inception the religion of Moses consisted of traditional Kenite forms infused with new charismatic substance. Both elements were present and significant. And this unstable fusion was destined to influence profoundly the subsequent history of the Hebrew people. From the time of Moses to the monarchy and beyond, it was the cause of almost continual tension and conflict in their life.

The Exodus Event

In the name of Yahweh Moses returned to Egypt to lead his people out of their enslavement. Since much of the material in Exodus 1–15 seems to have been used liturgically in connection with the Passover before being placed in its present context, one must exercise caution in arriving at historical conclusions. The present arrangement of the traditions depicts a dramatic conflict between Moses, as Yahweh's servant, and the Egyptian pharaoh. Ten plagues are brought by Yahweh upon the Egyptians in his effort to force them to release the Hebrew slaves. The plagues increase in intensity until finally the tenth—the death of the firstborn—causes the stubborn Pharaoh to let them go. They have

---

Exile (New York: G. P. Putnam's Sons, 1899), chapter 1. More recently it has been vigorously espoused by H. H. Rowley, *From Joseph to Joshua* (London: Published for the British Academy by the Oxford University Press, 1948), pp. 149 ff.

[15] Note that Exod. 18:24-26 states that certain judicial traditions of the Kenites were transmitted to Moses by Jethro.

scarcely set forth, however, when he changes his mind and sends his soldiers to bring them back. Soon the Hebrews are caught between the waters of the sea in front and the pursuing soldiers behind. Suddenly the wind blows, a path is opened in the waters which permits the Hebrews to pass through. When the Egyptians attempt to follow, they are caught by the returning flood and are drowned. The Hebrews view this event as an act of Yahweh and the joyous hymn of praise goes forth:

> Sing to Yahweh, for he has triumphed gloriously;
> the horse and his rider he has thrown into the sea.
>
> EXOD. 15:21

This hymn is generally recognized to be one of the oldest bits of poetry in the Old Testament and to preserve a reliable memory of the original event. The picture it suggests of the destruction of the threatening Egyptian soldiers and the deliverance of the threatened Hebrew slaves is authentic. The precise location of the incident cannot be determined with any certainty. The name of the body of water in the Hebrew text is "Reed Sea." It was undoubtedly a shallow, reedy lake on the eastern border of Egypt in the general area of the modern Suez Canal.

There is no reference in Egyptian records to the escape of this particular group of slaves. The Papyrus Anastasi VI describes the unsuccessful attempt of a similar group to escape from Egyptian bondage, at a somewhat later date.[16] The annals of Egyptian history are silent, however, about the event that became known as the exodus.

Although the latter incident was not remembered by the Egyptians, it was by the Hebrews themselves. It was remembered and its memory was preserved in poetry and prose never to be forgotten. This successful escape from Egypt was remembered because it was viewed from the moment of its occurrence as the work of Yahweh. And Moses, who had returned from Midian to Egypt under the compulsion of a divine commission to lead these people forth from their slavery, was un-

[16] See Noth, *History*, p. 112.

doubtedly the one who perceived in the event the power and purpose of Yahweh.

Concerning the events that preceded the passage through the sea there is less certainty. Moses would have been the leading spirit among the Hebrew slaves during the period that led up to the escape. He would have communicated to them the name "Yahweh," the God whose servant he was. He would have challenged and organized them as he prepared them to leave Egypt.

The traditions speak of direct negotiations between Moses and the Pharaoh while the plagues were occurring. The cultic character of the traditions suggests the possibility of a certain heightening of the events to make the conflict between the Hebrews and the Egyptians more dramatic. As the story was told in connection with the Passover it was necessary that the Pharaoh speak for the Egyptians just as Moses spoke for the Hebrews. It is of course impossible to determine the extent of the reigning Pharaoh's knowledge of this particular group of slaves. But that Moses came into conflict with certain Egyptian authorities in his efforts to free them is quite credible. The Egyptians would have been concerned to keep their slaves for continued labor on their building projects and would have resisted vigorously the attempted escape of any of them.

Most of the plagues are natural phenomena known to occur on occasion in Egypt. This would not be true of the death of the firstborn, of course, which is closely connected with a central motif of the Passover. It may well have developed in connection with the traditional custom by nomadic shepherds of sacrificing the firstborn at the Passover. The number "ten" of the plagues would also seem to be a later development, since none of the three sources of the Pentateuch has more than seven and only the first and the last are common to all. On the other hand, however, it is possible that the plague traditions do preserve an authentic memory of the times preceding the departure of the Hebrews from Egypt. A series of natural disasters struck Egypt, which Moses interpreted as evidencing the power of Yahweh. In the midst of the Egyptian consternation caused by the plagues the Hebrews slipped off the yoke of their bondage and fled toward the border and freedom.

Exodus 12–13 contains an account of a celebration of the Passover on the eve of their departure from Egypt. The Passover was a pre-Mosaic festival for shepherds, the original purpose of which probably was to protect family and flock at pasture changing time.[17] It was adapted to Yahwism by connecting it with the deliverance from Egypt. Later in Palestine it was joined with the agricultural feast of unleavened bread. Moses was probably responsible for reinterpreting the old pastoral festival and making it a celebration of the exodus event. The first observance of this reinterpreted Passover feast might have been more appropriate *after* the passage through the sea rather than *before,* as in the present arrangement of the traditions, since only then was the freedom of the people complete. It could be argued, though, that it was first celebrated in *anticipation* of their successful escape. Whether it was first observed before or after the deliverance at the Sea of Reeds, the Passover was established in the time of Moses and it continued to testify to subsequent generations of Hebrews the fact that they were a redeemed people:

And when in time to come your son asks you, "What does this mean?" [i.e., the rites of the Passover] you shall say to him, "By strength of hand Yahweh brought us out of Egypt, from the house of bondage." Exod. 13:14

Shortly after Yahweh had brought this people out of Egypt, and following a brief period of wandering, Moses led them to the mountain of his call.

The Mosaic Covenant

At Sinai these Hebrews entered into a solemn covenant with Yahweh. In the present arrangement of the traditions all the material from Exod. 19:1 to Num. 10:10 is associated with Sinai. Most of this, however, comes from the late Priestly Code. The early J and E traditions of the covenant are found in Exodus 19–24; 32–34 and in general can be said to reflect more fully the memory of the original event than P.[18]

---

[17] See especially Noth, *Überlieferungsgeschichte*, pp. 70-77 and *Das zweite Buch Mose. Exodus. Das Alte Testament Deutsch* (Göttingen: Vandenhoeck & Ruprecht. 1959), pp. 50 ff.

[18] The P material, however, should not be entirely disregarded in this respect. Although its present form is postexilic, the Priestly Code probably preserves the authentic

The E account of the covenant is found in chapters 19–24. Most of the J tradition is found in chapters 33–34, although there is some J material in chapters 19 and 24. These two accounts of the covenant are connected by the incident of the golden calf in chapter 32. Thus the present arrangement of the two traditions makes it appear as if the covenant was established once (chs. 19–24), it was broken (ch. 32), then it was made again (chs. 33–34). In all probability, however, both accounts ultimately reflect the same event.

In coming to conclusions concerning the character and significance of the Sinai event one should make use of both traditions. In general, it can be assumed that the points where the two versions agree preserve the memory of the original event most accurately. Points where the two differ must be evaluated with care to determine whether they actually belong to the original event or represent later developments of the traditions. What then can be said about the Sinai covenant on the basis of these two accounts?

1. The first thing to be said about this Sinai experience of the Hebrews is that it actually happened.[19] These Old Testament traditions are not referring to an *idea* of a covenant between God and man which could be merely the object of thought and speculation. They testify rather to the occurrence of a real historical event in which a real people and their real God were involved. At Sinai in the thirteenth century B.C. a group of Hebrews under the leadership of Moses actually entered into a covenant relationship with Yahweh. Just as the treaty that the great Hittite king established with his vassal marked the historical beginning of a special relationship between the two,[20] so the event at Sinai marked the historical beginning of a unique relationship between these Hebrews and their God. This relationship thus was radically different from the relationships that existed between other peoples of the ancient Near East and their gods. It was not a relationship

---

memory of certain Mosaic institutions, such as the ark of the covenant and the tent of meeting.

[19] Walther Eichrodt speaks of the "factual nature" (Tatcharakter) of God's revelation at Sinai. *Theology of the Old Testament*. Volume One (Philadelphia: The Westminster Press. 1961), p. 37. The following characterization of the covenant is especially dependent upon Eichrodt, pp. 36-45 and James Muilenburg, "The History of the Religion of Israel," *The Interpreter's Bible* (Nashville: Abingdon Press, 1952), I, 209-305.

[20] *Supra*, pp. 21-22.

of nature which bound the Hebrews to Yahweh, as was the case in religions of other cultures, but a historical relationship which had its beginning at a definite point in time.[21] This point was at Sinai in the thirteenth century B.C.

2. Further, the covenant was a relationship which was viewed as resulting from the *initiative of Yahweh*. The interior coherence of the events of the exodus and the covenant must be stressed: "I am Yahweh your God, who brought you out of the land of Egypt, out of the house of bondage" (Exod. 20:2 E). The two happenings are inextricably related. And both chronologically and theologically the exodus must be understood as the prior event. The covenant represented the *response* of the people to God's previous act of redemption. "You have seen what I did to the Egyptians, and how I bore you on eagles' wings and brought you to myself. Now therefore, if you will obey my voice and keep my covenant" (Exod. 19:4-5 E). Like the Hittite treaty,[22] the relation had as its foundation the gracious goodness of the One who offered it:

Yahweh passed before him, and proclaimed, "Yahweh, Yahweh, a God merciful and gracious, slow to anger, and abounding in steadfast love and faithfulness, keeping steadfast love for thousands, forgiving iniquity and transgression and sin. . . . Behold I make a covenant." Exod. 34:6, 7, 10 J

The spontaneous, unmotivated, unpredictable, and charismatic character of this initiative was undoubtedly perceived from the very beginning. It was not the people who first chose Yahweh, but Yahweh who chose the people. If the experience of Moses at the burning bush can be characterized as a new spiritual breakthrough not dependent upon any traditional religious or cultic forms, so also can the people's initial encounter by Yahweh. It is perhaps not fortuitous that the early poem in Exodus 15, which has preserved the memory of the passage of the Hebrews through the sea, relates the event to the activity of Yahweh's *ruach,* his wind, breath, spirit (vss. 8, 10).[23] The *ruach* is the living,

[21] On this point see especially G. Ernest Wright, *The Old Testament Against Its Environment* (London: SCM Press, 1950).

[22] Mendenhall, *op. cit.,* p. 32.

[23] On the idea of *ruach* in the Old Testament see Norman Snaith, *The Distinctive Ideas of the Old Testament* (Philadelphia: The Westminster Press, 1946), pp. 183-203.

spontaneous uncontrollable power of God which is particularly significant in the period of the Judges and the early prophetic movement. When the divine *ruach* is manifested, it is always clear that God, not man, is in control. The initiative is with him. When the Song of Miriam in Exodus 15, then, associates the *ruach* with the passage through the sea, it stresses the spontaneous initiative of Yahweh in the event. Because of Yahweh's sovereign act at the sea the covenant at Sinai was made.

3. The covenant was a relationship which began with a *vivid experience of Yahweh's personal presence*. This fact is frequently overlooked in studies of the Mosaic covenant.[24] It is one element which naturally is not found in the Hittite covenant form, but it was of great importance in the event at Sinai.

Just as he had appeared to Moses at the burning bush in connection with his call, so Yahweh personally manifested himself to the Hebrews at the holy mountain, the Old Testament traditions affirm. There was a theophany. There was *visible* and *audible* evidence of his real presence. This presence was perceived, on the one hand, by *all* the people:

16 On the morning of the third day there were thunders and lightnings, and a thick cloud upon the mountain, and a very loud trumpet blast, so that all the people who were in the camp trembled. 17 Then Moses brought the people out of the camp to meet God; and they took their stand at the foot of the mountain. 18 And Mount Sinai was wrapped in smoke, because Yahweh descended upon it in fire; and the smoke of it went up like the smoke of a kiln, and the whole mountain quaked greatly. 19 And as the sound of the trumpet grew louder and louder, Moses spoke, and God answered him in thunder. 20 And Yahweh came down upon Mount Sinai, to the top of the mountain. Exod. 19:16-20 JE

On the other hand, Moses is reported to have participated in the experience uniquely:

20:18 Now when all the people perceived the thunderings and the lightnings and the sound of the trumpet and the mountain smoking, the people were afraid and trembled; and they stood afar off, 19 and said to Moses,

---

[24] Eichrodt, for example, does not emphasize it sufficiently in his discussion.

"You speak to us, and we will hear; but let not God speak to us, lest we die." 20 And Moses said to the people, "Do not fear; for God has come to prove you, and that the fear of him may be before your eyes, that you may not sin." 21 And the people stood afar off, while Moses drew near to the thick cloud where God was. 20:1 And God spoke all these words, saying, "I am Yahweh your God." Exod. 20:18-21, 1 E

He is said to have seen evidence of God's presence not permitted to all the people:

33:18 Moses said, "I pray thee, show me thy glory." 19 And he said, "I will make all my goodness pass before you, and will proclaim before you my name 'Yahweh'; and I will be gracious to whom I will be gracious, and will show mercy on whom I will show mercy. 20 But," he said, "you cannot see my face; for man shall not see me and live." 21 And Yahweh said, "Behold, there is a place by me where you shall stand upon the rock; 22 and while my glory passes by I will put you in a cleft of the rock, and I will cover you with my hand until I have passed by; 23 then I will take away my hand, and you shall see my back; but my face shall not be seen." 34:5 and Yahweh descended in the cloud and stood with him there, and proclaimed the name of Yahweh. 6 Yahweh passed before him, and proclaimed, "Yahweh, Yahweh." Exod. 33:18-23; 34:5-6 J

For the most part, this theophanic language seems to suggest the phenomenon of a thunderstorm, "thunders," "lightnings," "thick clouds," although it is perhaps also possible to detect volcanic imagery. Whether in connection with a storm or volcano, however, the important fact was that at Sinai when the covenant was established the living presence of Yahweh, the God who transcended the forces of nature, was vividly apprehended by these Hebrews.

Particular note should be taken of the proclamation of God's name in connection with the theophany (20:2 E; 33:19; 34:6 J). In both traditions the announcement of the name "Yahweh" is a climactic moment of the theophany.[25] For the ancient Hebrews the name of a person was closely associated with his nature. The name was an ex-

[25] A classical treatment of the name of God in the Old Testament is Oscar Grether's *Name und Wort Gottes im Alten Testament* (Giessen: Alfred Töpelmann. 1934).

pression of his inmost being. The same was true of God. His name
stood for his reality. When Yahweh announced his name, therefore, he
was believed to be revealing his inmost nature to his people; he was
giving himself to them in a unique and intimate way. So it is that
when the traditions speak of the proclamation of Yahweh's name in the
covenant at Sinai, they point to the memory of an extremely vivid
experience of his presence. There must have been a climactic cultic
moment when God's presence was intensely experienced by these
people.

4. The covenant was a relationship in which *Yahweh was Lord and
Israel was servant.* This is one reason why a suzerainty type covenant
form was appropriate to express the relationship. A parity treaty form
would have been quite inappropriate because the Sinaitic covenant was
between unequals. Yahweh was Lord of the covenant:

Now therefore, if you will obey *my* voice and keep *my* covenant, you
shall be *my* own possession among all peoples; for all the earth is mine, and
you shall be to *me* a kingdom of priests and a holy nation. Exod. 19:5-6 E

Walther Eichrodt says that with the idea of a sovereign and his subjects
the concept of the kingdom of God was present even at Sinai.[26]

As Lord, Yahweh had no specific obligation, since that would in-
fringe upon his sovereignty.[27] He promised only to be God of Israel.
But Israel was responsible to obey Yahweh's will: "If you will obey
my voice and keep my covenant" (Exod. 19:5 E). "Observe what I
command you this day" (Exod. 34:11 J).

Like the vassal in the Hittite treaty,[28] the Hebrews, as Yahweh's
vassal, accepted certain obligations. These obligations were expressed
in the form of law. Precisely what law comes from the Mosaic period
cannot be said with certainty. That it was primarily apodictic law
seems a reasonable assumption in view of the research of Albrecht
Alt.[29] Apodictic law [30] is the terse, categorical type of law found in the

---

[26] Eichrodt, *op. cit.,* p. 40.
[27] See Mendenhall, *op. cit.,* p. 30.
[28] *Ibid.,* p. 33.
[29] Albrecht Alt, "Die Ursprünge des israelitischen Rechts" (*Kleine Schriften zur
Geschichte des Volkes Israel,* I, München: C. H. Beck, 1959, pp. 278-332).
[30] The other kind of law in the Old Testament Alt terms casuistic. Casuistic law is

decalogue: "You shall have no other gods before me." "You shall not make yourself a graven image." In its purest form it has an "I-Thou" style: Yahweh, in the first person, addresses the people, in the second person. Although some of the apodictic laws preserved in the Old Testament are positive in form, they were probably all negative originally. The setting of apodictic law is the covenant. Since the basic covenant of the Old Testament is that at Sinai, this kind of law is to be associated with the Sinaitic covenant.

It is unlikely that all the apodictic laws in the Pentateuch are Mosaic,[31] but many could be. That the *first* of the Ten Commandments is Mosaic would be conceded by almost all scholars who believe that the Old Testament traditions have preserved authentic information about Moses. It is the cornerstone of the Mosaic covenant: "You shall have no other gods before me" (Exod. 20:3 E). Or in another version: "You shall worship no other god, for Yahweh, whose name is Jealous, is a jealous God" (Exod. 34:14 J). Thus it appears in both the E and the J collections of law. In this connection it should be noted that the first stipulation of the Hittite treaty form was the explicit prohibition of other foreign covenants outside the Hittite empire.[32] No other sovereign but the Hittite was to be recognized.

Many believe that not only the first but all the commandments of the decalogue come from Moses.[33] If this is correct, they existed originally in a shortened form. One proposed reconstruction of the Mosaic decalogue is:

1. You shall have no other gods before me.
2. You shall not make for me any graven image or any likeness.
3. You shall not invoke the name of Yahweh your God in vain.
4. Remember the sabbath day to keep it holy.
5. Honor your father and your mother.

---

a type common to other cultures of the ancient world, e.g., the Code of Hammurabi. It is conditional in form, in the third person, and exclusively social. This type of law can be found, for example, in the E Covenant Code (Exod. 20:22–23:33).

[31] In addition to the decalogue, apodictic law is to be found in the J Covenant Code (Exod. 34:10-38), the early cursing code in Deut. 27:11-26, and is also scattered through the E Covenant Code and the book of Leviticus.

[32] Mendenhall, *op. cit.*, p. 33.

[33] H. H. Rowley defends this position in "Moses and the Decalogue," *Bulletin of the John Rylands Library*, Vol. 34, No. 1 (Sept. 1951). He includes a complete bibliography.

6. You shall not commit murder.
7. You shall not commit adultery.
8. You shall not steal.
9. You shall not bear false witness against your neighbor.
10. You shall not covet your neighbor's house.[34]

It need not be assumed that these were the only laws given by Moses. It is possible, for example, that there was a Mosaic commandment to observe the Passover (Exod. 34:25 J; cf. 12:21-27 J), but it has not been preserved in the decalogue.

In any event, Yahweh was recognized as Lord of the covenant and his will was expressed in terms of law. The people, as Yahweh's servant, voluntarily accepted their responsibility to obey Yahweh's law. At Sinai they gave their solemn oath: "All that Yahweh has spoken we will do" (Exod. 19:8 J; 24:3, 7 E).

5. The covenant was also a relationship that imparted *unity* to the Hebrews. In this event they became a people, the peculiar people of Yahweh. "You shall be my own possession among all peoples . . . you shall be to me a kingdom of priests and a holy nation" (Exod. 19: 5-6 E). Their relation to Yahweh in the covenant gave them a solidarity; it made a community out of a crowd.[35]

Among the many centrifugal elements in the subsequent centuries of Israel's history, the remembrance of the covenant was the primary centripetal element. Following the experience at Sinai on various occasions in the wilderness and later in Palestine other clans and tribes evidently joined these original adherents of Mosaic Yahwism. The new groups were of diverse social, economic and cultural levels. They brought with them a variety of customs and traditions. Some undoubtedly represented quite different racial streams. If the Hebrews who left Egypt were a "mixed multitude" (Exod. 12:38), those subsequently in Palestine were even more so. This great diversity inevitably led to frequent tension and division in Israel during the centuries from the conquest to the exile. The unity that did exist, however,

[34] Muilenburg, *op. cit.*, p. 303.
[35] Bernhard W. Anderson, *Understanding the Old Testament* (Englewood Cliffs, N.J.: Prentice-Hall, 1957), p. 53.

resulted from their common acknowledgment that they were the covenant people of Yahweh.

If it is true that only the Joseph tribes and a segment of the Levi tribe were involved in the event at Sinai, the Hebrews realized their basic unity not only before the emergence of the kingship but also before the organization of the twelve-tribe amphictyony (or theocratic confederation)[36] on Palestinian soil after the conquest under Joshua. The existence of a covenant faith and a covenant people antedated any kind of organization, either amphictyonic or monarchical, that we know in the Old Testament. There was presumably some kind of organization of the people at Sinai, but its memory has not been preserved.[37]

6. One final observation about the covenant is that it was a relationship which possessed a *binding character*. The rite which seals the covenant suggests this. Both J and E have preserved accounts of the sealing of the covenant. According to the E tradition (Exod. 24:3-8) burnt offerings and peace offerings were offered; then sacrificial blood was sprinkled first upon the altar, where Yahweh was present, and after that upon the people. Since blood represented life, Yahweh and the people were brought together by the sharing of common life. In the J tradition (Exod. 24:9-11) Moses, Aaron, Nadab, Abihu, and seventy of the elders ascended the sacred mountain, beheld God, and ate and drank a covenant meal. This account suggests that Yahweh and the people were bound together through the sharing of a common meal. It is of course impossible to determine with certainty which of the two preserves the original version of the ceremony. The important point is that there was such a ceremony which was viewed as bringing Yahweh and the people together in a deep interior psychic union.

The fact that Yahweh and the people were bound together in a covenant meant that they would share a common future. Just as the treaty between the great Hittite king and his vassal had an effect upon their future relations, so the covenant between Yahweh and these people promised the same. It would be too much to say that the cove-

---

[36] See below, Chap. Four, pp. 110-12 for a discussion of the twelve-tribe amphictyony.
[37] On this point see John Bright, *A History of Israel* (Philadelphia: The Westminster Press, 1959), p. 145.

nant could not be broken by the people or repudiated by Yahweh.[38] It was not a natural relationship and Yahweh was completely sovereign. Nevertheless, the histories of Yahweh and the Hebrews were bound together at Sinai, and their future history belonged together.

If the covenant was the result of an act of Yahweh in the past history of this people, it also looked forward to his acts in their future history. There is the suggestion of a promise for the future in the words of Yahweh in the E tradition: "Now therefore, if you will obey my voice and keep my covenant, you shall be my own possession among all peoples" (Exod. 19:5). The J tradition of course contains the explicit promise of Yahweh's activity in the conquest of the land:

10 Behold, I make a covenant. Before all your people I will do marvels, such as have not been wrought in all the earth or in any nation; and all the people among whom you are shall see the work of Yahweh; for it is a terrible thing that I will do with you. 11 Observe what I command you this day. Behold, I will drive out before you the Amorites, the Canaanites, the Hittites, the Perizzites, the Hivites, and the Jebusites. Exod. 34:10-11

Since all the Old Testament traditions indicate that the Hebrews left Sinai and journeyed toward Palestine for the explicit purpose of invading and possessing it, there is no reason to doubt that at this point J preserves an authentic memory of the faith of the people for the future at the time the covenant was sealed.

The covenant at Sinai thus was oriented toward the future. The future history of this people belonged to Yahweh to whom they had been sacramentally bound in the covenant.

---

[38] Eichrodt emphasizes the contingent character of the covenant, *op. cit.*, p. 44.

Chapter Two

Two Covenant Traditions
and
Two Mosaic Shrines

IT IS EXTREMELY SIGNIFICANT THAT TWO EARLY TRADITIONS HAVE BEEN preserved concerning the covenant at Sinai. Although the J and E covenant traditions are sufficiently similar to indicate that they both reflect the same historical event, the differences between them are striking. These differences are fully as important as their points of affinity. A consideration of the distinctive character of the two covenant traditions and their respective histories can greatly illuminate the history of the covenant people from Sinai to the division of the Davidic kingdom and beyond.

The difficulties of separating the J and E material in Exodus 19–24; 32–34 are well known. There can be no certainty in making a source division in these chapters, but it is possible to isolate two fairly well ordered and coherent narratives with few lacunae.[1]

---

[1] I have made a literary analysis of these chapters in *The Sinai Covenant Traditions*, pp. 90-142. The source division here is based on that analysis.

39

The Elohist's Version of the Covenant

1. *The Announcement for the People* (19:2b-6)

2b And there Israel encamped before the mountain. 3 And Moses went up to God, and God [2] called him out of the mountain, saying, "Thus you shall say to the house of Jacob, and tell the people of Israel: 4 You have seen what I did to the Egyptians, and how I bore you on eagles' wings and brought you to myself. 5 Now therefore, if you will obey my voice and keep my covenant, you shall be my own possession among all peoples; for all the earth is mine, 6 and you shall be to me a kingdom of priests and a holy nation. These are the words which you shall speak to the children of Israel."

2. *The Cultic Preparation of the People* (19:10-11a, 14-15)

10 And God [3] said to Moses, "Go to the people and consecrate them today and tomorrow, and let them wash their garments, 11a and be ready by the third day. 14 So Moses went down from the mountain to the people, and consecrated the people; and they washed their garments. 15 And he said to the people, "Be ready by the third day; do not go near a woman."

3. *The Theophany to the People* (19:16-17, 19)

16 On the morning of the third day there were thunders and lightnings, and a thick cloud upon the mountain, and a very loud trumpet blast, so that all the people who were in the camp trembled. 17 Then Moses brought the people out of the camp to meet God; and they took their stand at the foot of the mountain. 19 And as the sound of the trumpet grew louder and louder, Moses spoke, and God answered him in thunder.

4. *The People Make Moses Their Mediator* (20:18-21)

18 Now when all the people perceived the thunderings and the lightnings and the sound of the trumpet and the mountain smoking, the people were afraid and trembled; and they stood afar off, 19 and said to Moses, "You speak to us, and we will hear; but let not God speak to us, lest we die."

---

[2] Reading *'elohim* with the Septuagint rather than Yahweh of the MT.
[3] Reading *'elohim* with the Septuagint rather than Yahweh of the MT.

20 And Moses said to the people, "Do not fear; for God has come to prove you, and that the fear of him may be before your eyes, that you may not sin." 21 And the people stood afar off, while Moses drew near to the thick cloud where God was.

5. *God Announces His Name and Nature* (20:1-2)

1 And God spoke all these words, saying, 2 "I am Yahweh your God, who brought you out of the land of Egypt, out of the house of bondage.

6. *Yahweh Gives His Law* (20:3-17 [20:22–23:33])

3 "You shall have no other gods before me.

4 "You shall not make yourself a graven image, or any likeness of anything that is in heaven above, or that is in the earth beneath, or that is in the water under the earth; 5 you shall not bow down to them or serve them; for I Yahweh your God am a jealous God, visiting the iniquity of the fathers upon the children to the third and the fourth generation of those who hate me, 6 but showing steadfast love to thousands of those who love me and keep my commandments.

7 "You shall not take the name of Yahweh your God in vain; for Yahweh will not hold him guiltless who takes his name in vain.

8 "Remember the sabbath day to keep it holy. 9 Six days you shall labor, and do all your work; 10 but the seventh day is a sabbath to Yahweh your God; in it you shall not do any work, you, or your son, or your daughter, your manservant, or your maidservant, or your cattle, or the sojourner who is within your gates; 11 for in six days Yahweh made heaven and earth, the sea, and all that is in them, and rested the seventh day; therefore Yahweh blessed the sabbath day and hallowed it.

12 "Honor your father and your mother, that your days may be long in the land which Yahweh your God gives you.

13 "You shall not kill.

14 "You shall not commit adultery.

15 "You shall not steal.

16 "You shall not bear false witness against your neighbor.

41

17 "You shall not covet your neighbor's house; you shall not covet your neighbor's wife, or his manservant, or his maidservant, or his ox, or his ass, or anything that is your neighbor's."

7. *The Oath of the People* (24:3)

3 Moses came and told the people all the words of Yahweh and all the ordinances; and all the people answered with one voice, and said, "All the words which Yahweh has spoken we will do."

8. *The Sealing of the Covenant* (24:4-8)

4 And Moses wrote all the words of Yahweh. And he rose early in the morning, and built an altar at the foot of the mountain, and twelve pillars, according to the twelve tribes of Israel. 5 And he sent young men of the people of Israel, who offered burnt offerings and sacrificed peace offerings of oxen to Yahweh. 6 And Moses took half of the blood and put it in basins, and half of the blood he threw against the altar. 7 Then he took the book of the covenant, and read it in the hearing of the people; and they said, "All that Yahweh has spoken we will do, and we will be obedient." 8 And Moses took the blood and threw it upon the people, and said, "Behold the blood of the covenant which Yahweh has made with you in accordance with all these words."

The Jahwist's Version of the Covenant

1. *Yahweh Makes Moses the Mediator* (19:9a)

9a And Yahweh said to Moses, "Lo, I am coming to you in a thick cloud, that the people may hear when I speak with you, and may also believe you for ever."

2. *The Cultic Preparation of the People* (19:11b-13)

11b "For on the third day Yahweh will come down upon Mount Sinai in the sight of all the people. 12 And you shall set bounds for the people round about, saying, 'Take heed that you do not go up into the mountain or touch the border of it; whoever touches the mountain shall be put to death; 13 no hand shall touch him, but he shall be stoned or shot; whether beast or man, he shall not live.' When the trumpet sounds a long blast, they shall come up to the mountain."

3. *The General Theophany* (19:18)

18 And Mount Sinai was wrapped in smoke, because Yahweh descended upon it in fire; and the smoke of it went up like the smoke of a kiln, and the whole mountain quaked greatly.

4. *Moses Goes to the Top of the Mountain* (19:20; 34:1-4)

19:20 And Yahweh came down upon Mount Sinai, to the top of the mountain; and Yahweh called Moses to the top of the mountain, and Moses went up. 34:1 Yahweh said to Moses, "Cut two tables of stone. . . . 2 Be ready in the morning, and come up in the morning to Mount Sinai, and present yourself there to me on the top of the mountain. 3 No man shall come up with you, and let no man be seen throughout all the mountain; let no flocks or herds feed before that mountain." 4 So Moses cut two tables of stone . . . ; and he rose early in the morning and went up on Mount Sinai, as Yahweh had commanded him, and took in his hand two tables of stone.

5. *The Special Theophany to Moses* (33:18-23; 34:5)

33:18 Moses said, "I pray thee, show me thy glory." 19 And he said, "I will make all my goodness pass before you, and will proclaim before you my name 'Yahweh'; and I will be gracious to whom I will be gracious, and will show mercy on whom I will show mercy. 20 But," he said, "you cannot see my face; for man shall not see me and live." 21 And Yahweh said, "Behold, there is a place by me where you shall stand upon the rock; 22 and while my glory passes by I will put you in a cleft of the rock, and I will cover you with my hand until I have passed by; 23 then I will take away my hand, and you shall see my back; but my face shall not be seen. 34:5 And Yahweh descended in the cloud and stood with him there, and proclaimed the name of Yahweh.

6. *Yahweh Proclaims His Name and Nature* (34:6-8)

6 Yahweh passed before him, and proclaimed, "Yahweh, Yahweh, a God merciful and gracious, slow to anger, and abounding in steadfast love and faithfulness, 7 keeping steadfast love for thousands, forgiving iniquity and transgression and sin, but who will by no means clear the guilty, visiting the iniquity of the fathers upon the children and the children's children, to the third and the fourth generation." 8 And Moses made haste to bow his head toward the earth, and worshiped.

7. *Yahweh Offers His Covenant with His Law* (34:10-26)

10 And he said, "Behold, I make a covenant. Before all your people I will do marvels, such as have not been wrought in all the earth or in any nation; and all the people among whom you are shall see the work of Yahweh; for it is a terrible thing that I will do with you.

11 "Observe what I command you this day. Behold, I will drive out before you the Amorites, the Canaanites, the Hittites, the Perizzites, the Hivites, and the Jebusites. 12 Take heed to yourself, lest you make a covenant with the inhabitants of the land whither you go, lest it become a snare in the midst of you. 13 You shall tear down their altars, and break their pillars, and cut down their Asherim 14 (for you shall worship no other god, for Yahweh, whose name is Jealous, is a jealous God), 15 lest you make a covenant with the inhabitants of the land, and when they play the harlot after their gods and sacrifice to their gods and one invites you, you eat of his sacrifice, 16 and you take of their daughters for your sons, and their daughters play the harlot after their gods and make your sons play the harlot after their gods.

17 "You shall make for yourself no molten gods.

18 "The feast of unleavened bread you shall keep. Seven days you shall eat unleavened bread, as I commanded you, at the time appointed in the month Abib; for in the month Abib you came out from Egypt.

19 "All that opens the womb is mine, all your male cattle, the firstlings of cow and sheep. 20 The firstling of an ass you shall redeem with a lamb, or if you will not redeem it you shall break its neck. All the first-born of your sons you shall redeem. And none shall appear before me empty.

21 "Six days you shall work, but on the seventh day you shall rest; in plowing time and in harvest you shall rest.

22 "And you shall observe the feast of weeks, the first fruits of wheat harvest, and the feast of ingathering at the year's end. 23 Three times in the year shall all your males appear before Yahweh God, the God of Israel. 24 For I will cast out nations before you, and enlarge your borders; neither shall any man desire your land, when you go up to appear before Yahweh your God three times in the year.

25a "You shall not offer the blood of my sacrifice with leaven;

25b "Neither shall the sacrifice of the feast of the passover be left until the morning.

26a "The first of the first fruits of your ground you shall bring to the house of Yahweh your God.

26b "You shall not boil a kid in its mother's milk."

8. Yahweh's Covenant with Moses and the People (34:27-28)

27 And Yahweh said to Moses, "Write these words; in accordance with these words I have made a covenant with you and with Israel." 28 And he was there with Yahweh forty days and forty nights; he neither ate bread nor drank water. And he wrote upon the tables the words of the covenant, the ten commandments.

9. The Oath of the People (19:7-8)

7 So Moses came and called the elders of the people, and set before them all these words which Yahweh had commanded him. 8 And all the people answered together and said, "All that Yahweh has spoken we will do." And Moses reported the words of the people to Yahweh.

10. The Sealing of the Covenant (24:1-2, 9-11)

1 And he said to Moses, "Come up to Yahweh, you and Aaron, Nadab, and Abihu, and seventy of the elders of Israel, and worship afar off. 2 Moses alone shall come near to Yahweh; but the others shall not come near, and the people shall not come up with him." 9 Then Moses and Aaron, Nadab, and Abihu, and seventy of the elders of Israel went up,

10 and they saw the God of Israel; and there was under his feet as it were a pavement of sapphire stone, like the very heaven for clearness. 11 And he did not lay his hand on the chief men of the people of Israel; they beheld God, and ate and drank.

Distinctive Emphases of the Two Traditions

An analysis of these two covenant traditions reveals a number of points at which they sharply diverge in emphasis.

1. The two traditions begin with quite different emphases. The E account begins with a word for *all the people* (19:2b-6). What is about to happen to this group will establish them as "a kingdom of priests and a holy nation" (vs. 6). It is not an unconditional promise that they receive, however. This will come to pass only if they obey Yahweh's voice and keep his covenant (vs. 5).

The J version, on the other hand, begins with Yahweh's word to Moses which establishes an *office of covenant mediator*. "Lo, I am coming to you in a thick cloud, that the people may hear when I speak with you, and may also believe you for ever" (19:9a). The office is to be established "for ever," and presumably the promise is unconditional.

While the former version, then, stresses the contingent constitution of the life of the people in the covenant, the latter emphasizes the unconditional establishment of an office of covenant mediator "for ever."

2. The appointment of the covenant mediator differs strikingly in the two versions. According to E it is *the people themselves* who make Moses their covenant mediator (20:18-21). Their fear in the awesome presence of God prompts them to say to Moses: "You speak to us, and we will hear; but let not God speak to us, lest we die" (vs. 19).

In J, however, the people play no part at all in the appointing of the covenant mediator. It is *Yahweh himself* who speaks directly to Moses designating him to the office which is to continue for ever (19:9a). The people are merely to observe at a distance the coming of Yahweh in the cloud which confirms Moses in his office.

3. There is a significant divergence in the two versions concerning the preparation of the people for the covenant ceremony. E assumes the *full participation of the people* in the ceremony (19:10-11a, 14-15). Yahweh commands Moses to consecrate the people for two days;

on the third day the covenant is to be made. The cultic preparation consists of the washing of the garments of the people and their abstinence from sexual intercourse.

In J the cultic preparation does not consist of the consecration of the people, but rather of *the setting of bounds around the holy mountain* to prevent its profanation by the people (19:12-13; cf. 34:3). Only when the sanctity of the mountain has been ensured against any possible defilement will the trumpet sound, announcing the beginning of the processional toward the mountain.[4]

4. Of particular significance is the theophany in the two traditions. E has only one theophany and it is perceived by *all the people* (19:16-17, 19). The assumption of the tradition seems to be that Yahweh is present at the top of the mountain and thus it is necessary for Moses to go up to him (19:3, 16-17, 19; 20:21). There is no indication that Yahweh must come to the mountain. It might be said that God is viewed in some sense as being "enthroned" upon the mountain, although this particular expression is not used.

There are both visual and audible phenomena in E's description of the theophany. In general they suggest phenomena derived from a thunderstorm. Among the visual phenomena are "lightnings" (19:16; 20:18) and a "thick cloud" (19:16; 20:21). According to 19:16 all the people saw "the mountain smoking." The audible phenomena, however, are emphasized fully as much as the visual in this tradition. Accompanying the lightnings are "thunders" (*qoloth* 19:16; 20:18). God speaks in the "thunder" (*qol* 19:19), which is thus closely related to his voice. Associated with the thunder in the account is the "sound of the trumpet" (*qol shofar* 19:16, 19; 20:18).

The emphasis upon thunder and the voice of Yahweh in the description of the theophany underlines the importance of *speaking* and *hearing* in the E tradition. The sound of the trumpet grew louder and louder, then "Moses *spoke,* and God *answered* him in thunder" (19:19). When the people perceived the lightnings, thunderings, the sound of the trumpet, and the mountain smoking, they were frightened and said to Moses: "You *speak* to us, and we will *hear;* but let not God

---

[4] Since there is no record of the processional in the J tradition, it has presumably fallen out.

speak to us, lest we die" (20:19). Immediately following this passage comes 20:1: "And God *spoke* all these *words, saying.*" This all prepares for the key cultic word which is spoken: "I am Yahweh your God" (20:2). The name of God is proclaimed and heard. The E tradition has avoided the use of the name Yahweh to this point, having previously used only the more general word "God" (*elohim*); but now it is revealed. After this it appears a number of times in the narrative (20:5, 10, 11; 24:3, 4, 5, 7, 8). Thus this tradition is characterized by a kind of dramatic suspense. Only the word *"elohim"* is used until the climactic moment in the ceremony when God gives himself fully and intimately to his chosen people; this happens with the momentous proclamation of his name, Yahweh.

It is really necessary to speak of *two* theophanies in the J tradition. The first is a general theophany to the people (19:18). Its purpose is to confirm for them the fact that Yahweh has appointed Moses as the covenant mediator and that his office is to be continued for ever (19:9*a*). The second is the special theophany to Moses alone. Moses requests it, and it is granted (33:18-23; 34:5). The purpose of this theophany undoubtedly is to stress the intimacy of the relationship between Moses (and perhaps his successors) and Yahweh.[5]

If the E account suggests that Yahweh in some way is enthroned upon the mountain, J indicates clearly that he "comes down"[6] to it (19:11*b*, 18, 20; 34:5). His normal abode is in the heavens (24:10); so he must descend to meet with Moses.

Also unlike the E tradition, where the audible phenomena are as fully stressed as the visual, J's emphasis is exclusively upon the latter. For J it is *seeing* that is paramount. Yahweh comes down upon Mount Sinai in the *"sight* of all the people" (19:11*b*). Moses asks to *see* the glory of Yahweh (33:18).[7] When the covenant meal is eaten the leaders of the people *see* God (24:9, 11). There is no thunder in the J tradition; all the phenomena of the theophany are visual. Yahweh descends in "fire" (19:18). The mountain is "wrapped in smoke"

---

[5] It is perhaps possible to speak of three theophanies in J, since 24:9-11 says that Moses, Aaron, Nadab, Abihu, and seventy elders "saw the God of Israel."

[6] The Hebrew word *yarad* is a technical term of the Jahwist.

[7] The literal meaning of the Hebrew expression which the RSV translates "show me" is "make visible to me."

and its smoke "is like the smoke of a kiln" (19:18). Closely related to the smoke is the "cloud" in which Yahweh is present (19:9a; 34:5). The "glory" (*kabod*) of Yahweh which is manifested to Moses is also a visual phenomenon and in this tradition probably is to be associated with the fire.[8] Yahweh's "glory" is the bright, shining manifestation of his presence; it is his visible earthly form. In the E tradition the climactic cultic moment is the proclamation and hearing of Yahweh's name. This element does appear in J (33:19; 34:6), but much more important is the manifestation and seeing of Yahweh's glory.

5. Both covenant traditions contain law. The central law of E is the *decalogue*. These ten apodictic commandments are concerned with the cult (20:3-11) and society (vss. 12-17). Also incorporated into the E tradition is the covenant code in 20:22–23:33. Although there are a few apodictic laws scattered through this code, most of them are casuistic.[9] These casuistic laws, of course, are all social in character.

The law of the J covenant tradition is *exclusively apodictic and cultic* (34:10-26). It contains no casuistic law like the ones found in the E Covenant Code in 20:22–23:33. Nor does the J Covenant Code contain any law governing social relations of the people. Its exclusive orientation is cultic. 34:28 states that there are ten commandments in this code, but it is not easy to find ten. Since the purest form of the apodictic law is negative, it is interesting to note that there are *six* such laws here:

1. "You shall worship no other god." vs. 14
2. "You shall make for yourself no molten gods." vs. 17
3. "None shall appear before me empty." vs. 20*b*
4. "You shall not offer the blood of my sacrifice with leaven." vs. 25*a*
5. "Neither shall the sacrifice of the feast of the passover be left until morning." vs. 25*b*
6. "You shall not boil a kid in its mother's milk." vs. 26*b*

[8] On "glory" in the Old Testament see especially Gerhard von Rad's article in Kittel's *Theologisches Wörterbuch zum Neuen Testament* (Stuttgart: W. Kohlhammer, 1935), II, 240-45. A brief treatment of the concept in English is to be found in Arthur Michael Ramsey, *The Glory of God and the Transfiguration of Christ* (London, New York, Toronto: Longmans, Green & Co., Inc., 1949), pp. 9-18.

[9] See Chap. One, p. 34, n. 30 for a definition of casuistic law.

6. Another significant difference in the two traditions is their respective accounts of the sealing of the covenant. The *full participation of the people* in the E version is striking (24:3-8). When the covenant sacrifices are offered, not priests but rather "young men of the people" are called upon to perform the task (vs. 5). Then Moses takes the blood and puts half of it in basins; the other half he throws against the altar, where Yahweh is present (vs. 6). Following this he *reads* the book of the covenant in the *hearing* of the people and they take the oath of obedience to Yahweh (vs. 7). Finally he takes the blood in the basins and throws it upon *the people* with the words: "Behold the blood of the covenant which Yahweh has made with you in accordance with all these words" (vs. 8). Like the statement of Yahweh that stands at the beginning of the E tradition, this account of the sealing of the covenant also stresses the fact that the covenant is with *all the people.*

The J account of the sealing of the covenant differs radically. In J it is *not* participated in by all the people. They *do* take the formal oath to the covenant (19:8). They of course are under the obligation to observe the law (34:10-27). But the ceremony which seals the covenant is *attended only by a select group: Moses, Aaron, Nadab, Abihu,* and *seventy elders* (24:1-2, 9-11). They ascend the mountain where they are granted a heavenly vision. The covenant sealing itself consists of a sacramental meal, which is briefly stated but not described: "They beheld God, and ate and drank" (24:11).

The limiting of the participation of the people with the concomitant stress upon the leaders is a salient characteristic of the J tradition. The role of Moses as covenant mediator receives special stress in this tradition, an emphasis quite different from E. In the J account the covenant that Yahweh makes is not merely with Israel but rather with Moses *and* Israel (34:27). This is especially clear in the original Hebrew, a literal translation of which would be: "And Yahweh said to Moses, 'Write these words; in accordance with these words *I have made with you a covenant and with Israel.'*" Just as later Yahweh makes a covenant with David (II Sam. 23:5; Ps. 89:4, 29), in this tradition it is with Moses. In this connection the tradition in 19:9*a* concerning Yahweh's appointment of Moses as covenant mediator should be mentioned again: "And Yahweh said to Moses, 'Lo, I am coming to you in a thick cloud, that the people may hear when I speak with you, and may also believe you for ever.'" The expression "for ever" (le'olam) suggests a continuation and perpetuation of this office of covenant mediator to which Moses is appointed. It is the same expression which frequently is used in connection with Yahweh's promise of the continuation of the Davidic dynasty (II Sam. 7:29; I Kings 9:5; I Chron. 17:27; 28:4, 7; II Chron. 13:4; Ps. 89:29, 37), along with the synonymous expression 'ad 'olam (likewise translated "for ever") in II Sam. 7:13, 17, 25; 22:51; I Kings 2:33, 45; I Chron. 17:12, 14, 23; 22:10; Ps. 18:51; 89:5. If 19:9a suggests the establishment of a dynastic office of covenant mediator, the story of the sealing of the covenant in 24:1-2, 9-11 suggests the priestly dynasty appointed to carry on the office. Moses, Aaron, Nadab, Abihu and the seventy elders go up the mountain for the covenant meal. The seventy elders are obviously the representatives of the people. But the other names reveal the dynasty: Moses—Aaron—Nadab and Abihu. Moses is the first covenant mediator. Aaron, the brother of Moses, is the priest through whom the dynasty is to continue. Nadab and Abihu are the successors of Aaron. The covenant dynasty is established in the eating of the covenant meal itself.

In the J tradition, then, the covenant is made with Moses, the covenant mediator, and through him it is with the people (34:27). His office as covenant mediator is dynastic; it is to continue "for ever" (19:9a). This dynastic succession is traced from Moses to Aaron to Nadab and Abihu.

In brief these two traditions could be characterized as follows:

1. E is more congregational, democratic, prophetic, and ethical in tendency. It reflects a kind of "kingdom of priests" covenant theology.

2. J is more priestly, cultic, authoritarian, and dynastic in tendency. It reflects a "dynastic" covenant theology.

Cult Legends of Covenant Ceremonies

How are these two covenant traditions to be understood? Why is it that they have developed such distinct theological emphases? These questions can best be answered if the two traditions are viewed as cult

51

legends that were used in covenant ceremonies of the Hebrew people.[10] There are a number of elements in the two narratives which suggest that they were used in the cult.

One of the most obvious indications of a cultic usage of the E legend is the reference to the "trumpet" (*shofar* 19:16, 19; 20:18) in connection with the theophany. If the tradition is viewed simply as an account of the experience at Sinai, the loud trumpet blast with the thunders, lightnings, and thick cloud is most perplexing. Who, one might ask, was blowing the trumpet on the top of the mountain? Was it the Lord? But if the legend is associated with the cult, the trumpet can be understood as a cultic instrument which was blown in connection with a later covenant ceremony and was absorbed into the legend. Although its function is somewhat different, the same would presumably hold true for the "ram's horn" (*yobel* 19:13) in the J legend. Both of these instruments are associated with cultic activities in other parts of the Old Testament. The trumpet, for instance, was used in connection with David's removal of the ark to Jerusalem (II Sam. 6:15), and both the trumpet and the ram's horn are associated with the cultic activities of the Year of Jubilees (Lev. 25:8-10).

The appearance of codes of apodictic law in the two legends is another indication that they were used and formed in the cult (20:2-17 E; 34:10-26 J). In his creative study of Hebrew law Albrecht Alt stressed the relation between apodictic law and the cult.[11] With its terse, categorical style, apodictic law is ideally suited for liturgical recitation in the cult. Indeed it is only through repeated use in the life of the people that a literary form, such as apodictic law, receives its shape and content.[12] A clear illustration of a cultic setting for apodictic law elsewhere in the Old Testament is to be found in Deut. 27. The twelve apodictic laws which appear there in the literary form of curses are recited as part of a cultic ceremony which takes place in the neighborhood of Shechem between Mount Ebal and Mount Gerizim.

There are a number of other traces of cultic usage in the two legends. The sanctification of cult participants by means of rituals of

[10] *Supra*, Chap. One, p. 19.
[11] Alt, *op. cit.*, pp. 302-332.
[12] Alt, *op. cit.*, p. 325.

purification and sexual abstinence conforms to cultic custom (19:10, 14-15; cf. Lev. 16:4; I Sam. 21:5). The preservation of the holy mountain from profanation by people or animals is the expression of a cultic concern (19:12-13 J; cf. II Sam. 7:6-7; Exod. 28:43). The processional toward the sacred mountain, which appears in both E (19:13) and J (19:17), finds a parallel in the cultic processional at the time of the dedication of the Solomonic temple (I Kings 8:2-6; cf. II Sam. 6; I Chron. 13:5-14; II Chron. 5), as well as in a number of psalms such as Ps. 24:7-10.

This is the kind of evidence, then, that leads to the conclusion that the J and E traditions of the covenant at Sinai in their present form can be classified as cult legends which were used in covenant ceremonies. The definition of a cult legend as it is here understood is suggested by a comment that G. E. Wright makes on Deuteronomy 27:

For the understanding of the chapter it is important to recall that the rules for the observance of important ceremonies in the O.T. are nearly always presented by means of historical narration. The way in which the thing was originally done was the manner in which it was to be repeated [cf. the institution of the Passover in Exod. 12–13; the rules for the ordination of priests in Lev. 8–9; cf. the institution of the Lord's Supper in the N.T., e.g., Mark 14:1-26; I Cor. 11:23-26].[13]

This applies to the J and E traditions of the covenant. The rules for the observance of one covenant ceremony are presented in the form of J's historical narration. The rules for the observance of another covenant ceremony are presented in the form of E's historical narration.

In the case of these two cult legends, it must be emphasized that they both reflect an actual event. It is not that cultic rites have merely been historicized. Rather they both reflect the event at Sinai as outlined above.[14] They reflect the particular historical event in which a group of Hebrews voluntarily entered into a covenant relationship with Yahweh, the God who they believed had been gracious to them.

[13] G. Ernest Wright, "The Book of Deuteronomy," *The Interpreter's Bible* (Nashville: Abingdon Press, 1953), II, 488-89.
[14] *Supra*, pp. 29-38.

The event was characterized by a very vivid experience of Yahweh's presence in a theophany. It involved a formal commitment of the people to worship Yahweh alone, as well as to keep certain other unconditional laws. The relationship was sealed by a covenant rite which resulted in a feeling of being sacramentally bound to Yahweh and to one another.

They both can be called "legends" because in their present form they not only reflect the orginal event but also have absorbed other elements which were not part of the event. The original event can be dated in the thirteenth century B.c. The Jahwist epic can be dated in the tenth century B.c., and the Elohist epic not more than a century or so later. The development of the two covenant traditions took place during this general period of three or four centuries. Each tradition developed while used as the cult legend of a covenant ceremony. In the period nearer the event it would probably have reflected the event more accurately. The covenant event was re-enacted in the cult, and the cult legend both described and perpetuated the cult ceremony. Undoubtedly the legend was recited as part of the ceremony. Over a period of time new rites were introduced and new theological emphases developed, and these new elements were absorbed by the cult legend. It is probably correct to assume that the whole process was oral, since oral tradition lends itself to such flexibility.[15] One cannot determine at every point just which elements were assimilated later into the tradition and thus did not belong to the original event, but certain ones would seem to be obvious. In the E tradition, for example, the twelve pillars corresponding to the twelve tribes (24:4) could have been incorporated into the legend only after the establishment of the twelve-tribe amphictyony in Palestine at Shechem (Josh. 24). And in J the emphasis upon Moses as the all-important, covenant mediator from whom a priesthood traced its dynasty (19:9a; 24:1-2, 9-11; 33:18 ff.; 34:5 ff., 27) is probably the result of a later cultic development. In any event, the present forms of both traditions undoubtedly represent a stage of development close

[15] For suggestive treatments of oral tradition in the Old Testament see W. F. Albright, *From the Stone Age to Christianity* (Baltimore: The Johns Hopkins Press, 1946), pp. 33-43 and Eduard Nielsen, *Oral Tradition* (London: SCM Press, 1954), pp. 39-62.

to the tenth century. A more precise date for each will be considered later in this study.

Two Mosaic Shrines

If there are two early traditions concerning the covenant at Sinai, it is noteworthy that there are also early traditions concerning two important shrines at Sinai. The ark of the covenant and the tent of meeting both appear for the first time at Sinai. It seems probable that the E covenant legend is to be associated with the ark and the J legend with the tent.

The Priestly Code gives a complete description of the construction of the ark (*'aron*) in Exod. 25:10-22; 37:1-9 and the tabernacle (*mishkan*), which it equates with the tent of meeting (*'ohel mo'ed*), in Exod. 26, 27, 35–38. There is no J or E account of the construction of either the ark or the tent. The Jahwist [16] has preserved the tradition in Exod. 33:7-11 which describes the tent in use at Sinai. And the ark appears in the early[17] tradition of Num. 10:33-36 as the covenant people are preparing to leave the mountain. Thus there are early traditions which place both the ark and the tent at the covenant mountain. And it is not unreasonable to assume that originally there were early traditions concerning the construction of both sacred objects at Sinai, which have been replaced by P's more detailed accounts.[18]

The reliability of the traditions which ascribe the two shrines to the time of Moses is accepted by many scholars today, particularly as the result of archaeological studies. W. F. Albright writes:

After the demonstration by R. Hartmann and especially by H. Lammens of nomadic Arab parallels to the portable Tabernacle and Ark of the Covenant, some of them going far back into pre-Islamic times, it is captious to

---

[16] See *Infra* p. 63, n. 41.

[17] There is insufficient evidence to determine with certainty whether this passage belongs to J or E. Some, like George Buchanan Gray (*A Critical and Exegetical Commentary on Numbers.* [New York: Charles Scribner's Sons, 1920], p. 93), favor J. Others, like Bruno Baentsch (*Exodus-Leviticus-Numeri* [Göttingen: Vandenhoeck und Ruprecht, 1903], p. 501), incline toward E. Because the ark played a prominent role in the North before the time of David, the present writer prefers to assign it to the northern Elohist.

[18] This is suggested by most of the standard commentaries on Exodus. Of course there is such a tradition in Deut. 10:1-5.

refuse them Mosaic date, since they were completely foreign to sedentary Canaanite practice and since they were known to have persisted for some time after the Conquest of Palestine. The archaeologist no longer has any difficulty in proving the antiquity of many details in the description which is given in the Priestly Code.[19]

The Arab shrine most closely paralleling the ark and the tent is the pre-Islamic *qubbah*. The *qubbah* was a tentlike structure suitable for mounting on the back of a camel. It was made of red leather and contained two sacred betyls or tribal idols. It possessed a unique holiness and could be used as a place of worship and sacrifice. Some of its salient functions were the giving of oracles, guidance on tribal journeys, and usage in connection with battles. In these respects it parallels the ark and the tent. Although these parallels are clear and tend to support the nomadic origin of the two shrines of the Hebrews, and thus also the traditions concerning their Mosaic provenance, their distinctive usage in connection with Yahwism must not be overlooked. F. M. Cross, Jr., has a timely word of warning in this regard:

Thus it goes without saying that the Tabernacle and the Ark have historical connections with their Semitic past. On the other hand, we have no right to push such parallels too hard as has been the tendency of some scholars, particularly of Morgenstern. As the *qubbah* was radically reinterpreted by Mohammed, so no doubt the ancient Semitic tent-shrine was transformed under Moses to suit the purposes of Yahwism.[20]

One error of many Old Testament scholars who hold that the ark and the tent are Mosaic is the view that the former was housed in the latter from the very beginning and the two were never separated until the temple was built in the time of Solomon and the ark was

[19] *Op. cit.*, p. 293. The article by Hartmann is "Zelt und Lade," *Zeitschrift für die alttestamentliche Wissenschaft*, 37 (1917-18), 209 ff. and by Lammens, "Le culte des bétyles et les processions réligieuses chez les arabes préislamites," *Bulletin de L'Institut Francais d'Archéologie Orientale* (Cairo, 1919), XVII, 39-101. Two other important studies that should be mentioned in this connection are: F. M. Cross, Jr., "The Tabernacle," *The Biblical Archaeologist*, X (1947), 45-68 and Julian Morgenstern, "The Ark, the Ephod, and the Tent," *Hebrew Union College Annual*, XVII (1942-43), 153-265; XVIII (1943-44), 1-52.
[20] *Op. cit.*, p. 61.

placed in it. It is true that the late Priestly Code says that the ark was placed in the tabernacle, which it equates with the tent, at Sinai (Exod. 40:1 ff.). However, P probably reflects a later stage of cultic development, since the early traditions concerning the ark and the tent indicate that the ark was never kept in the tent of meeting. The two were separate.[21] They should be analyzed separately.

The Ark of the Covenant

The ark has a number of different names in the Old Testament. It is called variously "the ark of God" (I Sam. 3:3, et al.), "the ark of Yahweh" (Josh. 4:11, et al.), "the ark of the covenant" (Josh. 3:6, et al.), "the ark of the testimony" (Exod. 25:16, et al.), or simply "the ark" (Exod. 25:14, et al.).

Concerning its exact structure in the age of Moses one cannot be entirely certain. It is unlikely that the ark was a tent, as has been suggested.[22] Militating against this view is the Hebrew word for ark, 'aron, which has the basic meaning "chest" or "box." The description given by the Priestly Code in Exod. 25:10-22; 37:1-9 speaks against this position. According to P the ark was a chest two and a half cubits[23] in length, a cubit and a half in breadth, and a cubit and a half in depth. Made of acacia wood, it was overlaid without and within of gold and had a gold molding around it. On either side were two golden rings through which two poles of acacia wood overlaid with gold were put to carry the ark. The lid of the ark was of solid gold. Attached to it were two golden cherubim facing each other with their wings overshadowing the lid. Since the code which preserves this description is postexilic in its present form, these details cannot be accepted uncritically. The extensive use of gold by a group that had only recently been in slavery might be challenged, and the

[21] In many respects the best treatment of the ark and the tent of meeting still is the monograph by Gerhard von Rad, "Zelt und Lade" which appeared in 1931 (reprinted in *Gesammelte Studien zum Alten Testament* [München: Chr. Kaiser, 1958], pp. 109-29). He demonstrates that the two shrines belong to two separate cultic streams. It should be noted, however, that while in this work he felt that only the tent was nomadic in origin, now he believes that they both originated in the wilderness (*Theologie des Alten Testaments* [München: Chr. Kaiser, 1957], I, 235). He does not of course take the position that they both are Mosaic. On this point I would disagree.

[22] Morgenstern, *op. cit.*, VIII (1943-44), 55-71.

[23] A cubit is approximately eighteen inches.

cherubim may have been associated with it on Palestinian soil.[24] But the general picture of a portable shrine made of acacia wood in the shape of a chest is quite consonant with all the early passages in the Old Testament which pertain to the ark.

From the time of Moses the ark seems to have been regarded as the throne of Yahweh, as many passages in the Old Testament suggest (Num. 10:35-36; I Sam. 3:3, 10; 4:4, 7; II Sam. 6:2; II Kings 19:14-15; Jere. 3:16-17; Ezek. 43:7).[25] The technical Hebrew term which expresses this conception of Yahweh's relation to the ark is *yashab,* "to sit enthroned." It appears, for example, in the expression "the ark of the covenant of Yahweh of hosts, *who is enthroned* on the cherubim" (I Sam. 4:4; cf. II Sam. 6:2; II Kings 19:15, *et al.*). If the ark was viewed as a throne, as far as the human eye could tell, it was an *empty* throne upon which Yahweh was invisibly present. Thus it was the visible testimony to the invisible and continuing *presence* among the Hebrews of Yahweh, their God from Sinai. In this respect it parallels the mountain in the E covenant tradition where the view seems to obtain that Yahweh was enthroned on Sinai.[26] The ark was thus a kind of portable Sinai. Walther Eichrodt has suggested in this connection that theologically the ark, as the throne of the invisible Yahweh in the midst of his people, bore witness to the Mosaic experience of the immanence of God.[27]

The report that the tablets of law were kept in the ark (Deut. 10:1-5; Exod. 25:16, 21) is quite credible, although it is not attested by the earliest documents of the Pentateuch. Since the ark was a chest, it would have been a ready receptacle for such objects. If the ark was regarded as Yahweh's throne, the placing of the tablets of the law at his feet would have been entirely consonant with the practice in the ancient Near East of placing documents and treaties at the feet of the deity.[28]

The ark seems to have had at least two specific functions in the life

[24] Eichrodt, *op. cit.,* p. 109.
[25] See especially Martin Dibelius, "Die Lade Jahves," *Forschungen zur Religion und Literatur des Alten Testaments* (Göttingen: Vandenhoeck & Ruprecht, 1906), Heft 7.
[26] *Supra,* p. 47.
[27] Eichrodt, *op. cit.,* pp. 10-11.
[28] *Ibid.,* p. 108; Mendenhall, *op. cit.,* pp. 38-39.

of the people. During the wilderness period, like the *qubbah,* it served to guide the people in their journeys. This is indicated by Num. 10:33: "So they set out from the mount of Yahweh three days' journey; and the ark of the covenant of Yahweh went before them three days' journey, to seek out a resting place for them." The same function also seems to be suggested in Josh. 3 and 4:1-18, where the ark precedes the people as they cross the Jordan river. Closely connected with the function of the ark in leading the people through the wilderness is its usage in connection with war, also like the *qubbah.* The old poem in Num. 10:35-36 makes clear its significance in this respect:

> And whenever the ark set out, Moses said,
> "Arise, O Yahweh,
> and let thy enemies be scattered;
> and let them that hate thee flee before thee."
> And when it rested, he said,
> "Return, O Yahweh,
> to the ten thousand thousands of Israel."

From its first appearance in the wilderness, when it caused Yahweh's enemies to be scattered before him, through the conquest of Jericho (Josh. 6:1-20), the Philistine wars (I Sam. 4), and perhaps even in the time of David (II Sam. 11:11), its presence was deemed vital for victory in war.

Martin Noth has suggested that the ark was the central cult shrine of the twelve-tribe amphictyony which was organized at Shechem (Josh. 24). In a discussion of the "Confederation of the Tribes of Israel" he writes:

It follows that the shrine near Shechem was probably once the amphictyonic center of the Israelite association of tribes; and that appears to be the earliest state of affairs it is possible to discern with any certainty. According to what was said above, the Ark of Yahweh must have been set up on that spot at that time. Admittedly, there is no evidence that it was, but that is not surprising, since in the period of which we have direct historical records, the central shrine of the tribes, and therefore the Ark, had already been shifted from Shechem, and on the old spot only certain traditional ceremonies which derived from the one-time importance of the shrine near Shechem had been preserved because of the usual conservatism inherent in religious observances.[29]

It is not quite correct to say that there is "no evidence" for the presence of the ark at Shechem, since Josh. 8:30-35 places it there. In any event, the ark was probably at Shechem as the central cult shrine of the twelve-tribe confederation following its use during the wilderness wanderings of the Hebrews and its temporary residence at Gilgal, their encampment site while the invasion was being conducted under Joshua (Josh. 4:19-20; 5:9-10; 9:6; 10:16 ff., 43; Judg. 2:1). When the center of tribal power shifted from Manasseh to Ephraim,[30] the ark was removed from the Manassite city of Shechem.[31] It may have been at Bethel briefly (Judg. 20:26-27; cf. 20:18; 21:2),[32] but in the early chapters of I Samuel it is at Shiloh, the Ephraimite city which had become the new cultic center of the amphictyony.[33] It remained at Shiloh until its capture by the Philistines at Aphek (I Sam. 4). When they sent the terrifying ark back to the Hebrews, it was first at Bethshemesh (I Sam. 6:10-21) and then at Kiriath-jearim (I Sam. 7:1-2). There this sacred cultic object of the twelve-tribe amphictyony stayed during the long period when the Philistine pressure almost extinguished the life of the Hebrew people. David, who completely reversed the fortunes of Israel, found the ark and brought it to his newly established capital of Jerusalem (II Sam. 6). As the chief symbol of the old amphictyony, it lent to his new city a unique status. When the temple was built, the ark was placed in the holy of holies (I Kings 8) and evidently remained there until it was destroyed with the temple in 587 B.C.

[29] *History*, p. 93.

[30] Reflected in Jacob's blessing of Ephraim and Manasseh (Gen. 48:8-22).

[31] The destruction of Shechem by Abimelech (Judg. 9) perhaps also figured in this shift. See Walter Harrelson, *The City of Shechem: Its History and Importance* (New York: Union Theological Seminary dissertation, 1953), p. 487.

[32] This is Noth's view (*The History of Israel*, p. 95), but these traditions may have come from the tenth century when circles around Jeroboam I were attempting to magnify Bethel.

[33] See W. F. Albright's treatment in *Archaeology and the Religion of Israel* (3rd. ed. Baltimore: The Johns Hopkins Press, 1953), pp. 103 ff. His contention that Shiloh alone was the amphictyonic center seems to me not to take sufficiently into account the Shechem traditions in the Old Testament.

One thing seems clear concerning the ark throughout its history in the wilderness, at Shechem and Shiloh as chief cult shrine of the twelve-tribe amphictyony, and finally at Jerusalem: it was regarded as standing in a definite relation to the covenant at Sinai. The traditions which indicate that it was constructed at the covenant mountain, the report that the tables of law were kept in it, and the name "ark of the covenant" all suggest this. As the throne where Yahweh was present for his covenant people, the ark was indeed a kind of portable Sinai. Thus the ark continually bore witness to the covenant event and its meaning for the life of the people. Johannes Pedersen has stated it:

The chief thing was that the ark embodied the early history of Israel, and that the whole interaction of the people and its God was associated with it. Hence it is called the Ark of God or the Ark of Yahweh (I Samuel 3, 3; 4, 6 et al.); or the Ark of the covenant and the Ark of the covenant of Yahweh (Num. 10, 33; Josh. 3, 3, 6, 8; 4, 9; I Sam. 4, 3; I Kings 6, 19 etc.) but also the Ark of the testimony, the holy Ark, or "the Ark of thy Strength" (Ps. 132,8), all expressing that the holy strength of Yahweh and his covenant with the people were embodied in it.[34]

When one considers this significance of the ark, another possible function for the shrine suggests itself. *It might well have been used in the dramatic reproduction of the Sinai event in the cult.* If the ark did play a role in connection with a covenant ceremony of the Hebrew people, that ceremony would have been one in which the E rather than the J covenant legend provided the liturgy.

This is suggested first, of course, by the relation of Yahweh to the mountain in E and his relation to the ark. Unlike the J covenant legend, where Yahweh "comes down" to the mountain, in E it is evidently assumed that he is enthroned upon it.[35] Precisely the same picture obtains in the traditions concerning the ark.

Further, if the description of the theophany in the E covenant legend stresses the audible as much as the visual phenomena (unlike

[34] *Israel* (London: Oxford University Press; Copenhagen: Povl Branner, 1940), III-IV, 234-35.
[35] *Supra,* p. 47.

J),[36] it is significant that in the premonarchical period only audible indications of Yahweh's presence are associated with the ark.[37] Not until the ark is brought to Jerusalem, where it is related to another cultic tradition, are such phenomena as the "cloud" and "glory" associated with it (I Kings 8:10-11; cf. Ps. 24:7-10).

That which seems specifically to relate E's covenant legend to the ark is the "trumpet" (shofar). It has previously been suggested that the shofar represents a cultic coloration of the E tradition.[38] The "blast of the trumpet" (qol shofar 19:16, 19; 20:18) is associated with the "thunder" (qol 19:16, 19; 20:18), which represents Yahweh's voice. If the blowing of the shofar was a cultic phenomenon which was absorbed into the legend, it probably represented the thundering voice of Yahweh in the cult.

The cultic object with which the shofar is associated elsewhere in the Old Testament is the ark. When it was blown in connection with the ark, it must have had the same significance. The tradition in Joshua 6, for instance, depicts the ark as having been used in the conquest of Jericho. The ark was carried around the city and was accompanied by the blowing of the shofar (vss. 4, 6, 8, 13). If the ark represented Yahweh's presence in this holy war, the sound of the shofar represented the angry thunder of his voice. The blast of the shofar would have had the same significance when David brought the ark to Jerusalem in a solemn cultic processional (II Sam. 6:15). It was an audible sign to the people that he who was present and spoke in thunder at Sinai was also present upon the ark and continued to speak to them.[39]

The appearance, therefore, of the shofar in the E covenant legend and also with the ark makes plausible the hypothesis that the ark was used in connection with the covenant ceremony in which the E covenant legend was read and re-enacted. The further hypothesis suggests itself that the E covenant tradition was attached, for a time at least, to

[36] Supra, pp. 47-49.
[37] The only possible exception might be I Sam. 4:21-22.
[38] Supra, p. 52.
[39] Beyerlin (Herkunft und Geschichte der ältesten Sinaitraditionen, pp. 155-56) has reached the same conclusion.

the ark and developed its distinctive theological emphases in connection with the ark.

The Tent of Meeting

The second shrine associated with Sinai was the tent of meeting. The tent of meeting appears much less frequently in early traditions than the ark. It is found only in Exod. 33:7-11; Num. 11:16-17, 24-30; ch. 12; and Deut. 31:14-15,[40] all of which belong to J.[41] For this reason the tent is somewhat more obscure than the ark, although not thereby necessarily less important. The later Priestly Code makes much of the tabernacle, which it also calls the tent of meeting (Exod. 26-27, 35-38). However, a definite distinction must be made between the tent-tabernacle of P and its ancestor, the tent of meeting of the early J traditions. It is striking, and undoubtedly significant, that Deuteronomy makes nothing of the tent. The only reference to it in the entire book of Deuteronomy is in 31:14-15, which is generally regarded as being non-Deuteronomic in origin.[42]

Among the names of this shrine, "tent of meeting" ('ohel mo'ed) seems to have been original.[43] Frequently it is referred to merely

[40] Arnulf Kuschke adds II Sam. 7:6 to this list. "Die Lagervorstellung der priesterlichen Erzählung," *Zeitschrift für die alttestamentliche Wissenschaft*, 63 (1951), 82.

[41] Although many authorities assign these passages to E (Georg Beer, *Exodus. Handbuch zum Alten Testament* [Tübingen: J. C. B. Mohr, Paul Siebeck, 1939], p. 157; S. R. Driver, *The Book of Exodus* [Cambridge: At the University Press, 1929], pp. 359-60; A. H. McNeile, *The Book of Exodus. Westminster Commentaries* [New York: Edwin S. Gorham; London: Methuen & Co., 1908], Introduction, p. xxxii), I regard them as J traditions. My discussion of the problem is to be found in *Sinai Covenant Traditions*, pp. 132-36. It should be noted that there are some scholars who take this position: Hans-Joachim Kraus, *Gottesdienst in Israel* (München: Chr. Kaiser Verlag, 1954), p. 30; Arnulf Kuschke, *op. cit.*, p. 82; Martin Noth, *Überlieferungsgeschichte des Pentateuch*, p. 264; and especially Julian Morgenstern, "Biblical Theophanies," *Zeitschrift für Assyriologie*, XXV-XXVI (1911-12), 139-93.

[42] S. R. Driver, *A Critical and Exegetical Commentary on Deuteronomy. International Critical Commentaries.* (New York: Charles Scribner's Sons, 1895), p. 337; G. E. Wright, "The Book of Deuteronomy," *The Interpreter's Bible*, II, 513-14.

[43] It appears six times in the J traditions (Exod. 33:7 [2]; Num. 11:16; 12:4; Deut. 31:14 [2]). P makes extensive use of this name, employing it some 131 times for the tent-tabernacle. Elsewhere it is found in I Sam. 2:22 (LXX omits); I Kings 8:4; I Chron. 6:17; 23:32; II Chron. 1:3, 6, 13; 5:5.

as "the tent." [44] Two names that P uses for the tent-tabernacle are "tent of testimony" (Num. 9:15, *et al.*) and "tabernacle of testimony" (Exod. 38:21, *et al.*).

The Hebrew word *mo'ed* in the expression *'ohel mo'ed* is rendered "meeting." The word has a double meaning. It refers to the "meeting" between Yahweh and the cult official (or the people) at the tent. In P, for example, Yahweh says to Moses concerning the tent of meeting: "I will *meet* with you, to speak there to you. There I will meet with the people of Israel" (Exod. 29:42-43; cf. Exod. 25:22; 30:36). This indicates that the tent was a place of revelation, an oracle site. This is in accordance with the picture in the early traditions (e.g., Exod. 33:7-11). It also means "meeting" in the sense of "assembly," i.e., the meeting together or assembling together of the people. [45] Thus it was a shrine where the covenant people assembled; it provided a locus for the amphictyonic gatherings.

No description of the structure of the tent of meeting is given in the J traditions. The Hebrew word *'ohel* is the common expression for the dwelling of the nomad in the Old Testament (e.g., Gen. 4:20; 9:21, etc.); so it must have been literally a tent. In this respect it is parallel to the *qubbah*. The fact that it appears first at Sinai (Exod. 33:7-11) and then with the Hebrews after they have left the covenant mountain (Num. 11:16-17, 24-30; ch. 12) indicates its portable nature. P's tent-tabernacle, of course, was also a portable structure. Since the *qubbah* was made of red leather, in striking contrast to the ordinary black tents of the Bedouin, it has been plausibly suggested that the tent of meeting was red. [46] The Priestly Code says that "reddened rams' skins" (Exod. 25:5; 26:14, *et al.*) [47] were used in constructing the tent-tabernacle, so it is likely that its cultic ancestor, the tent of meeting, was made of the same material. Acacia wood, which is said to

[44] This is found thirteen times in the J traditions (Exod. 33:7, 8 [2], 9 [2], 10, 11; Num. 11:24, 26; 12:5, 10; Deut. 31:15 [2]), and nineteen times in P. It occurs elsewhere in II Sam. 6:17; 7:6; I Kings 1:39; 2:28-30; 8:4; I Chron. 9:19, 23; 15:1; 16:1;17:5; II Chron. 1:4; 5:5; 24:6.

[45] On this point see especially F. M. Cross, Jr., *op. cit.*, p. 65. Cross prefers the rendering "Tent of Assembly."

[46] Cross, *op. cit.*, pp. 60-61.

[47] The RSV translates the Hebrew expression *me'addim* "tanned," but the color red is clearly indicated.

have been employed in making the framework of the tent-tabernacle (Exod. 26:15, *et al.*), is native to the desert and would probably also have been used in the construction of the simple framework of the earlier tent. Beyond this it is impossible to come to any reasonably secure conclusions concerning the construction of the desert tent. Nothing is known of its arrangement, its dimensions, or its furnishings. Such things as the arrangement of the Priestly tent-tabernacle into a "holy place" and a "most holy place," its dimensions (45′ x 15′ x 15′), its cherubim decorations, etc., are the result of the influence of a Palestinian Canaanite environment.[48]

Nor is there any suggestion in the early traditions preserved by the Jahwist that the ark was kept in the tent of meeting during the wilderness sojourn of the Hebrew people. Moreover, the early ark traditions of the wilderness period do not indicate that it was kept in the tent. For that matter, there is no suggestion even in the ark traditions in I Samuel that it was protected by the tent. I Sam. 2:22 does place the tent of meeting at Shiloh, but this is a gloss dependent upon Exod. 38:8.[49] Even this tradition does not say the ark was in the tent. Not until the time of David did the ark find its resting place within the tent: "And, they brought *the ark of Yahweh,* and set it in its place, inside *the tent* which David had pitched for it; and David offered burnt offerings and peace offerings before Yahweh (II Sam. 6:17; cf. 7:2).

The only clear function of the tent of meeting in the early traditions is its use in connection with oracles. It was a tent of revelation, the place where one who sought the word of the Lord could go: "Now Moses used to take the tent and pitch it outside the camp, far off

[48] Cross, *op. cit.,* pp. 61-63.

[49] On I Sam. 2:22 Henry Preserved Smith comments: "The second half of the verse brings an additional accusation against the priests that they *used to lie with the women who ministered at the gate of the Tent of Meeting.* The sentence is suspicious; first, because it is lacking in LXXB. In the second place the original narrator has stated his accusation above and this should have been made a part of that accusation. Finally, the whole narrative, except in this verse, is ignorant of *women who ministered* and of the *Tent of Meeting* as established at Shiloh. The language is borrowed from the Priestly document of the Pentateuch, Ex. 38:8. For these reasons the half verse is to be regarded as a later interpolation (We., Kl., Dr., Bu.)." *A Critical and Exegetical Commentary on the Books of Samuel, International Critical Commentaries* (New York: Charles Scribner's Sons, 1902), p. 20.

from the camp; and he called it the tent of meeting. And every one who sought Yahweh would go out to the tent of meeting, which was outside the camp" (Exod. 33:7). Although Moses pitches the tent and presumably is in charge, it seems to be available to everyone. In the subsequent verses of the passage, however, Moses alone goes to the tent where Yahweh speaks to him face to face (vss. 8-11). These verses would seem to have been influenced by circles that desired to magnify Moses as a priestly figure and in their present form probably represent a subsequent although early development. In any event, Exod. 33:7-11 reveals clearly the early oracular function of the tent of meeting. The same is true of Num. 11:16-17, 24-30 and ch. 12. The Priestly author too has preserved traditions concerning the oracular function of the tent-tabernacle (Exod. 29:42-43; Num. 14:10, 26 ff., et al.).

In these traditions it is clear that Yahweh's relationship to the tent of meeting is quite different from his relationship to the ark. He is not enthroned upon it. Rather from time to time he "comes down" (yarad Exod. 33:9; Num. 11:17, 25; 12:5) in a "cloud" ('anan Num. 11:25; 12:10) or "pillar of cloud" ('ammud 'anan Exod. 33:9; Num. 12:5; Deut. 31:15) to the tent to meet with Moses. This, of course, is precisely the same picture that is found in the J covenant tradition. There too he is depicted as being enveloped in a "cloud" ('anan Exod. 19:9a; 34:5) and "coming down" (yarad Exod. 19:11, 18, 20; 34:5) to the mountain. Thus the tent of meeting, like the ark, was a kind of miniature and portable Sinai. It was the shrine where the Sinai theophany was subsequently repeated in the cultic life of the covenant people.[50] If the ark testified to the Mosaic experience of the nearness and immanence of Yahweh whose presence dwelt in the midst of his people, the tent testified to the Mosaic experience of the distance and transcendence of Yahweh who descended from above to appear to his people.[51]

In regard to the history of the tent of meeting between the wilderness period, where it first appeared, and its presence at Jerusalem in

[50] Martin Noth makes this point in his discussion of the tent traditions. *Überlieferungsgeschichte des Pentateuch*, p. 265.
[51] Eichrodt, *op. cit.*, pp. 110-11.

the time of David there is a good deal of obscurity. If it is recognized that before the ark was brought to Jerusalem it was not kept in the tent, there is little reason to think that the tent was ever at the cult site of Shiloh, in spite of I Sam. 2:22 and Josh. 18:1. Its appearance in the former passage is evidently a gloss.[52] The latter represents the only occurrence of the tent in the book of Joshua and it attributes no function or significance to the shrine. It too is a gloss, inserted by a later "priestly hand," [53] and undoubtedly resulted from the later assumption that if the ark was at Shiloh in the past the tent too must have been there. Nor is the Chronicler's report reliable which places the tent at Gibeon (II Chron. 1:3, 13; cf. I Chron. 16:39, 21:29). Martin Noth has shown that this tradition rests on Exod. 25 ff. and I Kings 3:4 ff., and developed from the assumption that Solomon could only have made his Gibeon sacrifice at the great cult object which had been constructed under Moses at Sinai, viz., the tent of meeting.[54]

If Shiloh and Gibeon are thus excluded, there is no evidence that the tent was ever north of Jerusalem. And since the early traditions concerning the tent of meeting have all been preserved by the *southern* Jahwist, one would suspect that its residence was located at some cult center in the southern part of Palestine before the time of David. In the Jahwist, the dominant cultic site in the South is *Hebron*. According to J Hebron was a site where Abraham built an altar (Gen. 13:18) and it is subsequently associated closely with this patriarch (Gen. 15:1 ff.; 18:1 ff.). This is precisely where Gerhard von Rad has suggested that the tent of meeting was at home:

The distinctively alien character of the few passages about the Tent of Meeting within the other old Hexateuch traditions prompts the question whether an addition from some quite different sphere of tradition is not present here. Is it not possible that the Tent, which was obviously foreign

[52] *Supra*, p. 65.

[53] John Bright, "The Book of Joshua," *The Interpreter's Bible* (Nashville: Abingdon Press, 1953), II, 546.

[54] Noth, *Überlieferungsgeschichtliche Studien* (Halle [Saale]: Max Niemeyer, 1943), p. 137, n. 6.

to the Shechem amphictyony, belonged originally to the south, perhaps as the sanctuary of the old amphictyony of the six tribes in or near Hebron? [55]

If the tent of meeting was at Hebron, it was evidently brought there from the wilderness area south of Judah. The Hebrews are said to have spent most of the time after the exodus and before the conquest in the area around Kadesh-barnea; so presumably the tent was with them there before it was removed to Hebron. From Hebron it was brought to Jerusalem by David where the ark was placed in it (II Sam. 6:17). Undoubtedly the tent of meeting at Jerusalem in David's time was a highly developed cult object and much more elaborate than the old desert shrine. F. M. Cross, in fact, has plausibly suggested that the tent-tabernacle described in the Priestly Code was in reality the tent of David's Jerusalem.[56] When the temple was built by Solomon, and the ark placed within it (I Kings 8), the tent was superseded and was evidently no longer used.[57]

If the ark of the covenant was used in the dramatic reproduction of the Sinai event in the cult, and the Elohist covenant legend was attached to it, a similar function for the tent of meeting suggests itself, as well as a similar relation between the tent and the Jahwist covenant legend.

Although found in three different books of the Pentateuch, the four tent traditions are all characterized by essentially the same language and theological concerns. Exod. 33:7-11 depicts the tent as a shrine located outside the camp to which Moses goes to consult Yahweh. When Moses goes out to the tent, Yahweh comes down in the pillar of cloud and speaks with him face to face. Num. 11:16-17, 24-25 is an account of the sharing of the spirit which is upon Moses with the seventy elders at the tent. Numbers 12 contains the story of the challenge to the authority of Moses by Miriam and Aaron:[58] "Has Yahweh indeed spoken only through Moses? Has he not spoken through us also?" When Yahweh descends to the tent in the pillar of cloud, the

---

[55] *Studies in Deuteronomy* (Chicago: Henry Regnery Co., 1953), p. 43. Arnulf Kuschke too believes the tent of meeting was at Hebron, *op. cit.*, pp. 104-5.

[56] Cross, *op. cit.*, p. 63.

[57] See especially I Kings 8:4.

[58] In the orginal form of the tradition it was probably Miriam alone who was involved.

controversy is decided in Moses' favor. In Deut. 31:14-15 the transfer of authority from Moses to Joshua takes place at the tent when Yahweh again descends in the pillar of cloud.

There are a number of affinities of language and thought between these four traditions and the J covenant legend. The most obvious point of contact between them is the theophany, as has already been suggested.[59] The picture of Yahweh "coming down" in a "cloud" or a "pillar of cloud" to the mountain and to the tent is the same.

Further, the tent of meeting in these traditions is regarded in somewhat the same way as the holy mountain in the J covenant tradition. In the latter Sinai is set apart from the people by the placing of bounds (Exod. 19:12-13; 34:3). Only Moses and the select few have full access to the mountain. Similarly the tent is "outside the camp, far off from the camp" (33:7). The people remain at their own tents while Moses goes to the cultic tent to meet Yahweh (vss. 8-11).[60] In the other traditions too the tent is apart from the people; only Moses and the seventy elders (Num. 11:16-17, 24-25), Moses, Aaron and Miriam (Num. 12), or Moses and Joshua (Deut. 31:14-15) go out to this shrine where Yahweh comes down to meet them.

The emphasis upon Moses and his unique relation to Yahweh is fully as striking in the tent traditions as in the J covenant tradition. The Jahwist legend depicts Moses as the great priestly covenant mediator appointed by Yahweh (Exod. 19:9a), with whom Yahweh makes a covenant (34:27), and whose office will continue "for ever" (19:9a). He is granted a special theophany (33:18-23; 34:5), and to him alone is God's name proclaimed (Exod. 33:17; 34:6). Similarly in Exod. 33:7-11 Moses pitches the tent and is the key figure in relation to it. Only when he enters the tent does the theophany occur; then the cloud descends and Yahweh speaks with him "as a man speaks to his friend" (vs. 11). Joshua is in attendance at the tent, but he is only a young man who is Moses' servant. Num. 11:16-17, 24-25 stresses the authority of Moses in relation to the seventy elders. In this tradition

[59] *Supra,* p. 66.
[60] It is true than in Exod. 33:7 the tent seems to be accessible to anyone who seeks Yahweh. But in vss. 8-11, which reflect a subsequent but early development, the tent is evidently accessible only to Moses and his servant Joshua.

the "spirit" does not come directly from God to the elders; rather some of the "spirit" that is upon Moses is withdrawn and placed upon them. He is, as it were, a channel of the spirit of God. Numbers 12 too underscores Moses' authority. The key question is: "Has Yahweh indeed spoken *only* through Moses?" (vs. 2). Yahweh's answer at the tent of meeting is unequivocal:

6 Hear my words: If there is a prophet among you, I Yahweh make myself known to him in a vision, I speak with him in a dream. 7 Not so with my servant Moses; he is entrusted with all my house. 8 With him I speak mouth to mouth, clearly, and not in dark speech; and he beholds the form of Yahweh. Why then were you not afraid to speak against my servant Moses? Num. 12:6-8

Deut. 31:14-16 agrees. Joshua derives his authority over the covenant people from Moses who commissions him at the tent of meeting.

Finally, a point of contact between the J covenant legend and the tent tradition in Num. 11:16-17, 24-25 is the appearance of the seventy elders. Nowhere else in the Old Testament do seventy elders appear. In the latter tradition the seventy elders are the recipients of the spirit of Moses; in the former they accompany Moses, Aaron, Nadab, and Abihu up the mountain to see God and to partake of the covenant meal (Exod. 24:1-2, 9-11).[61]

These several points of similarity between the tent of meeting traditions and the J covenant legend, then, are good evidence for the plausibility of the hypothesis that the tent was used in a covenant ceremony in which the J covenant legend was read and re-enacted. It would, further, seem likely that the J covenant tradition for a time was attached to the tent and developed its distinctive theological emphases in connection with the tent.

If the E covenant tradition is to be associated with the ark and the J covenant tradition with the tent, we have some indication of the

---

[61] In this connection it should also be noted that there is a definite relation between the rare verb *'atsal* "lay aside, reserve, withdraw, withhold" in Num. 11:17, 25 and the equally unusual noun *'atsil* "noble, chief man" in Exod. 24:11. The seventy elders are "chief men" only because they have been privileged to share some of the spirit "withdrawn" from Moses. On this point see Gray, *op. cit.*, p. 116.

time when the two covenant traditions with their distinctive covenant theologies emerged in the life of the covenant people. Since both the ark and the tent were evidently with the Hebrews in the wilderness after the exodus under Moses, but after that were separated, the ark being at Shechem and Shiloh before it was removed to Jerusalem and the tent at Hebron before it was taken to Jerusalem, the wilderness period suggests itself as the time when the two traditions first emerged. The central site of the Hebrews during their wilderness wanderings was Kadesh-barnea, where they are said to have remained "many days" (Deut. 1:46). Thus Kadesh presents itself as the possible site where these two covenant traditions and theologies first came to expression.

Chapter Three

Controversy
at
Kadesh

KADESH-BARNEA was located in the northeastern section of the Sinaitic peninsula. Since the last century it has generally been identified with 'Ain Kedeis, the site of a good spring, or with 'Ain Qudeirat, an even more copious spring three miles northwest.[1] Another spring in the immediate area is 'Ain Qoseimeh. Thus Kadesh was evidently some fifty miles south of Beersheba, the city which traditionally marked the southern boundary of Palestine. With its adequate water supply Kadesh was an attractive area for wandering nomadic groups.

The name "Kadesh" in Hebrew means "sacred," so it was evidently regarded as a holy site. In Gen. 14:7 Kadesh is also called "En Mishpat" ("Well of Judgment"). Another name which the site bears is "Meri-

[1] H. Clay Trumbull in his work *Kadesh-barnea* (Philadelphia: John D. Wattles & Co., 1895) established with some certainty this area as the site of Kadesh-barnea; cf. Emil G. Kraeling, *Rand McNally Bible Atlas* (New York: Thomas Nelson & Sons, 1956), p. 117, and George Ernest Wright and Floyd Vivian Filson, *The Westminster Historical Atlas to the Bible* (Philadelphia: The Westminster Press, rev. ed., 1956), p. 68.

bah" ("Strife, Contention, Litigation"). This word is found in the expression "Waters of Meribah of Kadesh" (Num. 27:14; Deut. 32:51; Ezek. 47:19; 48:28; cf. Deut. 33:2), in the shorter form "Waters of Meribah" (Num. 20:13, 24; Deut. 33:8; Ps. 81:7; Heb. vs. 8; 106:32); and alone (Exod. 17:7; Ps. 95:8). "Massah" ("Testing, Trial") is sometimes equated with Meribah (Exod. 17:7; Deut. 33:8; Ps. 95:8; cf. Deut. 6:16; 9:22), so it is undoubtedly yet another name for Kadesh. These several names, Kadesh, En Mishpat, Meribah, and Massah, would seem to indicate that the site must have been a sacred shrine which was the center of divine law and legal decisions.[2]

In the books of Exodus and Numbers there are several traditions which probably are to be associated with Kadesh. Not until Num. 13:26 is it specifically stated that the Hebrews are at Kadesh after the covenant at Sinai. It is the Priestly writer [3] who states: "And they [the spies] came to Moses and Aaron and to all the congregation of the people of Israel in the wilderness of Paran, at Kadesh." This refers to the return of the spies who had been sent out by Moses to explore Canaan, so it must be assumed that the Hebrews had arrived at Kadesh previously. In Num. 13:3 P speaks of the Wilderness of Paran as being the point of departure for the spies and thus regarded Kadesh as located in that region.[4] It might be concluded from Num. 12:16 [5] that the spies were sent out immediately after the arrival and encampment in the Wilderness of Paran. But Num. 10:12 (P) places the arrival in Paran *before* the incidents in Numbers 11–12. In their present form the traditions in these latter two chapters are actually not firmly attached to any geographical site. It is with the tent of meeting that they are associated. Even though there is some uncertainty in the present arrangement of the traditions as to just when the Hebrews

[2] See Gerhard von Rad, *Theologie*, I, 21; cf. R. Brinker, *The Influence of Sanctuaries in Early Israel* (Manchester: University Press, 1946), p. 139; Theophile James Meek, *Hebrew Origins* (New York: Harper & Brothers, rev. ed., 1950), p. 37.

[3] The source analysis of Numbers in this section in general follows that of George Buchanan Gray, *A Critical and Exegetical Commentary on Numbers*. Divergences will be noted.

[4] The exact extent of the Wilderness of Paran is uncertain. It is not impossible that the Wilderness of Paran included Kadesh. See Kraeling's discussion of the problem, *op. cit.*, p. 116.

[5] Gray terms 16*b* an "editorial link," *op. cit.*, p. 128.

arrived at Kadesh, Num. 20:22 (P) definitely notes their *departure*: "And they journeyed from Kadesh, and the people of Israel, the whole congregation, came to Mount Hor." It would therefore not be unreasonable to conclude that most of the traditions in Numbers 11-20 are to be connected with Kadesh.[6] This would include such narrative traditions as the manna and quail (ch. 11), the seventy elders at the tent of meeting (ch. 11), the complaint of Miriam and Aaron against Moses (ch. 12), the abortive invasion (14:39-45; cf. 21:1-3), the rebellion of Korah (ch. 16), the death of Miriam (20:1), and the miraculous flow of water from the rock (20:2-13).

There are other traditions too which must be considered as possibly standing in some relation to Kadesh. This would seem to be the case with most of the traditions in Exod. 15:23–ch. 18.[7] It is likely, for instance, that Exod. 17:1-7 is a parallel account of the water incident at Kadesh which is found in Num. 20:2-13. The names Massah and Meribah (Exod. 17:7) and the motif of "proving" (vss. 2, 7) suggest this, as well as the fact that Kadesh was the appropriate place for the wonder of water from the rock.[8] If this is the case, the reference to Horeb in vs. 6 would be a later addition to the text.

Also the battle with the Amalekites (Exod. 17:8-16) can best be understood as occurring in the vicinity of Kadesh. Gen. 14:7 associates this tribe with the area of En Mishpat-Kadesh, and Num. 14:45 preserves the memory of a conflict the Hebrews had with the Amalekites north of Kadesh. In fact it has been suggested that the tradition in Exod. 17:8-16 reflects a battle the Hebrews fought with the Amalekites for the possession of Kadesh.[9]

Since both traditions in Exodus 17 are evidently to be associated

[6] Bernhard Anderson takes the position that all the JE material in Num. 11-20 had its original setting at Kadesh. *Understanding the Old Testament,* pp. 63-64; cf. Robert H. Pfeiffer, *Religion in the Old Testament* (New York: Harper & Brothers, 1961), p. 51.

[7] It has frequenly been pointed out that these traditions are evidently to be associated with Kadesh, e.g., Elias Auerbach, *Moses* (Amsterdam: G. J. A. Ruys, 1953), pp. 78-104; Hugo Gressman, *Die Anfänge Israels. Die Schriften des Alten Testaments* (Göttingen: Vandenhoeck & Ruprecht, 1922), pp. 86-94; Pfeiffer, *op. cit.,* p. 51; Ernst Sellin, *Geschichte des israelitisch-jüdischen Volkes* (Leipzig: Quelle & Meyer, 1924), I, 65-73, *et al.*

[8] See especially Trumbull, *op. cit.,* p. 273.

[9] Sellin, *op. cit.,* p. 69.

with Kadesh, it is probable that the Jethro traditions in the following chapter are also to be connected with that site. The Jethro incident is not likely to have occurred at the "mountain of God" (vs. 5), since the Hebrews are not said to have arrived at Sinai until 19:1-2. Chapter 18 suggests no movement of the people after the events of chapter 17, so evidently it is assumed that the Jethro visit occurred at the same site. The lengthy section in this chapter concerning the administration of law (vss. 13-26) definitely suggests a cultic site with a judicial orientation. This could be Kadesh. Moreover, the appointment of judges in vss. 25-26 is paralleled by the tradition in Num. 11:16-17, which we have already suggested probably belongs to Kadesh.

In addition to Exod. 17–18, it is not impossible that the J material in chapter 16 concerning the manna and quails is also to be related to Kadesh. The same phenomena in Numbers 11 probably are to be associated with the site.

Finally, it is likely that Exod. 15:23-26 is a Kadesh tradition.[10] The giving of law in vss. 25b-26 fits in well with the reputation of Kadesh as a judicial site and the reference to Yahweh's "proving" the people (vs. 26b), as the Hebrew verb makes clear,[11] is a clear allusion to Massah, one of the names of Kadesh. Also the phenomenon of the spring called Marah (vss. 23-25a) fits in well with a Kadesh location. In fact, it has frequently been suggested that the three names, Meribah, Massah and Marah, refer to the three springs at Kadesh.[12]

To Kadesh, then, can be assigned most of the traditions in Exod. 15:23–ch. 18 and Num. 11–20. These form the core of the Kadesh traditions for the Mosaic period.

Southern Tribes at Kadesh

It has previously been concluded that the Joseph tribes were the dominant Hebrew tribes in Egypt, and that they, along with some Levites, experienced the event of the exodus and concluded the covenant at Sinai. The Joseph tribes, of course, were Rachel tribes,[13] who

[10] See Rowley, *From Joseph to Joshua,* p. 104; Auerbach, *op. cit.,* pp. 78-82.

[11] The noun "Massah" ("Testing, Try") is derived from the verb *"nissah"* ("to test, try, prove") which appears here.

[12] E.g., Sellin, *op. cit.,* p. 71. Rowley, in fact, says there is a fourth spring in the vicinity which was named En Mishpat. *Op. cit.,* p. 104.

[13] Rachel is the mother of Joseph in Gen. 30:22-24.

later settled in the central mountain range of Palestine. From Sinai these Hebrews went to Kadesh.[14] Thus Rachel tribes must have been at Kadesh during the Mosaic age, i.e., in the first half of the thirteenth century B.C.

On the other hand, however, there are a number of traditions which persistently connect certain *southern tribes* with Kadesh and its general vicinity.[15] There is the early tradition of the spies sent out from Kadesh, in which *Caleb* is dominant and gives the minority report (Num. 13:17b-20, 22-24, 26b-31, 33; cf. Deut. 1:19-36).[16] Caleb is the eponymous ancestor of the Calebites and is closely associated with Judah, historically the most important of the Leah tribes (Num. 13:6; Judg. 1:11 ff.; I Sam. 3:14).[17] He is said to have occupied Hebron, the primary cult center in the South (Judg. 1:20; Josh. 14:13; 15:13-14; 21:9-12).[18]

If Caleb is to be connected with Kadesh, the same would seem to be the case with the other southern tribes with which Caleb is associated in Judg. 1:1-21: *Judah* and *Simeon* (vss. 3 ff., 8-10, 16 ff.), *Othniel* (vss. 11-15), and the *Kenites* (vs. 16). The striking similarity between vss. 16-17 of Judg. 1 and Num. 21:1-3 has long been recognized.[19] The former reads:

16 And the descendants of the Kenite, Moses' father-in-law, went up with the people of Judah from the city of palms into the wilderness of Judah, which lies in the Negeb near Arad; and they went and settled with the people. 17 And Judah went with Simeon his brother, and they defeated

---

[14] In the light of the present arrangement of the Pentateuchal traditions it might be concluded that these Hebrews went immediately to Kadesh from Egypt (Exod. 15:23–ch. 18), then to Sinai (Exod. 19–Num. 10), and returned to Kadesh (Num. 11–20). This seems unlikely, especially if the traditional location of Sinai at Jebel Musa is assumed. It is more probable that the Kadesh traditions in Exod. 15:23–ch. 18 and Num. 11–20 belong together and reflect events that occurred *after* the Sinai experience.

[15] By "southern tribes" is meant tribes which occupied the southern part of Palestine after the time of the conquest.

[16] For a literary analysis of Num. 13–14 see Gray, *op. cit.,* pp. 130-32; cf. also Rowley, *From Joseph to Joshua,* p. 105.

[17] The Leah tribes are those born to Leah according to Gen. 29:31-35; 30:14-20, i.e., Reuben, Simeon, Levi, Judah, Issachar, and Zebulun.

[18] See Noth, *History,* p. 76 on Caleb.

[19] See, for example, C. F. Burney's treatment of the two passages in *Israel's Settlement in Canaan* (London: Oxford University Press, 1921), pp. 28-30.

the Canaanites who inhabited Zephath, and utterly destroyed it. So the name of the city was called Hormah.

The latter passage reads:

1 When the Canaanite, the king of Arad, who dwelt in the Negeb, heard that Israel was coming by the way. of Atharim, he fought against Israel, and took some of them captive. 2 And Israel vowed a vow to Yahweh, and said, "If thou wilt indeed give this people into my hand, then I will utterly destroy their cities." 3 And Yahweh hearkened to the voice of Israel, and gave over the Canaanites; and they utterly destroyed them and their cities; so the name of the place was called Hormah.

The reference to Arad in both passages and the explanation of the name Hormah mark them as parallel accounts of the same incident. And Num. 21:1-3 is undoubtedly correct when it indicates that the occupation of this area was from the south after the Hebrews left Kadesh.[20] Thus one can conclude that Num. 21:1-3 and Judg. 1:1-21, along with Num. 13–14 and Josh. 15:14-19, reflect an invasion of Palestine from Kadesh on the part of these southern tribes.[21] This means that Judah, Simeon, Othniel, and Kenites, as well as Caleb, were connected with Kadesh at some time.

In addition to Judah and Simeon, another Leah tribe that is related to Kadesh is *Levi*. The blessing of Moses in Deuteronomy 33 places Levi at Massah-Meribah, i.e., Kadesh:

> 8 And of Levi he said,
> "Give to Levi thy Thummim,
> and thy Urim to thy godly one,
> whom thou didst test at Massah,
> with whom thou didst strive at
> the waters of Meribah;
> 9 who said of his father and mother,
> 'I regard them not';
> he disowned his brothers,
> and ignored his children.

[20] *Ibid.*, p. 29.
[21] As many scholars have held, e.g., Burney, *op. cit.*, pp. 27-34; Meek, *op. cit.*, pp. 40-41; Noth, *History*, pp. 76-77; Rowley, *op. cit.*, pp. 101 ff.

For they observed thy word,
    and kept thy covenant.
10 They shall teach Jacob thy ordinances,
    and Israel thy law;
    they shall put incense before thee,
    and whole burnt offering upon
    thy altar.
11 Bless, O Yahweh, his substance,
    and accept the work of his hands;
    crush the loins of his adversaries,
    of those that hate him, that they
    rise not again."

DEUT. 33:8-11

These scattered traditions which relate Judah, Simeon, Levi, Caleb, Othniel, and Kenites to the area of Kadesh have been dealt with in a variety of ways by those scholars who have taken them seriously. Generally, they are interpreted as reflecting some kind of a confederation at Kadesh in which southern tribes were involved, as well as an invasion by these tribes from the south. Beyond that there is much diversity of opinion.[22] One thing which seems to be fairly certain is that Kadesh was not an important cultic site for any Hebrews much before the Mosaic age. This sanctuary has no significance in the patriarchal legends of Genesis and not until after the exodus event are Hebrews specifically said to have come there. If only the Joseph tribes and a few Levites were in Egypt, it is probable that some Hebrews had already been at Kadesh for a time before their arrival. These would have been Judah, Simeon, and other Levites, along with Kenites, Calebites, and Othnielites.

The Judahites, Simeonites, and Levites at Kadesh in the thirteenth century may have represented remnants of a six-tribe amphictyony which flourished for a time in Palestine during the previous century.

[22] Among the more recent works that have dealt with the Kadesh traditions in some detail are Meek, *op. cit.,* pp. 35-41; Rowley, *op. cit.* (a succinct outline of his position is to be found on p. 164); C. A. Simpson, *The Early Traditions of Israel* (Oxford: Basil Blackwell, 1948), pp. 419 ff. The following historical reconstruction has been influenced to some extent by these three works, but even more so by Burney, *op. cit.,* and Otto Procksch, *Theologie des Alten Testaments* (Gütersloh: C. Bertelsmann, 1950), pp. 55 ff.; 93 ff.; 99 ff.; 103 ff.

This amphictyony would have been comprised of the six Leah tribes: Reuben, Simeon, Levi, Judah, Issachar, and Zebulun (Gen. 29:31-35; 30:17-20; cf. Gen. 49:4-15).[23] That it existed before the Mosaic age is evident from the fact that Reuben, Simeon, and Levi, although pictured as the three eldest sons of Leah and thus at some time dominant tribes, did not possess such significance during the Mosaic age or subsequently.[24] The late patriarchal period would be the most probable time for its existence. Shechem was probably the cult center of this confederation, as is suggested by such passages as Gen. 33:18-20; ch. 34; 35:1-4.[25]

Gen. 33:18-20 may reflect the movement of these Hebrews into Palestine from the east:

18 And Jacob came safely to the city of Shechem, which is in the land of Canaan, on his way from Paddan-aram; and he camped before the city. 19 And from the sons of Hamor, Shechem's father, he bought for a hundred pieces of money the piece of land on which he had pitched his tent. 20 There he erected an altar and called it El-Elohe-Israel.

The word which the RSV renders "safely" might better be translated "peace-minded" or "peacefully." [26] It indicates that the settlement of the Hebrews in this area was without violence. Their relations with the "sons of Hamor" were originally amicable.[27] That there was some

[23] A six-tribe amphictyony antedating the later twelve-tribe amphictyony seems first to have been proposed by Martin Noth in *Das System der zwölf Stämme Israels, Beiträge zur Wissenschaft vom Alten und Neuen Testament* (Stuttgart: W. Kohlhammer, 1930), Vierte Folge, Heft 1, pp. 92 ff. It has been accepted by a number of other scholars since, e.g., Harrelson, *Shechem,* pp. 223 ff.; Procksch, *Theologie,* p. 59, *et al.*

[24] See Noth's argument in this regard, *History,* pp. 88-89; cf. Procksch, *op. cit.,* p. 106.

[25] Harrelson's treatment of these passages is especially suggestive from this standpoint. *Op. cit.,* pp. 223-83

[26] This is the suggestion of Eduard Nielsen, *Shechem: A Tradition-Historical Investigation* (Copenhagen: G. E. C. Gad, 1955), pp. 223-24.

[27] On the expression "sons of Hamor," i.e., "sons of [the] Ass" see Albright, *Archaeology and the Religion of Israel,* p. 113. Since in the Mari texts "killing an ass" is equivalent to "making a covenant," it has frequently been suggested that some kind of covenant tradition obtained among the Shechemites before the Hebrews arrived there. They may have viewed themselves as being in a covenant relation with their god. This old Shechemite covenant tradition might have influenced the later Sinaitic covenant tradition of the Hebrews at certain points when Shechem became their chief cult site in the early period of the twelve-tribe confederation. See below, Chap. Four, pp. 112, n. 28, 116-17.

kind of treaty between the Hebrews and the native Shechemites is evident from this passage, as well as chapter 34. Although the relations between the Shechemites and the Hebrews were close, the latter undoubtedly had their own traditions and cultic concerns.[28] The name given to the altar reveals both the name of the six-tribe amphictyony and the name of its God: "El-Elohe-Israel" ("El, the God of Israel" vs. 19). The amphictyony was thus called "Israel," which later became the name of the twelve-tribe confederation at Shechem (Josh. 24). The God of this group was simply "El," i.e., "God," or "El, the God of Israel."

Shechem was the cultic center of this league, but its individual members must have ranged north and south in the hill country of Palestine. Perhaps Simeon and Levi were in the more immediate vicinity of Shechem, and thus close enough for the incident of Genesis 34 to have occurred. This would have been the area occupied by the Joseph tribes in the next century. Zebulun and Issachar probably were in the region immediately to the southwest of the Sea of Galilee, the same general area that is said to have belonged to them from the time of Joshua. Reuben must have been *west* of the Jordan during this period, probably in the territory northwest of the Dead Sea.[29] Judah then would likely have been farther south, in the neighborhood of Bethlehem. It was this same area, of course, that Judah reoccupied by force in the next century in connection with the invasion led by Joshua.

It is possible that the Tell el-Amarna letters have preserved the memory of the incursion of these Hebrews into Palestine during the first half of the fourteenth century.[30] Written by native kings of cities in Palestine, Phoenicia, and Syria to the Egyptian pharaohs, Amenophis III (1406-1370 b.c.) and Amenophis IV (Akhenaton) (1370-53 b.c.), these letters reflect the unrest and instability of this part of the Egyptian

[28] A massive temple has been discovered by archaeologists at Shechem which was certainly in use during this period. It continued to stand until the 12th century b.c. destruction of the city, evidently by Abimelech (Judg. 9). See the report on the 1960 excavations at Shechem in the *Bulletin of the American Schools of Oriental Research* (No. 161, Feb., 1961, especially pp. 28-39). Whether the Hebrews themselves made regular use of this particular temple is uncertain.

[29] As Noth has plausibly conjectured. *History,* pp. 63-65.

[30] Procksch explicitly relates the six-tribe Leah amphictyony to the 'Apiru movement of the Amarna texts. *Op. cit.,* pp. 58, 69.

empire during the period.[31] They specifically mention a group of troublesome people called 'Apiru who are making incursions into the general area. While the Hebrews cannot be simply equated with the 'Apiru of these letters, the two groups may be related. It is perhaps best to think of the biblical Hebrews as being part of a larger 'Apiru movement.[32] In any event, there is possibly a parallel between Hamor and sons who make a treaty with the Hebrews at Shechem (Gen. 33:18-20; ch. 34) and Labayu and sons, of Shechem, who likewise reach an agreement with the 'Apiru in the Amarna letters.[33] Of course, the 'Apiru are not only in the Shechem area but also farther south in Palestine. The communications of Milkilu of Gezer, 'Abdu-Heba of Jerusalem and Shuwardata of Hebron refer to the 'Apiru as being in their territory. This would be in accordance with our previous suggestion that some of the Leah tribes were located in the southern part of Palestine. The picture that the Amarna letters suggest in this period in Palestine is not that of a devastating conquest of key towns, as is found in Joshua 1-12. It is rather one of gradual infiltration by nomadic groups who are troublesome, to be sure, but are frequently willing to enter into treaties with the native inhabitants of the land. It is the same general kind of picture that Genesis gives of the patriarchs.

Sometime in the fourteenth century B.C., perhaps toward the middle of it, this Leah amphictyony was broken up. The occasion of its disruption can possibly be seen in Genesis 34.[34] Simeon and Levi sought to avenge some actual or presumed wrong on the part of the native Shechemites. This was a violation of the covenant the Leah group had with the people of Shechem and it made the Hebrews "odious to the inhabitants of the land" (vs. 30). The result was the scattering of those two tribes, of which the blessing of Jacob speaks:

[31] Some of the more important Amarna letters appear in James B. Pritchard (ed.), *Ancient Near Eastern Texts* (Princeton, New Jersey: Princeton University Press, 1950), pp. 483-90.

[32] This is Rowley's position. *Op. cit.*, pp. 55-56; cf. Albright, *From the Stone Age to Christianity*, pp. 182-83.

[33] Rowley speaks of the Labayu incident as being "reminiscent of the story recorded in Genesis xxxiv." *Op. cit.*, p. 44.

[34] The present writer follows Harrelson's position. *Op. cit.*, pp. 272-73.

> 5 Simeon and Levi are brothers;
>   weapons of violence are their swords.
> 6 O my soul, come not into their council;
>   O my spirit, be not joined to their company;
> 7 Cursed be their anger, for it is fierce;
>   and their wrath, for it is cruel!
> I will divide them in Jacob
>   and scatter them in Israel.
>
> GEN. 49:5-7

Reuben too seems to have suffered some catastrophe about this time. Its exact nature cannot be determined, but it evidently involved some kind of tribal conflict (Gen. 35:22).[35] Both Reuben's past pre-eminence and subsequent downfall are referred to in the blessing of Jacob:

> 3 Reuben, you are my first-born,
>   my might, and the first fruits of my strength,
>   pre-eminent in pride and pre-eminent in power.
> 4 Unstable as water, you shall not
>   have pre-eminence
>   because you went up to your father's bed;
>   then you defiled it—you went up to my couch!
>
> GEN. 49:3-4

The other tribes would necessarily have been weakened by the dissolution of their amphictyony. Their residence in the land, which at best had probably been tenuous, became even more precarious. Adding to their troubles during this period was the rapid increase of the native princes of the land. As the Canaanite rulers moved out from the larger towns to the more sparsely settled areas, they must have displaced some of the Leah tribes, particularly those in central and southern Palestine.[36]

So the second half of the fourteenth century saw the Leah tribes fairly well scattered. Perhaps Issachar and Zebulun alone were able to remain without interruption in the region they had occupied. And

---

[35] See Burney, *op. cit.*, pp. 50-51.

[36] See W. F. Albright, *The Biblical Period* (Pittsburgh: Biblical Colloquium, 1950), p. 14 and Procksch, *op. cit.*, p. 70.

they must have continued to maintain friendly relations with the Shechemites. This would account for the peaceful occupation of central Palestine by other Hebrews under Joshua in the next century. Reuben, greatly reduced in size and influence, may have moved to the eastern side of the Jordan, in the general region occupied by this tribe from the conquest of Joshua.

The other tribes, Simeon, Levi, and Judah, were pushed far southward to the arid Negeb, where they evidently resumed a nomadic existence after a period of seminomadic life in Palestine. Since Simeon and Levi had been fairly well decimated, it was only natural that Judah should become the dominant tribe. In the vicinity were other nomadic groups with which these displaced Hebrews came into friendly association. Among them were Calebites, Othnielites, and Kenites. The cultic center of these various tribes now in the Negeb was probably Kadesh.

Soon after these remnant Hebrew tribes established themselves around Kadesh, a segment of the tribe of Levi may have migrated to Egypt, where they joined with the Joseph tribes who were already there.[37] This would account for the tradition which makes the family of Moses members of the tribe of Levi. It could also explain why Moses, a Levite, led the Joseph tribes to Kadesh from Sinai: fellow Levites were there.

Yahwism at Kadesh

During the period when Judah, Simeon, and Levi came into association with Kenites at Kadesh, they may have become Yahweh worshipers.[38] The Yahwism accepted by these Hebrews at this time, however, was *Kenite* rather than Mosaic.

The Kenites, whose ancestor was Cain (Gen. 4), were a nomadic clan of the Midianites.[39] Since the word "Kenite" means "smith," they were evidently roving coppersmiths somewhat like modern gypsies. Copper

[37] This is essentially the position that Procksch takes. *Op. cit.*, p. 70; cf. Burney, *op. cit.*, pp. 44 ff. and Rowley, *op. cit.*, pp. 122-23.

[38] This position was suggested to the writer by Rowley, *op. cit.*, pp. 149-56, but is not identical with his view in all details.

[39] On the Kenites see W. F. Albright, *Archaeology and the Religion of Israel*, pp. 98-99; Budde, *The Religion of Israel to the Exile*, pp. 19 ff.; Rowley, *op. cit.*, p. 152; and G. Ernest Wright, *Biblical Archaeology* (Philadelphia: The Westminster Press, 1957), p. 65.

mines are known to have existed in Midian, in the Arabah, and in the Sinaitic peninsula,[40] so the biblical traditions that place the Kenites in those areas are quite credible. During the thirteenth century B.C. the Kenites probably ranged from Kadesh southeastward to the area directly north of the Gulf of Aqaba.[41] This would place them in contact with the Midianites east of the Gulf of Aqaba, to whom they were connected racially, as well as with the Hebrews in the Kadesh area, with whom they had established friendly relations.

The Kenites were particularly close to the southern Hebrew tribes. According to Judg. 1:16, "the decendants of the Kenite, Moses' father-in-law," invaded Palestine with Judah and settled in the area southeast of Hebron. Josh. 15:57 refers to a town called Kain, which was probably located some three or four miles from Hebron.[42] It was possibly occupied by Kenites. In the time of Saul, Kenites were to the south of Palestine among the Amalekites. Because of the kindness they had shown to the people of Israel when they came out of Egypt, Saul urged the Kenites to separate themselves from the Amalekites before the latter were exterminated by the Hebrews (I Sam. 15:6 ff.). In other traditions from the same period, the Kenites are specifically related to the tribe of Judah. For example, when the Philistine Achish would ask David against whom he had been conducting raids, the deceptive vassal would reply: "Against the Negeb of Judah," or "Against the Negeb of the Jerahmeelites," or "Against the Negeb of the Kenites" (I Sam. 27:10; cf. 30:29).

That the Kenites were the original Yahweh worshipers seems quite probable. Exodus 18 can be viewed as evidence for this position, as has already been suggested.[43] If it is assumed that the Kenites were the original Yahweh worshipers, then the southern Jahwist's ascription of

[40] Wright, *Biblical Archaeology*, p. 65.

[41] Kraeling makes this suggestion. See the map on pages 232-33 of his *Bible Atlas;* cf. Rowley, *op. cit.,* p. 152, n. 7.

[42] According to L. H. Grollenberg, *Atlas of the Bible* (New York: Thomas Nelson & Sons, 1956), p. 154; see map 13, p. 60.

[43] Chapter One, pp. 25-26. In addition to Exodus 18, the mark of Yahweh borne by Cain, the eponymous ancestor of the Kenites (Gen. 4:15), can be interpreted to support such a view, as does Rowley, *op. cit.,* p. 153. Also the great zeal for Yahwism by the Kenite Rechab and the later Rechabites might point to the same conclusion. (See Budde, *op. cit.,* pp. 30-31.)

the beginning of Yahweh worship to Enosh, the first man [44] (Gen. 4:26), is quite explicable.[45] For the southern Hebrew tribes there was no dramatic adoption of Yahweh worship, as was the case with the Joseph tribes under Moses who accepted Yahweh as God in connection with the miraculous event of the exodus. The southern clans rather came to the worship of Yahweh by the "gradual penetration" [46] of the faith after they had come into association with the Kenites in the Kadesh area. Since the Kenites had worshiped Yahweh from time immemorial, this tradition was incorporated into J: "To Seth also a son was born, and he called his name Enosh. At that time men began to call upon the name of Yahweh" (Gen. 4:26). The northern Elohist, on the other hand, ascribed the introduction of Yahweh worship to Moses (Exod. 3:13 ff.), which was true for the Joseph tribes.

The Kenites, as the original Yahweh worshipers, would have been the source of priestly traditions connected with Yahweh worship.[47] If Moses mediated Kenite priestly traditions to the Hebrews who were in Egypt,[48] the Hebrews who came into contact with the Kenites at Kadesh may have become the recipients of some priestly traditions even before the time of Moses. It is possible that the Kenite understanding of the priesthood itself was one of these elements. Since the Kenites continued to maintain relations with the southern tribes for several centuries, it would be expected that these priestly traditions would have been entrenched with special firmness among them. Among the northern Hebrew tribes in Palestine subsequently these traditions would not have been taken quite as seriously.

When in the thirteenth century B.C., then, Moses brought the Joseph tribes to Kadesh with *Mosaic* Yahwism, other Yahweh worshipers were already there. Judah, Simeon, Othniel, Caleb, some Levites, and of course Kenites, had a previous allegiance to *Kenite* Yahwism. The relations between these two groups during a period of nearly forty years is reflected in Exod. 15:23–ch. 18; Num. 11–20.

---

[44] Since in Hebrew the word "Enosh" means man, it seems likely that in some early circles the first man was "Enosh" rather than "Adam."

[45] On this point the writer is dependent upon Rowley, *op. cit.*, pp. 153-54.

[46] This is Rowley's expression. *Op. cit.*, p. 153.

[47] Eichrodt, *Theology*, p. 393; Rowley, *op. cit.*, p. 151.

[48] Chap. One, p. 26.

One of the reasons why Moses brought the Hebrew tribes to Kadesh was undoubtedly the fact that he was a Levite and fellow Levites were there. Another reason for Moses' coming would seem to be that he had agreed to meet Jethro there. If Exodus 18 is a Kadesh tradition, Jethro would have arrived at this cult site soon after Moses did.[49] In some way the message concerning the exodus of Moses and his fellow Hebrews from Egypt had come to Jethro: "Jethro, the priest of Midian, Moses' father-in-law, heard of all that God had done for Moses and for Israel his people, how Yahweh had brought Israel out of Egypt" (Exod. 18:1). It is possible that Hobab, the brother-in-law of Moses, was instrumental in the communications between Moses and Jethro, since Num. 10:29-32 seems to indicate that Hobab was with the Hebrews at Sinai and afterwards.[50] Upon hearing the news, Jethro came to Kadesh bringing Moses' wife and children. It is possible that the Kenites associated with the southern Hebrew tribes were of the same stock as Moses' father-in-law.[51] This would make Jethro's presence at Kadesh quite natural. His coming to Kadesh from the region around the northern part of the Gulf of Aqaba, the main area of Midianite life, would have been in no way unusual, since, as we have already suggested, the Kenites connected with the Hebrews were moving about in this general area.

Not only because he was Moses' father-in-law, but also because he was a priest of the Kenite God Yahweh did Jethro play a prominent role on this occasion at Kadesh.[52] After the two met and greeted each other, they entered "the tent" (vs. 7). There Moses recounted to Jethro Yahweh's mighty act in bringing the people out of Egyptian servitude. Jethro rejoiced at all that Yahweh had done and exclaimed:

10 Blessed be Yahweh, who has delivered you out of the hand of the Egyptians and out of the hand of Pharaoh. 11 Now I know that Yahweh

[49] It is assumed that the events of Exodus 18 occurred *after* the covenant at Sinai. See Procksch, *op. cit.*, p. 99.

[50] The writer accepts that the expression "Moses' father-in-law" in vs. 29 refers to Hobab rather than Reuel (i.e., Jethro), although the Hebrew permits the alternate interpretation.

[51] This is Rowley's position. *Op. cit.*, pp. 152-53.

[52] See Chap. One, pp. 25-26.

is greater than all gods, because he delivered the people from under the hand of the Egyptians, when they dealt arrogantly with them. Exod.18:10-11

Karl Budde comments on this passage:

This has generally been interpreted to mean that Jethro, the heathen, now recognizes the true God in Yahweh, the God of Israel, and does him homage. The contrary, however, is the fact. He rather gives expression to his proud joy that his God, Yahweh, the God of the Kenites, has proved himself mightier than all other gods.[53]

It is possible, however, to interpret the passage to mean that on this occasion Jethro, the priest of Kenite Yahwism, actually accepted Mosaic Yahwism; and not only in his own behalf but also in behalf of all the tribes at Kadesh who had been devoted to Kenite Yahwism, i.e., Judah, Simeon, Othniel, Caleb, some Levites, *and* Kenites. One might, therefore, conclude that at Kadesh in the thirteenth century B.C. the southern Hebrew tribes received the tradition of Yahweh's wondrous act in the exodus.[54]

In connection with the acceptance of this tradition a covenant ceremony was consummated: "And Jethro, Moses' father-in-law, offered a burnt offering and sacrifices to God, and Aaron came with all the elders of Israel to eat bread with Moses' father-in-law before God" (vs. 12). Budde explains this covenant ceremony as sealing "an alliance of Israel with the nomad tribe of the Kenites at Sinai, which had as its self-evident condition the adoption of their religion, Yahweh-worship."[55] The other Old Testament traditions, he says, speak of this covenant merely as one between Israel and Yahweh at Sinai, the Kenite association having been dropped. However, it is unlikely that the Kenites were involved in the covenant at Sinai. The covenant at Sinai

[53] *Op. cit.*, pp. 22-23.

[54] In this connection it is interesting to observe the comment of John Bright: "According to the Bible, the group formed in covenant at Sinai moved to Kadesh, at which great oasis it established itself for a considerable period of time. There it doubtless was in contact with other groups frequenting the area, perhaps including some who had left Egypt in various ways, as well as some already familiar with the cult of Yahweh in its pre-Mosaic form. We may suppose that numerous conversions to the new faith took place." *History*, p. 126.

[55] Budde, *op. cit.*, p. 24.

rather was the immediate response of the Hebrews who came out of Egypt to Yahweh. The covenant ceremony in Exodus 18, therefore, must have a somewhat different significance from that which Budde ascribes to it.

That this passage[56] stands in some relation to J's version of the covenant ceremony in Exod. 24:1-2, 9-11 seems probable. It has already been suggested that both the Jahwist and the Elohist traditions reflect the original event of the covenant at Sinai, but that they also have been formed and colored by later historical events and cultic practices. It is important for this conclusion to be kept in mind in interpreting the relation between Exod. 24:1-2, 9-11, and Exod. 18.

Those who partake of the covenant meal in the latter passage are (1) Jethro, (2) Aaron, and (3) all the elders of Israel. In the former passage the participants are (1) Moses, (2) Aaron, (3) Nadab and Abihu, and (4) seventy of the elders of Israel. The participants that the two traditions have in common are *Aaron* and *elders of Israel*. Exodus 18, of course, refers to "all the elders of Israel," while Exodus 24, with greater precision, speaks of "*seventy* of the elders of Israel." In the Sinai passage it is Moses who presides at the covenant ceremony. In the Kadesh passage, however, it is Jethro who presides, although the presence of Moses during the ceremony probably can be assumed. Nadab and Abihu, who participate in the covenant meal at Sinai in the J tradition, do not appear in the E tradition of the covenant meal at Kadesh.

It seems probable, as frequently has been suggested,[57] that the figures of Aaron, Nadab, and Abihu, and the seventy elders in the J covenant tradition represent later cultic officials. None of them is to be found in the Elohist's narrative of the Sinai covenant. This fact clearly calls into question their presence at Sinai. One would hesitate to deny that Aaron was in any way associated with Moses;[58] but in this tradition the figure does seem somewhat artificial. The same would be true of the "seventy" elders, as their appearance in Numbers 11 might suggest.

[56] It is the general consensus of Old Testament scholarship that Exodus 18 belongs to E. Beer, *Exodus*, p. 93; McNeile, *The Book of Exodus*, pp. 104-8, *et al.*

[57] Martin Noth, *Überlieferungsgeschichte des Pentateuch*, pp. 203-5; Hans-Joachim Kraus, *Gottesdienst in Israel*, p. 66.

[58] As does Noth, *Überlieferungsgeschichte*, pp. 195 ff.

Nadab and Abihu too must have been important cultic names only after the time of Moses. The appearance of Moses himself in this passage is historically accurate in regard to the event at Sinai, but his position as the head of a covenant dynasty probably should be viewed as a later development.

If these are accurate observations concerning the figures in Exod. 24:1-2, 9-11, the significance of Exod. 18:12 becomes clearer. "Aaron" could represent the priesthood of the tribes at Kadesh when Moses arrived. The "elders of Israel" were the representatives of the tribes themselves. Jethro was a priest of Kenite Yahwism, the religion of these tribes. So it was he who officiated at the cultic meal which sealed the covenant of the tribes with Yahweh on the basis of the newly accepted exodus tradition. In entering this covenant they were united with the Joseph tribes. Now all were the covenant people of Yahweh, who had acted in the event of the exodus.

Since the ceremony at Kadesh was the one which marked the entrance of the southern tribes into Mosaic Yahwism, it was of great importance in the development of their covenant tradition. They accepted the Sinai covenant form from Moses, with its basic elements of: (1) Theophany, (2) revelation of Yahweh's name and nature, (3) revelation of Yahweh's will in the form of law, (4) oath of the people, (5) sealing of the covenant. But this covenant form was influenced by the Kadesh event. This would seem to be the reason, therefore, for the close affinity between Exod. 18 and Exod. 24:1-2, 9-11.

In the official covenant tradition of the southern tribes, of course, Moses was the chief figure rather than Jethro. But the influence of Kenite priestly traditions would have been strong among the southern tribes, and the dynastic principle especially important. A covenant priesthood emerged which traced its succession from Moses. Moses was viewed as the first covenant mediator (which historically was true), and his office had been established "for ever" (Exod. 19:9). Aaron derived his authority from Moses; and Nadab and Abihu were the successors of Aaron. The official covenant priesthood among the southern tribes, consequently, was that which derived its authority from this line. And this priestly succession was undoubtedly viewed subsequently as forming the center of the life of the covenant people. The perpetuation of this priesthood was the basis of the continuing life of the people. All religious authority was vested in this hierarchy.

Not only was Jethro responsible for a priestly dynasty among certain of the Hebrew tribes, but he also seems to have given advice concerning the organization of the people. According to Exod. 18:13-16 Jethro admonished Moses to decide himself all major matters affecting the people before God, but to relinquish minor decisions to selected men. Moses accepted the advice and organized the people accordingly. It seems probable that involved here was the formulation and administration of casuistic law. The tradition in Exod. 15:25 states that at Kadesh Moses (or Yahweh) "made for them a statute and an ordinance." The Hebrew word for ordinance is the technical expression in the Old Testament for casuistic law. So it is possible that casuistic law was first introduced into the life of the covenant people of Yahweh at Kadesh.[59]

It is possible that "the tent" referred to in Exod. 18:7 is the tent of meeting. This would mean that the tent of meeting played a part in the covenant ceremony at Kadesh.

Controversy at Kadesh

Kadesh, then, became the central cultic site of these Hebrews who worshiped Yahweh in accordance with the Mosaic traditions. The tribes were Joseph, Judah, Simeon, Levi, Othniel, Caleb, and the Kenites. Presumably this group spent some thirty-eight years in the Kadesh area.[60] It is clear from the traditions in Num. 11–20 (cf. Exod. 16–17) that this was a period of controversy. The traditions preserve the memory of three related problems. (1) There was the complaint concerning food. (2) There was the controversy concerning the invasion of Palestine. (3) There was the question of leadership.

The agricultural resources of the region around Kadesh were limited. With the advent of a new group, the problem of food intensified. The diet was meager, and many were unhappy. P preserves this bitter complaint of the Hebrews to their leaders: "Would that we had died by the hand of Yahweh in the land of Egypt, when we sat by the fleshpots and ate bread to the full, for you have brought us out into this

[59] See Bright, *History*, p. 150.
[60] Deut. 1:46; 2:1, 14.

wilderness to kill this whole assembly with hunger" (Exod. 16:3; cf. Num. 11:4-6). The traditions state that God's answer to this problem came in the miraculous bestowal of manna and quail upon the people (Num. 11:7-9, 18-23, 31-34; Exod. 16). Thus they were sustained during these difficult years.[61]

Closely connected with the problem of food was the question of the invasion of Palestine. Even though the Hebrews had sufficient nourishment to maintain an adequate physical existence at Kadesh, the much more fertile land to the north beckoned invitingly. Moreover, some of the traditions in their possession at the time contained divine promises of this land to their forefathers.[62] It belonged to them.

The traditions concerning the problem of invading Palestine from the south are preserved in Num. 13–14. There is general agreement among scholars that these chapters contain an earlier and a later tradition concerning the invasion.[63] In the Priestly account [64] Yahweh commands Moses to send twelve spies, one from each tribe, to traverse the land and to return with a report on the possibility of conquering it. In accordance with this command, the twelve move from the wilderness of Paran northward. During a period of forty days they pass through the whole country from its southern extremity to its northernmost point. At the end of this time they report to Moses and Aaron that it would be futile to attack the land because its inhabitants are men of such great stature. Joshua and Caleb, however, submit a minority report: "The land, which we passed through to spy it out, is an exceedingly good land" (14:7). But the people reject this report. Because of the murmurings of the people, the glory of Yahweh appears at the tent of meeting and Yahweh condemns all those over twenty years of age to death in the wilderness. Only Joshua and Caleb are excepted.

In the earlier narrative that J has preserved [65] there are some marked differences. Here the spies (it is never stated that there are twelve)

[61] See the recent comments on the manna and quail by G. E. Wright, *Biblical Archaeology*, pp. 64-65.

[62] The classical study of the promise of the land in the patriarchal traditions of Genesis is Albrecht Alt's "Der Gott der Väter," *Kleine Schriften zur Geschichte des Volkes Israel* (München: C. H. Beck, 1959), I, 1-78.

[63] On the literary analysis see especially Gray, *op. cit.*, pp. 129-33.

[64] 13:1-17a, 21, 25-26a, 32; 14:1-2, 5-7, 10, 26-28.

[65] 13:17b-20, 22-24, 26b-31, 33; 14:3-4, 8-9, 11-24, 39-45.

go up from Kadesh to the Negeb. They travel as far as Hebron or the Valley of Eshcol. Then they return to Kadesh with a great cluster of grapes, some pomegranates and figs to illustrate their report concerning the fertility of the land. They also bring back stories of giants and strong cities. In this narrative it is Caleb *alone* who is optimistic: "Let us go up at once, and occupy it; for we are well able to overcome it" (13:30). But the other spies voice their opposition: "We are not able to go up against the people; for they are stronger than we" (13:31). The people oppose Caleb and side with the majority. At the same time they complain bitterly concerning their lot. Yahweh is angry and threatens to punish them. When Moses intercedes, Yahweh forgives them but says that only Caleb will be permitted to enter the promised land. After this, the people change their minds and determine to conquer the land. Neither the ark of the covenant nor Moses accompany them, however, and they are driven back by the Amalekites and the Canaanites.

It is noteworthy that in this early tradition only Caleb brings back the report favorable to an immediate invasion from the south. Since Caleb was probably one of the tribes at Kadesh when the Joseph group arrived, it can probably be concluded that in this tradition he represents the interests of these tribes. The three Leah tribes, Judah, Simeon, and Levi, had been pushed out of Palestine not too many years before. It is understandable that they were eager to return by the same route that they left. The element of vengeance upon those who were responsible for their expulsion was perhaps an important factor in their attitude. They brought pressure to invade. On the other hand, the tribes who had just come from Egypt were more cautious. They were probably quite eager to gain possession of this fertile country, but their interest was in the *best* invasion route rather than the nearest one. The obstacles to a conquest of the land from the south seemed too great and they resisted the movement to invade from this direction. The result was serious tension between the tribes affiliated with Judah and those associated with Joseph.

According to Num. 14:39-45 some of the people attempted an invasion at this time in spite of the difficulties. They were unsuccessful in their effort, however. The reason given for their lack of success is that "neither the ark of the covenant of Yahweh, nor Moses, departed out of the camp" (vs. 44). Since from the period of the conquest under Joshua until the time of David the ark of the covenant was in the area of Palestine controlled by the Joseph tribes, this notice might be interpreted to confirm the suggestion that the Joseph group did not favor this expedition.

The position that Moses took in this invasion controversy is difficult to determine. As leader of both groups, he would have tried to reconcile their differences, and it is possible that in the process he vacillated somewhat. Perhaps he originally was in favor of the invasion and interpreted the refusal of the majority to participate as an act of apostasy against Yahweh which necessitated a prayer of intercession (14:11-24). Later he may have changed his views and refused to participate in the abortive invasion (14:39-45).

One can surmise that, although they failed in this attempt, the southern tribes continued to nourish the desire to invade the land from this direction. They were determined that some time in the future they would do so.

A third problem which emerged at Kadesh was the question of leadership. Numbers 11, 12, and 16 preserve traditions which are concerned with Moses' authority over the covenant people of God. It is to be recognized, of course, that these traditions not only reflect a situation that obtained at Kadesh, but they also have been colored by the rivalries and claims of subsequent religious groups that preserved and transmitted them. Since Moses was the dominating figure of the most decisive age in the development of Israel's faith, it would be expected that later groups would claim him for their special interests.[66] Caution must therefore be exercised in drawing conclusions concerning the situation at Kadesh.

Num. 11:16-17, 24-25 is a tradition in which the authority of Moses is unequivocally asserted over the seventy elders. The elders prophesy only when some of the "spirit" upon Moses is withdrawn and is placed upon them. Lay authority is subordinate and dependent upon Moses' authority. This passage has probably been shaped by certain interests

[66] On this point see especially von Rad, *Theologie*, I, 289.

in a post-Mosaic period. And that it belongs to the Jahwist [67] would seem to mean that it was preserved and used by a *southern priesthood* which traced its dynasty back to Moses. In asserting so unequivocally the authority of Moses, the tradition was also asserting the authority of this priestly line. On the other hand, the fact that the incident is associated with Kadesh must indicate that the tradition has preserved the memory of a burning issue there. Through whom does Yahweh exercise his authority? Is religious authority to be limited to the few or extended to the many?

Numbers 12 is concerned with essentially the same question, although in this chapter there is a specific challenge to Moses' authority. "Has Yahweh indeed spoken only through Moses?" (vs. 2.) Thus Miriam [68] challenges Moses' status as the unique mediator between Yahweh and the covenant people. The answer of Yahweh at the tent of meeting is in the affirmative:

6 Hear my words: If there is a prophet among you, I Yahweh make myself known to him in a vision, I speak with him in a dream. 7 Not so with my servant Moses; he is entrusted with all my house. 8 With him I speak mouth to mouth, clearly, and not in dark speech; and he beholds the form of Yahweh. Why then were you not afraid to speak against my servant Moses?

Like the tradition in Numbers 11, which also associates Moses' authority with the tent of meeting, Numbers 12 belongs to J.[69] And it too seems to have been preserved and shaped by southern priestly circles interested in asserting the unique authority of Moses and thus their own. The prominence of the tent of meeting in this passage, as well as in chapter 11, could mean that it was the central cult object of these southern priests. Although colored by later interests, Numbers 12 must also reflect the conflict among the Hebrew worshipers of Yahweh at Kadesh. Through whom is the will of Yahweh revealed? Is it through official priestly channels alone? Or does he make known his purposes directly to those outside the official circles? That Miriam is

[67] Chap. Two, p. 63.
[68] Aaron is secondary in this passage.
[69] Chap. Two, p. 63.

elsewhere called a "prophetess" (Exod. 15:20; cf. Judg. 4:4) might suggest a kind of prophetic-priestly clash at Kadesh.[70]

Numbers 16 also depicts a controversy over authority. It is generally recognized that several traditions have been combined in this chapter.[71] Two of them seem to be early and two later traditions. The two later traditions seem to be two strata of the P writing.[72] In the earlier stratum preserved by P [73] a certain Korah, at the head of 250 leaders of the congregation, instigates a rebellion against Moses and *Aaron* in the interest of *all* the people. "All the congregation are holy," they insist, "every one of them, and Yahweh is among them; why then do you exalt yourselves above the assembly of Yahweh?" (vs. 3). Moses challenges them to settle the matter by bringing their censers the next day to offer incense. "Yahweh will show who is his, and who is holy" (vs. 5). The challenge is accepted and the next day they come to the tent of meeting where the "glory of Yahweh" appears. The issue is decided in Moses' favor when fire comes forth from Yahweh consuming Korah and the 250 men. Because of this incident the people murmur against Moses and Aaron. The rebellion precipitates a plague which is stayed only by the atoning offering of Aaron.

A later writer of the Priestly school made certain additions to the earlier stratum[74] which changed the story greatly. According to this version, Korah, at the head of 250 *Levites,* challenges the exclusive prerogatives of the *Aaronic* priesthood. The test in this narrative is the same as the one proposed in the earlier P version. The fate of the rebels too is the same as in the earlier story; they are consumed by fire which comes forth from Yahweh. Afterwards Moses commands Eleazar, the son of Aaron, to hammer the censers of the rebels into plates as a covering for the altar "to be a reminder to the people of Israel, so that no one who is not a priest, who is not of the descendants of Aaron, should draw near to burn incense before Yahweh, lest he

[70] On this point see Noth, *Überlieferungsgeschichte,* pp. 199-200.
[71] See especially Gray, *op. cit.,* pp. 186 ff. and S. R. Driver, *An Introduction to the Literature of the Old Testament* (New York: Charles Scribner's Sons, rev. ed., 1913), pp. 62-64.
[72] Driver, *op. cit.,* p. 63.
[73] 16:1a, 2b-7a, 18-24, 27a, 32b, 35, 41-50; cf. ch. 17.
[74] Vss. 7b-11, 16-17, 36-40.

become as Korah and as his company" (vs. 40). This tradition almost certainly reflects the situation which obtained in the priesthood of the postexilic temple in Jerusalem.

It seems likely that Numbers 16 contains two early traditions too, one of which can be assigned to E and the other to J.[75] The Elohist tradition reads:

1 Dathan and Abiram, the sons of Eliab . . . sons of Reuben rose up [against Moses]. 12 And Moses sent to call Dathan and Abiram the sons of Eliab; and they said, "We will not come up." 14b "You have [not] given us inheritance of fields and vineyards. Will you put out the eyes of these men? We will not come up." 25 Then Moses rose and went to Dathan and Abiram; and the elders of Israel followed him. 27 . . . Dathan and Abiram came out and stood at the door of their tents. . . . 32a And the earth opened its mouth and swallowed them. . . . 33b And the earth closed over them, and they perished from the midst of the assembly. 34 And all Israel that were round about them fled at their cry; for they said, "Lest the earth swallow us up!"

This story involves a rebellion of Dathan and Abiram, two Reuben-ites. Their complaint is that Moses has not given them their inheritance of fields and vineyards. Presumably they are referring to his failure to lead in the conquest of Palestine. When Moses summons them, they refuse to come. So Moses takes "the elders of Israel" (evidently repre-sentatives of the whole people) and goes to them. Moses' position is vindicated when the earth opens up and swallows the rebels. This narrative (which is referred to in Deut. 11:6) seems not to involve any questions of religious authority. Rather, like Num. 13-14, it is concerned with the question of the invasion. Two members of the tribe of Reuben (a Leah tribe) rebel, and Moses and the elders stand firmly against them.

The J tradition, however, is much closer to the early stratum of P:

1 On, the son of Peleth . . . [said to Moses]: 13 "Is it a small thing that you have brought us up out of a land flowing with milk and honey, to kill us in the wilderness, that you must also make yourself a prince over us?"

---

[75] See Gray, op. cit., pp. 190-91.

14a Moreover you have not brought us into a land flowing with milk and honey. . . . 15 And Moses was very angry, and said to Yahweh, "Do not respect their offering. I have not taken one ass from them, and I have not harmed one of them." 26b [Moses addresses the people]: "Depart, I pray you, from the tents of these wicked men [On, and his followers], and touch nothing of theirs, lest you be swept away with all their sins. . . . 27 [along with] their wives, their sons, and their little ones. 28 And Moses said, "Hereby you shall know that Yahweh has sent me to do all these works, and that it has not been of my own accord. 29 If these men die the common death of all men . . . then Yahweh has not sent me. 30 But if Yahweh creates something new, and the ground opens its mouth, and swallows them up, with all that belongs to them, and they go down alive into Sheol, then you shall know that these men have despised Yahweh." 31 And as he finished speaking all these words, the ground under them split asunder. 33a So they and all that belonged to them went down alive into Sheol.

Here the chief rebel is On, the son of Peleth. And the controversy clearly concerns religious authority. The charge brought against Moses is not only that he has not brought the people to the promised land, but also that he has made himself a prince over them (vs. 13). And Moses, in his prayer to Yahweh, urges: "Do not respect their offering" (vs. 15). When On and his party are swallowed up and descend into Sheol, Moses' status as prince over the people is vindicated. And even more, the claim of the rebels to exercise sacrificial functions is rejected; it is the sacrifice of Moses that Yahweh will regard.

This J tradition is thus quite similar to Numbers 11 and 12 in that it strongly affirms the authority of Moses. It must also have been preserved by the same priestly circles which preserved them. In stressing Moses' authority, they were stressing their own authority.

That the traditions in Numbers 16 are placed at Kadesh can also be interpreted to mean that they too reflect the controversy over authority that took place at that cultic site. But these traditions add a new element to the controversy: the violent death of some of those involved in the struggle. *This would seem to indicate that the controversy at Kadesh ended in some sort of open conflict.*

When it is observed that the early traditions which stress the authority of Moses all belong to J, it can be concluded that the southern tribes at Kadesh represented the priestly and authoritarian side of the controversy. The fact that the Kenites, the original Yahweh worshipers, were closely associated with the southern tribes would tend to confirm this conclusion. As the group that contributed the priestly traditions of Yahwism to the Hebrews, they would have been quite interested in stressing their importance and centrality. Although the Kenites at Kadesh had accepted the exodus-covenant traditions of Moses, they nevertheless continued to feel that the authority of the Kenite priesthood should be primary. Siding with the Kenites, then, would have been Judah, Simeon, Caleb, and Othniel.

If these southern tribes stood on the side of religious authoritarianism in the dispute, it would seem natural to conclude that the Joseph tribes took the opposite position. Since this group had experienced Yahweh's presence and power in the event of the exodus apart from any priestly control or direction, they resisted the movement to restrict religious authority to one priestly dynasty, even though it was derived from Jethro the priest of Yahweh. The Joseph tribes had a less restricted and more charismatic understanding of Yahwism. Their general position is undoubtedly reflected accurately by the tradition preserved by P: "All the congregation are holy, every one of them, and Yahweh is among them" (Num. 16:3; cf. 12:2).

And if Numbers 11, 12, 16 have preserved traditions reflecting the southern side of the controversy, it is possible that Deut. 33:8-11 and Exod. 32:25-29 are traditions preserved by circles on the other side. Deut. 33:8-11, the blessing of Moses on Levi, is set at Kadesh, as the references to Massah and Meribah reveal. It speaks of a testing of Levi at Kadesh which resulted in Levi's being entrusted with the task of teaching Yahweh's law and offering of sacrifice. Since Exod. 32:25-29 seems to reflect the same event as does Deut. 33:8-11, it too should probably be associated with Kadesh.[76]

25 And when Moses saw that the people had broken loose . . .[77] 26 then Moses stood in the gate of the camp, and said, "Who is on Yahweh's side?

[76] I have treated Exod. 32:25-29 in greater detail in *The Sinai Covenant Traditions*, pp. 124-26, 273-74.

[77] Vs. 25b is probably secondary. *Ibid.*, p. 125.

Come to me." And all the sons of Levi gathered themselves together to him. 27 And he said to them, "Thus says Yahweh God of Israel, 'Put every man his sword on his side, and go to and fro from gate to gate throughout the camp, and slay every man his brother, and every man his companion, and every man his neighbor.' " 28 And the sons of Levi did according to the word of Moses; and there fell of the people that day about three thousand men. 29 And Moses said, "Today you have ordained yourselves for the service of Yahweh, each one at the cost of his son and of his brother, that he may bestow a blessing upon you this day."

Gerhard von Rad has demonstrated the close connection between the Levites and the covenant tradition among the northern tribes of Israel after the conquest.[78] In charge of the ark of the covenant, the Levites played a prominent role in the cult at Shechem, as is suggested by such passages as Deut. 27; 31:9-11 and Josh. 8:30-35. Since the Levitical priests were later active in the cultic life which centered in the area occupied by the Joseph tribes, it is natural to conclude that Exod. 32:25-29 and Deut. 33:8-11 preserve the memory of the participation of at least a sizable group of Levites on the side of the Joseph tribes in the Kadesh controversy.[79] One would assume that the Levites who sided with Joseph in the struggle concerning religious authority were those who had themselves been in Egypt and had experienced the event of the exodus and the covenant at Sinai. They were thus the Levites from whom the family of Moses came. This group of Levites evidently took a vigorous part in the conflict. The references to Levi's disregard of his own kindred on this occasion in Exod. 32:27-29 and Deut. 33:7 perhaps refer to an especially bitter fight between these Levites who had been to Egypt and those who had been at Kadesh ever since the breakup of the old Leah amphictyony at Shechem and were closely aligned with the southern tribes.

As a consequence of this strong stand for the Joseph tribes and their understanding of Yahwism, these Levites were invested with special

[78] Von Rad, *Studies in Deuteronomy*, pp. 66 ff.; cf. *Theologie*, I, pp. 79 ff.

[79] The position taken here concerning the Levites at Kadesh has been influenced by Eichrodt, *op. cit.*, pp. 392-402 and Meek, *op. cit.*, pp. 127 ff., but is identical with neither. For example, Eichrodt thinks that the secular tribe of Levi was in no way related to the priestly tribe, and Meek contends that the Levites were exclusively associated with Judah.

cultic responsibilities: "Today you have ordained yourselves for the service of Yahweh" (Exod. 32:29). This was true at least as far as the Joseph tribes were concerned; the southern tribes clung tenaciously to the centrality of the Kenite priestly dynasty in Yahwism. The two primary functions of the Levitical priests were to be: (1) Teaching of the law; (2) offering of sacrifice.

> They shall teach Jacob thy ordinances,
>   and Israel thy law;
> they shall put incense before thee,
>   and whole burnt offering upon thy altar.
>   DEUT. 33:10

Since the Yahwism with which they aligned themselves was more congregational and democratic in tendency, the Levitical priesthood seems subsequently not to have been confined to those who were Levites by blood. This priesthood was by no means a closed and tightly knit group, at least not until near the exilic period. The Levitical priesthood seems to have been rather loosely organized, accepting into its membership people of other tribes, such as Samuel who was an Ephraimite of the Zuphite clan.[80]

It is impossible to determine with any certainty just what role Moses himself played in this controversy over religious authority. Since he had originally sought to combine a more charismatic understanding of Yahwism with traditional Kenite priestly forms, it is likely that he did his utmost to keep the two groups together, albeit in tension. He could appreciate the importance of a central priestly dynasty to express the historical continuity of a people who were to take seriously the fact that their God was acting uniquely in their history. But at the same time he knew that Yahweh, the God of history, was not bound by any historical considerations, not even by a sacred priesthood of his chosen people; so Moses also had a deep appreciation of discontinuity, of the charismatic element in the life of the covenant people. Possibly Moses

---

[80] See Albright, *Archaeology and the Religion of Israel*, p. 109. If Albright intends to deny that there was ever a secular tribe of Levi, the present writer would disagree. Both Gen. 34 and Gen. 49:5-7 are strong evidence to the contrary. See Rowley, *From Joseph to Joshua*, pp. 8-9 and Meek, *op. cit.*, pp. 121 ff.

took positions at different times in the struggle which made it possible for each side to believe that he was *really* with them. This would explain why subsequently both groups could confidently claim his blessing upon their separate positions.

Division at Kadesh

In any event, Moses' efforts in this respect were ultimately futile. The final result of the various controversies at Kadesh that culminated in the violent clash over religious authority was a separation of the two groups. The group dominated by Joseph, a Rachel tribe, broke off from that dominated by Judah, a Leah tribe.[81] Accompanying Joseph were most of the Levites. They were to form the nucleus of the northern priesthood. With the Joseph tribes also was the ark of the covenant. The Levites were in charge of it. Moses evidently went with this group, since the tradition says that he died in the land of Moab opposite Jericho just before the invasion of Palestine under Joshua (Deut. 34).

Remaining at Kadesh with Judah were Simeonites, Calebites, Othnielites, Kenites, and some Levites. The priesthood of this group was derived from Kenite Yahwism, with a strong authoritarian and dynastic tendency, and with which the figure of Aaron was closely identified. Also with this group was the tent of meeting. The "Aaronic" priesthood was in charge of it.

These were the circumstances, then, out of which two covenant traditions emerged in the life of the Hebrew people. As a result of a separation at Kadesh, there were two groups of Hebrews who were worshipers of Yahweh and who accepted the traditions of the exodus and the Sinaitic covenant. Each of these groups was in possession of a cult shrine. The northern tribes had the ark of the covenant, while those in the South had the tent of meeting. Each group evidently used its palladium in connection with a covenant ceremony in the cult. It was in connection with this usage that both the J and E covenant legends developed their distinctive characteristics. The J legend with its special emphases was attached to the tent and the E legend with its theology was attached to the ark.

---

[81] Note that Burney's position in this regard is quite similar. *Op. cit.*, pp. 48-49; cf. Sellin, *op. cit.*, pp. 70-71.

Chapter Four

The Twelve-Tribe Amphictyony

SOON AFTER THE SEPARATION OF THE TWO GROUPS AT KADESH, THE conquest of Palestine occurred, probably beginning a few years after 1250 B.C. This conquest of course was not the first penetration of the land by Hebrews. For many years nomadic Hebrew clans evidently had been moving in and around Palestine. One group was the six-tribe Leah amphictyony which had centered at Shechem more than a century earlier.[1] It is clear to Old Testament scholarship that the occupation of Canaan by the Hebrews was a long and complicated process continuing over several centuries.[2] Before the thirteenth century it consisted primarily of peaceful penetrations of sparsely populated areas not controlled by the Canaanite city states. But the thirteenth century invasion was different. As the traditions in Numbers 20-24; Joshua 1–12 and Judges 1 indicate, this entry into Palestine was anything but peaceful. This was Holy War.[3]

[1] See Chap. Three, pp. 78 ff.

[2] This point has been particularly stressed by Albrecht Alt ("Die Landnahme der Israeliten in Palästina," *Kleine Schriften,* I, 89-125; "Erwägungen über die Landnahme der Israeliten in Palästina," *Kleine Schriften,* I, 126-75) and Martin Noth, *History,* pp. 68-84; cf. John Bright, *History,* pp. 117-20 and G. E. Wright, *Biblical Archaeology,* pp. 69-84.

[3] On the idea of Holy War in the Old Testament see Gerhard von Rad, *Der Heilige Krieg im alten Israel* (Göttingen: Vandenhoeck & Ruprecht, 1958); cf. *idem, Studies in*

The leaders in this invasion were the Joseph tribes. With the ark of the covenant and traditions concerning the exodus and the covenant, these charismatic worshipers of Yahweh left Kadesh and moved through Transjordan in order to attack the land of Canaan from the east. Refused transit through Edom, they circumvented that land and moved northward (Num. 20:14 ff.). Soon they encountered the kingdoms of Sihon (Num. 21:21-32) and Og of Bashan (Num. 21:23 ff.), whom they defeated. They also came into conflict with Balak, king of Moab (Num. 22-24). Thus the Joseph tribes were able to establish themselves in the "plains of Moab" to the east of Jericho. It was here, immediately before the invasion of the Palestinian hill country under Joshua, that Moses is said to have died (Deut. 34).

The Conquest Under Joshua

Joshua 1-12 preserves the memory of the next events. These chapters contain a number of etiological [4] and cultic legends set in a later Deuteronomic framework.[5] The etiological and cultic character of these traditions means that they must be used cautiously in coming to historical conclusions; they are not the reports of eyewitnesses, but were preserved partially for the purpose of explaining certain customs and unusual landmarks of the Hebrew people in Palestine.[6] On the other hand, just because a tradition has etiological or cultic significance does not necessarily mean that it thereby has no historical significance.[7] The J and E covenant traditions, as we have seen, are cult legends, but also preserve the memory of the original event at Sinai. It must be recognized, of course, that later generations at times tended to ascribe to Joshua a conquest of Palestine more far-reaching than he

---

Deuteronomy, pp. 45-59. That Holy War was always defensive, as von Rad maintains, seems unlikely to me.

[4] An etiological legend is a story which seeks to explain the cause or origin of a custom or landmark. On the etiological character of various traditions in Josh. 1-12 see especially Martin Noth, *Das Buch Josua. Handbuch zum Alten Testament* (Tübingen: J. C. B. Mohr, 2nd ed. 1953), pp. 20-73.

[5] Josh. 1 and 11:15-12:24 are mostly Deuteronomic. A recent treatment of the composition of the Book of Joshua is that by John Bright, "The Book of Joshua," *Interpreter's Bible*, II, 541-46.

[6] Josh. 6 would be an illustration of the former and Josh. 7 of the latter.

[7] This point Bright makes strongly in *Early Israel in Recent History Writing* (London: SCM Press, 1956), pp. 91-100.

actually achieved (e.g., Josh. 11:16-20). It must also be acknowledged that not all twelve tribes of Israel were involved in this conquest. Those primarily involved were the Joseph tribes. Further, the possibility of a certain amount of conflation of the traditions of the Joseph tribes with those of other groups must be reckoned with.[8] At the same time, in view of a number of modern archaeological excavations in Palestine, it is quite credible that Joshua 1–12 preserves the authentic memory of a major thirteenth-century assault on Palestine by Hebrew tribes which resulted in the establishment of a decisive beachhead in the land.

The leader of this assault was Joshua the son of Nun of the clan of Ephraim of the tribe of Joseph.[9] The name Joshua in Hebrew means "Yahweh is salvation." It is one of the two earliest names found in the Old Testament which are compounded with the name "Yahweh."[10] Thus Joshua clearly came from a tribe of Yahweh worshipers. Since Yahwism was introduced to the Joseph tribes by Moses and Moses was evidently associated with them until his death in Transjordan, the Old Testament traditions which make Joshua the successor of Moses are quite credible.

This decisive penetration of Palestine by the Joseph tribes under Joshua began after a scouting party had been sent forth (Josh. 2). The Jordan was crossed and a camp established at Gilgal, a site not far from Jericho (chs. 3–5). Gilgal evidently remained the base of these invaders during the whole period of their conquest. Before they could move with any safety from the Jordan valley up into the hills, it was necessary for them to control Jericho. The tradition that pre-

---

[8] W. F. Albright, *The Biblical Period*, p. 16.

[9] Albrecht Alt (followed by his influential school) does not associate Joshua with the kind of conquest that seems to be reflected in Josh. 1–12 ("Josua," *Kleine Schriften*, I, 176-92). Alt views him as merely a local leader of the clan of Ephraim. Only the traditions in Josh. 10:1-15; 17:14 ff. and chapter 24 were originally associated with Joshua. His name has been introduced secondarily into the other traditions in the Book of Joshua.

[10] The other is Jochebed, the mother of Moses according to P (Exod. 6:20; Num. 26:59). Some scholars, however, question whether Jochebed is a Yahweh name. (Martin Noth, *Die israelitischen Personennamen im Rahmen der gemeinsemitischen Namengebung. Beiträge zur Wissenschaft vom Alten und Neuen Testament.* Dritte Folge. Heft 10. [Stuttgart: W. Kohlhammer, 1938] p. 111) If it is not, Joshua would be the earliest. There are no names in the book of Genesis compounded with Yahweh.

serves the memory of the conquest of Jericho (ch. 6) seems to be cultic in character and probably was used in a regularly observed ceremony that celebrated the taking of Palestine by the Hebrews. Jericho was the first important site west of the Jordan and its conquest symbolized the conquest of the whole land. If the tradition was so used, many features in chapter six may have resulted from later cultic practices. The original event shines only dimly through the cult legend. Any battle that the Joseph tribes under Joshua may have fought for possession of Jericho presumably was minor, since it was evidently a small place at this time.[11] In any event, the site was certainly taken by these Hebrews.

From Jericho, Joshua led his fighting men up into the mountains. Their first objective was an area in which were located Ai and Bethel, two sites only a mile and a half apart. According to Josh. 7:1-8:29, Ai was conquered by this group under Joshua. Excavations, however, have shown that Ai had been destroyed a thousand years earlier. In Joshua's day it was still a "ruin," which interestingly is the meaning of the word "Ai" in Hebrew. But excavations have also revealed that the neighboring site of Bethel *was* devastated in the thirteenth century B.C. This is in accordance with the tradition in Judg. 1:22-26 (cf. Josh. 12:16), which attributes the conquest of Bethel to the house of Joseph. Control of Bethel would have been indispensable to any group, such as the Joseph tribes under Joshua, seeking to control the Palestinian hill country. It seems likely, therefore, that the tradition in Josh. 7:1-8:29 originally referred to Bethel, and later was associated with Ai in order to explain the origin of the age-old "ruin." [12]

When the inhabitants of Gibeon (a city located a few miles southwest of Bethel) learned of this successful invasion of the land, they succeeded, by means of a ruse, in establishing a treaty with the invaders (Josh. 9). This treaty resulted in the sparing of their city, but it also meant the acceptance of an inferior status in relation to the Hebrews.

[11] Recent excavations at Jericho have revealed that the destruction of Jericho formerly associated with the conquest under Joshua is to be dated centuries earlier and had nothing to do with the Hebrews. See Kathleen Kenyon, *Digging Up Jericho* (London: Ernest Benn, 1957), ch. XI; cf., Bright, *History*, pp. 118-19.

[12] Wright, *Biblical Archaeology*, pp. 80-81.

Now the Joseph tribes had a firm foothold in the Palestinian mountains and were ready to extend their conquests to the south and north. Joshua 10 contains an account of their conquest of key cities in the southern part of Palestine.[18] These initial victories of the Hebrews resulted in the establishment of a coalition of the kings of Jerusalem, Hebron, Jarmuth, Lachish, and Eglon to stop the invaders (vss. 1-27). Joshua defeated these Canaanite kings decisively, however, and then led his men in a campaign to conquer and destroy as many cities in the South as he was able. The conquered cities included Makkedah (vs. 28), Libnah (vss. 29-30), Lachish (vss. 31-32), Eglon (vss. 34-35), Hebron (vss. 36-37), and Debir (vss. 38-39). Of these six cities, Lachish, Eglon, and Debir have been excavated. All three suffered violent destruction in the second half of the thirteenth century B.C., evidently at the hands of the Hebrews under Joshua, as the Book of Joshua contends. It should be noted that Joshua 10 contains no reference to a conquest either of Gezer or Jerusalem, two formidable Canaanite city states which were not taken until after the emergence of the Davidic monarchy in the tenth century B.C.

After this southern venture, Joshua led a campaign in extreme northern Palestine (Josh. 11:1-15). Another coalition was formed against the invaders, this one led by Jabin, king of Hazor, a city some ten miles north of the Sea of Galilee. This coalition was also defeated and the victory was followed up by the conquest and sacking of Hazor. Recent excavations have shown that this site too, like those in southern Palestine, suffered violent destruction in the latter part of the thirteenth century B.C.

It is, of course, clear that the whole land of Palestine was not taken by the Hebrews under Joshua at this time. Any number of Canaanite cities, especially on the coastal plain and in the Valley of Jezreel, were not conquered until much later, some as late as the early period of the monarchy. On the other hand, however, it also seems clear that the second half of the thirteenth century B.C. did see a violent invasion of Palestine by a group of Hebrews under Joshua that resulted in a firm foothold in the mountains. These were the charismatic Joseph

---

[18] On this invasion see especially Bright, *History*, pp. 119-20 and Wright, *Biblical Archaeology*, pp. 81-83.

tribes who believed this holy war of conquest was in accordance with the will, promises and purposes of Yahweh, the God who had delivered them from Egyptian bondage and had covenanted with them at Sinai.

One puzzling aspect of this conquest is that, while the Joseph tribes evidently *conquered* southern Palestine, they did not occupy it; they settled in central Palestine. The tribes associated with Judah settled in the southern part of Palestine. It is probable that Judges 1 [14] preserves the memory of the occupation of southern Palestine by these tribes who moved north from Kadesh in this general period. For this reason it is not necessary to think of Judges 1 as reflecting an invasion from the south in a different period.[15] For some time the tribes with Judah had been desirous of conducting the invasion from this direction. This was evidently one of the reasons for the earlier tension between them and the Joseph group. Now was their opportunity to move. When the Joseph tribes under Joshua for strategic reasons conquered a number of cities in southern Palestine, their fellow Hebrews and Yahweh worshipers were able to advance northward and occupy them. According to Judges 1 the key southern tribes involved in this military thrust from the south were Judah (vss. 2, 3, 4, etc.), Simeon (vss. 3, 17), Caleb (vss. 12, 14, 20), Othniel (vs. 13), and the Kenites (vs. 16). They are said to have taken the cities of Hebron (vs. 10; cf. Josh. 15:13-14), Debir (vss. 11-15; cf. Josh. 15:15-19), Arad (vs. 16; cf. Num. 21:1), and Hormah (vs. 17; cf. Num. 21:3). Although this southern tradition does acknowledge that the northern "house of Joseph" conquered Bethel (vss. 22-26), it is particularly concerned to stress the failures of northern tribes (vss. 21, 27-36). In general, it can

[14] Judg. 1 belongs to the J epic.

[15] H. H. Rowley, for example (*From Joseph to Joshua*, pp. 111 ff.), thinks that the invasion from Kadesh by the southern tribes reflected in Judg. 1 occurred during the Amarna age, while the invasion under Joshua took place in the thirteenth century. Theophile J. Meek (*Hebrew Origins*, Ch. One) believes that the Joshua invasion took place during the Amarna age and that in the thirteenth century Moses led the southern tribes directly north from Kadesh in a conquest of southern Palestine. And G. E. Wright ("The Literary and Historical Problem of Joshua 10 and Judges 1," *Journal of Near Eastern Studies*, V (1946), 105-14) holds that the conquest under Joshua was conducted in the thirteenth century and suggests that the traditions in Judg. 1 refer to the reconquest of these cities in the period of the Judges after they had been lost to later enemies.

be said that Judges 1 gives as little credit to those who were primarily responsible for the conquest of southern Palestine as presumably did the Russian reports concerning areas in Germany they occupied during World War II only after Allied troops had made it possible.[16]

It was in this manner that both groups of Hebrews formerly at Kadesh established themselves firmly in Palestine during the latter part of the thirteenth century. The Joseph tribes occupied the central part of the country with their new Levitical priesthood. In the South were Judah, Simeon, Caleb, Othniel, and the Kenites.

The Amphictyony at Shechem

Joshua 24 suggests that Shechem was a significant site for the Hebrew people in the period following the invasion of Palestine under Joshua.[17] Located in the narrow pass between Mount Gerizim and Mount Ebal in central Palestine, Shechem had been an important city since the nineteenth century B.C. This chapter preserves the memory of an assembly of Hebrew tribes called by Joshua at Shechem.[18] After rehearsing Yahweh's mighty acts from the call of Abraham to the conquest of Canaan, he challenged his hearers to put away other gods and give themselves in unqualified commitment to Yahweh. To this challenge they responded and gave their formal oath of allegiance: "Yahweh our God we will serve, and his voice we will obey." The ceremony was then concluded with the sealing of a covenant, the giving of law and the erection of a great stone under a sacred oak.

This tradition of the assembly of Hebrew tribes at Shechem is important for a number of reasons.[19] For one thing, it reflects the memory of the extension of Mosaic Yahwism to Hebrew tribes which had not

[16] Or conversely!

[17] Two recent treatments of Shechem are: Walter Harrelson, *The City of Shechem: Its History and Importance*, 1953, and Eduard Nielsen, *Shechem. A Tradition-Historical Investigation*, 1955. Reports of the Drew-McCormick archaeological expeditions at Shechem, which began in the summer of 1956 and have continued intermittently since then, are to be found in various issues of the *Biblical Archaeologist* and the *Bulletin of the American Schools of Oriental Research* beginning in 1957.

[18] Josh. 24 is mostly E material, although there are some evidences of a Deuteronomic hand and possibly traces of a second early source. On literary problems connected with the chapter see especially Noth, *Das Buch Josua*, pp. 105-6.

[19] The basic work on Josh. 24 is Martin Noth's *Das System der zwölf Stämme Israels*. His position is summarized in English in his *History*, pp. 85-109. In the following section the writer is greatly dependent upon Noth's work.

been in Egypt nor experienced the events of the exodus and the covenant at Sinai. That Shechem was used for this convocation, even though the Book of Joshua records no conquest of it or the area in central Palestine surrounding it, would seem to suggest that this territory was already in the hands of people who were friendly to the invaders.[20] If the six-tribe Leah amphictyony had been organized around Shechem in the previous century, as we have suggested, it is quite possible that the general area was still occupied by Hebrews and others friendly to them. This would provide the context for an interpretation of Joshua's statement in vss. 14-15:

Now therefore fear Yahweh, and serve him in sincerity and in faithfulness; put away the gods which your fathers served beyond the River, and in Egypt, and serve Yahweh. And if you be unwilling to serve Yahweh, choose this day whom you will serve, whether the gods your fathers served in the region beyond the River, or the gods of the Amorites in whose land you dwell; but as for me and my house, we will serve Yahweh.

The words "as for me and my house" could refer to Joshua's tribe, i.e., Joseph. Joseph was the charismatic tradition-bearing "house" which on this occasion was offering Mosaic Yahwism to other Hebrew tribes that had gathered at Shechem.

Which tribes were these? We have already concluded that Judah and Simeon accepted Mosaic Yahwism at Kadesh shortly after the events of the exodus and covenant at Sinai. Their allegiance to Mosaic Yahwism had not been unqualified, however, since they sought to interpret it in terms of Kenite priestly forms. This, of course, was a basic reason for the split at Kadesh. After the Joseph tribes had succeeded in conquering a major portion of the Palestinian hill country and freeing southern Palestine for occupation by the tribes associated with Judah, it is possible that Judah and Simeon were less hesitant to acknowledge some validity in the more charismatic understanding of the covenant people than they had been before. Since Judah and Simeon were probably represented at Shechem on this occasion, it might be said that in this sense they accepted Yahwism from the

[20] See the comments by G. E. Wright, *Biblical Archaeology*, pp. 76-78.

Joseph tribes. At least they were compelled to recognize the dynamic of this kind of Yahwism. Those who accepted the Mosaic faith and entered into the covenant relationship with Yahweh for the first time at the Shechem assembly, however, would have been the rest of the tribes which claimed descent from the ancestor Jacob-Israel (Gen. 29:16–30:24; 35:16-20). These would have been Reuben, Issachar, Zebulun (Leah tribes), Benjamin (a Rachel tribe), Gad, Asher (Zilpah tribes), Dan, and Naphtali (Bilhah tribes).[21]

Joshua 24 also preserves the memory of the establishment of a twelve-tribe amphictyony at Shechem.[22] An amphictyony is a confederation of tribes organized around a central cult site. Such confederations existed not only in the Middle East in ancient times, but also in Greece and Italy. At times comprised of six tribes and at other times of twelve tribes, such confederations had a common form of worship at the central cult site and held special festivals there. Each tribe was responsible for the upkeep of the cult center for one month of the year in the twelve-tribe amphictyony and for two months in the six-tribe confederation. There is evidence in the Old Testament that some of Israel's neighbors were similarly organized (Gen. 25:13-16; 36:10-14; 36:20-28), and it is reasonable to assume that the twelve-tribe division of the Hebrews reflects the same phenomenon. The twelve-tribe system of the Hebrews has been preserved in two forms. In one form the tribe of Levi is included and Joseph appears as *one* tribe, e.g., Gen. 29:31–30:24 and Gen. 49:1b-27. In the other form Levi is omitted and Joseph is divided into Ephraim and Manasseh, e.g., Num. 26:4b-51. In both forms there is a persistent six-tribe division within the twelve-tribe system. In the earlier form it consists of Reuben, Simeon, Levi, Judah, Issachar, and Zebulun. In the other Gad replaces Levi.

[21] The question of the ultimate origin of these various tribes is most difficult. Reuben, Issachar, and Zebulun presumably had been in Palestine since the Amarna age. Benjamin may have entered the land not too long in advance of the Joseph tribes. The four concubine tribes may have been primarily of Canaanite composition and thus indigenous to Palestine. On this whole problem see Noth, *History*, pp. 53-84 and Bright, *Early Israel in Recent History Writing*, pp. 115-19.

[22] The key work in this regard is Noth, *Das System;* a summary of his position in English is in his *History*, pp. 85 ff.; cf. Bright, *History*, pp. 142 ff.

At Shechem, therefore, during the second half of the thirteenth century Joshua organized the Hebrews into a twelve-tribe amphictyony. On this occasion the people made the solemn oath, "Yahweh our God we will serve, and his voice we will obey" (vs. 24), and thus bound themselves into a sacred confederation. The God of this amphictyony was Yahweh, "a holy God" (vs. 19) and "a jealous God" (vs. 19; cf. Exod. 20:5; 34:14). The name of the amphictyony was "Israel" ("may God rule"). It is probable that this was the name first used by the six-tribe Leah amphictyony at Shechem in the fourteenth century. This would indicate some kind of continuity between the earlier and later confederations. The holy shrine of this amphictyony was the ark of the covenant. It was regarded as the throne of Yahweh and formed the center of the worship of the Hebrew tribes.

Comprising the original membership of this loosely organized confederation of twelve tribes were the Leah tribes, Reuben, Simeon, Levi, Judah, Issachar, and Zebulun, the two Rachel tribes, Joseph and Benjamin, and the four concubine tribes, Dan, Naphtali, Gad, and Asher. It would seem, however, that Levi's inclusion as a full member of the amphictyony was mostly a gesture of recognition of the seniority of the earlier six-tribe Leah amphictyony upon which the later twelve-tribe confederation was in part based.[23] There is little evidence that Levi ever functioned as a full tribe during this time. So it must have been relatively early in the period of the Judges that Levi was withdrawn and Joseph was divided into the two tribes, Manasseh and Ephraim. After this, Levi was to continue only as the name of a priesthood.

Although Judah and Simeon were members of this twelve-tribe amphictyony centering at Shechem, it seems likely, as Martin Noth has plausibly suggested,[24] that at the same time they were also part of a six-tribe amphictyony which was organized at Hebron in this period. This confederation was comprised of Judah and Simeon (also members of the twelve-tribe amphictyony),[25] as well as Caleb, Othniel,

---

[23] See Noth, *Das System*, pp. 33 ff.; *idem, History*, pp. 88 ff.

[24] Noth, *Das System*, pp. 107-8; cf. *idem, History*, pp. 181-2.

[25] In Greece and Italy it was quite common for a tribe to belong to more than one amphictyony.

THE PEOPLE OF THE COVENANT

Kenites (Cain), and Jerahmeel. The fact that the twelve-tribe amphictyony was rather loosely organized and left the individual tribes
a great deal of freedom would explain why this smaller amphictyony
could exist along with the larger one. The continuing existence of
this six-tribe confederation with its special theological and cultic concerns would also seem to explain why Judah always appears only
partially committed to the larger group.[26] The life of this southern
amphictyony will be considered more fully in the next chapter.

Covenant Ceremony at Shechem

A third reason for the significance of Joshua 24 is that it sheds light
on the worship of the twelve-tribe amphictyony. It preserves the
memory of a single historical event at Shechem in the time of Joshua,
but it is also the etiological story for a regularly observed covenant renewal ceremony there.[27] Other passages that are generally recognized
as belonging with Joshua 24 in this connection are Deut. 11:26-32;
27:1-26; 31:9-13; and Josh. 8:30-35. They all had their origin in a
regularly observed covenant renewal ceremony of the Israelite amphictyony at Shechem which began in the time of Joshua.[28] In addition
to these five traditions, it also seems likely that the E covenant legend
in an early oral stage can be connected with this ceremony at
Shechem.[29] It provided the basic liturgy of the cultic rite. It would

[26] Note the comments of Harrelson, *Shechem*, p. 357.

[27] Hugo Gressmann seems to have been one of the first to suggest that Josh. 24
reflects the memory of a covenant ceremony regularly observed at Shechem (*Die
Anfänge Israels. Die Schriften des Alten Testaments* [Göttingen: Vandenhoeck & Ruprecht,
1922.] p. 163). Ernst Sellin viewed it as a certainty (*Geschichte des israelitisch-jüdischen
Volkes*, I, 101). Subsequently this position has been accepted by any number of Old
Testament scholars, including Noth (*Das System*, pp. 72 ff.), Alt ("Die Ursprünge," pp.
325 ff.), von Rad (*Das formgeschichtliche Problem*, pp. 33-34), Artur Weiser (*Die
Psalmen. I. Das Alte Testament Deutsch*. [Göttingen: Vandenhoeck & Ruprecht, 1950.]
13 ff.), and Kraus (*Gottesdienst*, pp. 49 ff.). In English see especially Anderson,
Understanding the Old Testament, pp. 85 ff., and Wright, "The Book of Deuteronomy,"
pp. 325-26, 488 ff., 501 ff., 512-13.

[28] It is likely that there was some kind of a covenant tradition at Shechem even
before it became the chief cult site of this amphictyony. This is indicated, for one
thing, by the name of the principal deity of the Canaanite inhabitants of Shechem,
"Baal berith" (i.e., "Baal of the covenant" Judg. 8:33; 9:4; cf. 9:46). A number of the
traditions of this older Shechem cult seem to have been appropriated by the Israelites.
See my remarks in *Sinai Covenant Traditions*, pp. 317-21.

[29] I have sought to relate the E covenant legend to the ceremony at Shechem in my
Sinai Covenant Traditions, pp. 295-316. James Muilenburg has connected Exod. 19:4-6

have been read and re-enacted as representatives of the twelve tribes made their annual pilgrimage in the autumn [30] to Shechem to renew their covenant vows to Yahweh.

1. They appeared before the ark of the covenant which would have been used in the ceremony.[31] We have already suggested that the ark was used in connection with the E covenant tradition.[32] If this conjecture is correct, the ark must have been used in the dramatic reproduction of a theophany in the cult. Just as Yahweh had been present in the thunderstorm at Sinai when the original covenant was made, so his presence was enthroned upon the ark when succeeding generations of Hebrews renewed that covenant. The blast of the *shofar* represented his voice in this ceremony (Exod. 19:16, 19; 20:18); it was the audible indication of his invisible presence.

2. Also in the rite Yahweh's name would have been announced: "I am Yahweh your God" (Exod. 20:2; cf. Josh. 24:2). The proclamation of God's name must have been a dramatic moment. It was fraught with meaning, for God's name was closely associated with his inmost being. Yahweh, of course, was continually present on the ark. But when his name was announced at the decisive moment in the liturgy, he was uniquely and intimately giving himself anew to his covenant people. He was God *for them.*[33] It was thus a moment of surpassing significance in the life of Israel, and it kept before the people continually the importance of the Divine Name.[34] Because the name "Yahweh"

(E) with the Shechem ceremony ("The Form and Structure of the Covenantal Formulations," *Vetus Testamentum,* IX (1959), 347-65), and Walter Beyerlin, *op. cit.,* pp. 171 ff., associates both the J and E covenant legends with the Shechem cult.

[30] That the covenant ceremony is to be associated with the annual feast of Ingathering in the autumn seems likely. See especially Kraus, *Gottesdienst,* pp. 49-66.

[31] There is only one explicit reference to the ark at Shechem, and it would seem to be authentic (Josh. 8:33; cf. Deut. 31:9-13). Although there is only this one *definite* allusion to the ark at Shechem, it is probable, as Noth suggests (*History,* p. 97), that the expression "before God" in Josh. 24:1 refers to it, because as Yahweh's throne the ark was the place of his presence (cf. Judg. 20:26-27).

[32] Chap. Two, pp. 61-62.

[33] The third commandment (Exod. 20:7) guarded against misuse of God's gift of himself in his name.

[34] It seems likely that what Gerhard von Rad terms "Name" theology in Deuteronomy (*Studies in Deuteronomy,* pp. 38 ff.) is related to this part of the covenant ceremony at Shechem. Von Rad distinguishes between the "Name" theology in Deuteronomy and the "Kabod-Moed" theology of the Priestly Code. That which constitutes the "Kabod-Moed" theology is the occasional descent of the "glory of Yahweh" to the tent of

was proclaimed over the ark in this way, II Sam. 6:2 calls it: "The ark of God, over which is called the name, the name of Yahweh of hosts who sits enthroned upon the cherubim." [35]

3. With the name of Yahweh was coupled a recapitulation of his great deeds: "I am Yahweh your God, who brought you out of the land of Egypt, out of the house of bondage" (Exod. 20:2). What Yahweh does testifies to what Yahweh is. Thus his nature is revealed. Because he has shown himself in his actions to be gracious to her, Israel is called to respond by accepting anew his covenant and its obligations. This element is quite clear in Joshua 24. Verses 2b-13 recount Yahweh's activity in the history of the Patriarchs (vss. 2b-4), in the exodus (vss. 5-7), and in the conquest (vss. 8-13). This passage is thus merely an expansion of the tradition in the E covenant legend of the basic act of Yahweh for Israel, the event of the exodus (Exod. 20:2; 19:4).

The cultic character of this recital of Yahweh's deeds can be seen clearly in the alternation between "you [we]" and "your fathers":

5 And I sent Moses and Aaron, and I plagued Egypt with what I did in the midst of it; and afterwards I brought *you* out. 6 Then I brought *your fathers* out of Egypt, and *you* came to the sea; and the Egyptians pursued *your fathers* with chariots and horsemen to the Red Sea. 7 And when *they* cried to Yahweh, he put darkness between *you* and the Egyptians, and made the sea come upon *them* and cover *them;* and *your eyes* saw what I did to Egypt; and *you* lived in the wilderness a long time. Josh. 24:5-7; cf. vss. 16-17

This alternation is not evidence of two different sources;[36] rather it is cultic language which identifies later generations with the one that

meeting. It probably originated at Hebron, according to von Rad. "Name" theology, on the other hand, probably originated at Shechem. It is characterized by the idea of the continuing presence of Yahweh's "Name" in the cult. The characteristic expression of this theology is that Yahweh will choose a place and cause his name "to dwell" or "put" his name, there (Deut. 12:5, 11, 21; 14:24, etc.). The root of this theology von Rad sees in the ark which was viewed as the throne of the invisibly present God. I would merely go a bit further and specifically root "Name" theology in this part of the covenant renewal ceremony.

[35] This is a literal rendering of the original Hebrew.
[36] So Noth, *Josua*, pp. 106-7.

114

experienced the original events. In the cult the later generations could affirm: "This is *our* life-story too." [37]

4. Then Yahweh's law would have been proclaimed. Israel's obligation as the covenant people of Yahweh was to keep his law. The fundamental law of the covenant was apodictic law, the basic purpose of which was "to preserve Israel's relationship to God intact and to prevent its possible disturbance in all departments of life by the prohibition of unlawful acts." [38] Because of its literary form and categorical character apodictic law was particularly suitable for recitation in the cult when the representatives of the twelve tribes annually committed themselves anew to the sovereign and absolute will of their covenant God. The fundamental apodictic law of Israel was the first commandment: "You shall have no other gods before me" (Exod. 20:3). This law was undoubtedly recited on each occasion when the covenant was renewed at Shechem, as Josh. 24:19-23 indicates.

The twelve apodictic laws in the form of curses in Deut. 27:11-26 can also be related to the covenant ceremony at Shechem.[39] The number twelve obviously corresponds to the twelve tribes of the amphictyony. These laws were evidently taken from a larger body of apodictic law [40] and used to form a code which was recited at Shechem in connection with the renewal of the covenant. It is noteworthy that this code of twelve curses is like the decalogue of the E covenant legend not only in that both are comprised of apodictic law, but also both contain *cultic* and *social* law. They regulate the relation of the Israelites to their God and to one another. In this respect they differ from the early collection of apodictic law preserved in the J covenant legend

[37] Anderson, *op. cit.*, p. 87.

[38] Noth, *History*, p. 104.

[39] Rituals of blessing and cursing are peculiarly associated with the two mountains on either side of Shechem, Gerizim and Ebal (Deut. 11:29; Josh. 8:33-34).

[40] The fact that the first commandment does not appear in the twelve curses, but was undoubtedly known and used at Shechem (Josh. 24:19-23), would seem to suggest that they must have been taken from a larger body of apodictic law. Only three of the commandments of the decalogue are found in the twelve curses (Deut. 27:15—Exod. 20:4; Deut. 27:16—Exod. 20:12; Deut. 27:24—Exod. 20:13). One can probably assume, however, that all of the commandments of the decalogue were known at Shechem. Gerhard von Rad specifically associates the decalogue with the Shechem cult (*Theologie* I, 27). See the writer's further comments in *Sinai Covenant Traditions*, pp. 305-7.

(Exod. 34:10-26). It contains exclusively *cultic* law and thus expresses a different theological concern.

Josh. 24:25 shows that casuistic law was also in use at Shechem: "So Joshua made a covenant with the people that day, and made statutes and *ordinances* for them at Shechem." The word "ordinance" [41] is the technical term for casuistic law. Although it is probable that some casuistic law was already a part of the tradition of the Hebrews even in the nomadic stage of their development, it is likely that most of the casuistic law of the E Covenant Code (Exod. 20:23-23:33) was incorporated into the life of the Yahweh-worshiping amphictyony during this period.[42] The casuistic law of the Covenant Code presupposes a sedentary, agricultural society, and was the kind of law that was indispensable for the Hebrews in their new environment. It was thus borrowed by Israel from her neighbors;[43] but it was adapted to the unique spirit of Mosaic Yahwism.[44] Since the law came to be viewed as Yahweh's law, it was naturally associated with the covenant he made with Israel at Sinai. It was not, however, the kind of law that was appropriate for recitation in the cult as part of the covenant ceremony, both because of its content and literary form. Nevertheless, the casuistic law in the E Covenant Code must have been known and preserved by the same circles that transmitted the E covenant legend.

5. After the proclamation of Yahweh's law, the people would have taken the oath of obedience to the covenant. According to Josh. 24:24, when Joshua admonished the people to put away their foreign gods and incline their hearts to Yahweh, they responded: "Yahweh our God we will serve, and his voice we will obey." This corresponds to the oath of the people in the E covenant legend (Exod. 24:3, 7). In addition to this oral oath at Shechem, there also seems to have been a symbolic action to express the commitment of the people to Yahweh.

[41] The Hebrew expression is *mishpat*.

[42] Albrecht Alt is one who takes this position ("Die Ursprünge," p. 302, n. 1); cf. Anderson, *op. cit.*, pp. 90-91 and Mendenhall, *Law and Covenant*, p. 42. Otto Procksch (*op. cit.*, p. 114) thinks that the casuistic law of the E Covenant Code comes from the older Shechemite Leah amphictyony.

[43] Not from the Canaanites, however. It was ultimately of Mesopotamian origin. See Bright, *History*, pp. 150-51.

[44] See especially Procksch, *op. cit.*, pp. 116-18.

This was a "ritual of renunciation of foreign gods." [45] Joshua's exhortation to the people to put away the foreign gods (Josh. 24:24; cf. vss. 14-15) is evidently an allusion to this rite. Another tradition which would seem to reflect this same ritual is in Gen. 35:2-4:

2 So Jacob said to his household and to all who were with him, "Put away the foreign gods that are among you, and purify yourselves, and change your garments; 3 then let us arise and go up to Bethel, that I may make there an altar to the God who answered me in the day of my distress and has been with me wherever I have gone." 4 So they gave to Jacob all the foreign gods that they had, and the rings that were in their ears; and Jacob hid them under the oak which was near Shechem.

This ritual in which foreign gods were renounced and buried seems to have been indigenous to the Shechem cult. It was possibly first used by the Canaanite inhabitants of Shechem against their traditional enemies.[46] It may also have been employed by the old six-tribe Leah amphictyony at Shechem. When the Israelites under Joshua occupied Palestine and selected Shechem as the central cult site of the twelve-tribe amphictyony, the ritual was appropriated for Yahwism. It was quite compatible with the demand for exclusive worship of Yahweh which characterized the Mosaic faith. Consequently it became the negative part of a ceremony that had as its positive expression the oath of allegiance to Yahweh.

6. Finally, in this ceremony at Shechem there would have been a sacrificial rite which sealed the covenant. In Joshua 24 it is simply stated that "Joshua made a covenant with the people that day" (vs. 25). But both Josh. 8:30-31 and Deut. 27:5-7 speak of "burnt offerings" and "peace offerings" in connection with the Shechem ceremony. The E covenant legend also tells of "young men of the people of Israel" who offer to Yahweh "burnt offerings" and "peace offerings of oxen" (Exod. 24:5), after which the blood is sprinkled on the altar and the people (Exod. 24:6-8). The "burnt offering" was one which was completely

---

[45] See especially Alt, "Die Wallfahrt von Sichem nach Bethel," *Kleine Schriften* I, 79-88; cf. also Kraus, *Gottesdienst*, pp. 58-59; and Nielsen, *Shechem*, pp. 234-39; *idem*, "The Burial of the Foreign Gods," *Studia Theologica*, VIII (1955), 103 ff.

[46] Nielsen, *Shechem*, p. 238. Mendenhall (*op. cit.*, pp. 33, 41) points to a similar motif in the Hittite covenant form.

consumed by sacrificial fire and thus was wholly offered to God.[47] The "peace offering" was a communion sacrifice.[48] In it the fat of the sacrificial animal was consumed on the altar, while the rest was eaten by worshipers who knew that God was invisibly present at the meal. With its communion character, the "peace offering" was thus peculiarly suitable for the sacramental sealing of the covenant relation.[49]

It has been plausibly suggested that the custom of having "young men of the people of Israel" (Exod. 24:5) offer the covenant sacrifices began at Shechem.[50] Each year a new generation of young men would have offered the sacrifices at the annual covenant ceremony. This cultic activity marked their full incorporation into the life of the covenant people. They were subsequently recognized as mature sons of the covenant.

The Levitical Priesthood of the Amphictyony

Those in charge of the celebration of the covenant festival, as well as those responsible for the preservation and transmission of its traditions, seem to have been Levites. We have already suggested that at Kadesh the Levites received the priestly office and were subsequently recognized as official priests by the powerful Joseph tribes.[51] Deut. 33:8-10 preserves the memory of this event and also states the functions of the Levitical priests as teaching law and offering sacrifices. Since they were recognized by the Joseph tribes, who were dominant during most of the life of the twelve-tribe amphictyony, it was natural that the Levites had this privileged position at the central cult. Three passages explicitly connect Levites with the covenant festival at Shechem. Deut. 27:14 states that they were involved in the proclamation of the law: "And the Levites shall declare to all the men of Israel with a loud voice." Then follow the twelve apodictic laws in the form of curses. This involvement of the Levites with Yahweh's law is in complete accordance with their function as indicated in Deut. 33:10. Josh. 8:33 and Deut. 31:9 report that the Levites carried the ark as it was

[47] See von Rad, Theologie, I, 254-55.
[48] Ibid., pp. 255-56.
[49] Eichrodt, op. cit., pp. 156-57.
[50] Beyerlin, op. cit., pp. 46-48, 174-75.
[51] Chap. Three, pp. 98-100.

used in the covenant ceremony (cf. Deut. 10:8). Since they are thus explicitly connected with both the ark, on which the cult theophany occurred, and the proclamation of the law, it can probably be assumed that Levites were in general charge of the entire ceremony as it was observed annually.

Although the traditions are silent on the point, it is not improbable that a Levite usually functioned as "covenant mediator" in the ceremony. The E etiological story for the institution of the office of covenant mediator, as we have seen, is in Exod. 20:18-20 (cf. Deut. 18:15-18).[52] The covenant mediator took the role of Moses in the covenant ceremony. Joshua 24 would indicate that Joshua fulfilled this function. Subsequently a Levite may have presided over the ceremony. If certain Levites did function in this way, it was probably not because they had a special claim as priests but merely because it was practical for them to do it.

The Levites in this period, like the twelve-tribe amphictyony itself, were evidently a very loosely organized group. If they were scattered through the various tribes, as a number of passages suggest (Josh. 21:20 ff.; Deut. 12:12, 18-19; 14:27, 29, et al.), a closely knit organization would have been impossible. Nor do they seem to have had any tightly drawn genealogical lines. As W. F. Albright observes: "One could either be born into the Levite tribe or one could be adopted as a full member of it." [53] It would have been merely a small group of Levites that were formally involved in the annual covenant ceremony and in the preservation and transmission of its legal and narrative traditions and cult objects. Others carried on their priestly duties at tribal cult sites in a variety of ways (e.g., Judg. 17-18; 19-20).

The most important cult object in charge of this special group of Levites, of course, was the ark. A very important tradition they evidently preserved was the E covenant legend.[54] The latter was presum-

---

[52] On the covenant mediator see especially Kraus, *Gottesdienst*, pp. 60-66; cf. also my article, "The Prophetic Call of Samuel," in *Israel's Prophetic Heritage: Essays in Honor of James Muilenburg* (New York: Harper & Brother, 1962).

[53] *Archaeology and the Religion of Israel*, p. 109.

[54] Another significant tradition stream that seems to have emerged in connection with the covenant ceremony at Shechem and to have been preserved and transmitted by Levites was that which eventually became the book of Deuteronomy (see especially von Rad, *Studies in Deuteronomy* and Wright, "The Book of Deuteronomy," pp. 315-16,

ably the official covenant legend of the twelve-tribe amphictyony and reflected its *official theology*. It was the covenant theology favored by the dominant Joseph tribes.

The theology of the E covenant legend is quite in accordance with what is generally known about the amphictyony. Indeed it is much more compatible with the picture of the Hebrew tribes given in the Book of Judges than would be the theology of the J covenant tradition. The latter suggests a strongly centralized organization of the covenant people centering in an authoritarian priestly line. In the former there is little indication of a concentration of authority in the hands of the few. The covenant is with *all* the people; they are a "kingdom of priests." In the E tradition the people themselves are consecrated for the ceremony; they all experience the theophany; they appoint the covenant mediator; and "young men" from the people offer the covenant sacrifices. The whole story points to a kind of "universal priesthood of believers" theology. There is no centralized religious authority and the laity participate fully.

Since the twelve-tribe amphictyony was very loosely organized with no strong, centralized government the E legend was quite appropriate theologically. These tribes did know themselves as the covenant people of Yahweh and they were committed to his will, but they recognized no authoritarian human government. In a time of crisis they could be summoned in the name of Yahweh of Sinai to follow a leader in meeting a threat to the national existence, as in the time of Deborah (Judg. 4-5). But the authority of the leader was limited to the crisis. There was no succession of authority. When the idea of a king emerged in

---

323-36). The oldest traditions in Deuteronomy consist of homilies preached at the covenant ceremony. They expound the covenant faith and exhort the covenant people to obedience to the covenant law. So, if the E covenant tradition can be understood as the basic *liturgy* of the covenant ceremony at Shechem, the earliest traditions of Deuteronomy can be viewed as a *collection of sermons* preached on the occasion. The writer would suggest that this Deuteronomic tradition flowed from Shechem with the ark to Shiloh when that city became the cult center of the twelve-tribe amphictyony and the site of the annual covenant renewal ceremony (see below). Subsequently, after the division of the Davidic kingdom in 922, the traditions were at Bethel (see especially Fritz Dummermuth, "Zur deuteronomischen Kulttheologie und ihren Voraussetzungen," *Zeitschrift für die Alttestamentliche Wissenschaft*, 70 [1958], 59-98). Finally, after the fall of the northern kingdom in 722, this stream flowed to Jerusalem where it became the basis of Josiah's reformation in 621 B.C.

this period, the official view was that it was incompatible with Yahwism. When he is offered the kingship, Gideon says: "I will not rule over you, and my son will not rule over you; Yahweh will rule over you" (Judg. 8:23).[55]

Moreover, it is clear that the "spirit" of Yahweh could come upon a layman investing him with divine authority as fully as upon a priest. It possessed Gideon (Judg. 6:34), Jephthah (11:29), and Samson (14:6, 19; 15:14), none of whom was a priest. And the action of God was direct upon these men, with no mediation through a priest or cult functionary, not even a Levite. This is quite a different picture from that given by the J tradition in Num. 11:16-17, 23-25, where there is a definite attempt to control the "spirit" of Yahweh by channeling it through the official priestly line.

This "kingdom of priests" theology evidently resulted in a certain religious tolerance. Such tolerance was confined to Yahwism, to be sure. The first commandment obtained: "You shall have no other gods before me." At the same time, however, there was considerable freedom throughout the land in regard to the forms of worship of Yahweh and the organization of the tribes. There was no national authority to enforce complete religious uniformity. This official tolerance probably explains why the smaller six-tribe amphictyony at Hebron with its more intolerant theology was permitted to carry on its distinctive life. The southern group worshiped Yahweh, but with a very different interpretation of his relation to the covenant people.

The Amphictyony at Shiloh

Some time during the amphictyonic period of Israel's life Shiloh replaced Shechem as the central cult site. This is the situation reflected in the early chapters of I Samuel. Shiloh was a city which evidently had possessed no significance previously. According to Judg. 21:19 it was located "north of Bethel, on the east of the highway that goes up from Bethel to Shechem, and south of Lebonah." It was thus in a rather secluded area in the territory of Ephraim. In modern times Shiloh has been identified with *Seilun,* which is some ten miles north of Bethel.[56]

---

[55] Abimelech's attempt to establish a kingship, of course, was abortive (Judg. 9).

[56] Excavations were carried on at this site by a Danish expedition under H. Kjaer and A. Schmidt in 1926-29 (H. Kjaer, *JPOS,* X [1930]). The writer has not had access

Just why Shiloh replaced Shechem as the cult center of the amphictyony is not completely clear. It is quite possible, as Noth suggests,[57] that it was a general policy to change the central place of amphictyonic worship from time to time; in the wilderness the ark had been a traveling shrine and it must not become a cult object in the manner of the Canaanites. The controversies at Shechem during the period of Abimelech which ended in its destruction too probably figured in this particular change.[58] If the change can be associated with the activity of Abimelech, it may have occurred around 1150 B.C.[59] Another factor might have been that the tribe of Ephraim surpassed the tribe of Manasseh in power and significance during this period.[60] When Ephraim clearly became superior, Shechem of Manasseh had to yield to Shiloh of Ephraim.[61]

In any event, by the second half of the eleventh century Shiloh had become the cult center of the amphictyony. The ark was there, as was also the priest Eli who was assisted by his two sons Hophni and Phinehas. The traditions in I Samuel give no clue as to the ancestry of Eli. It is only the Chronicler who relates the line of Eli to Aaron through the latter's fourth son Ithamar (I Chron. 24:1-6). However,

---

to this work, but is dependent upon Albright, *From the Stone Age to Christianity*, pp. 103-4 and Kraeling, *Bible Atlas*, p. 172. The excavations revealed that the city was inhabited in the Middle Bronze Age, but apparently not in the Late Bronze Age. In the Early Iron Age the site was again occupied, when there was evidently a rather extensive settlement. There is evidence that the city suffered violent destruction during the middle of the eleventh century B.C. and was not again occupied until the Hellenistic period. This destruction of Shiloh is generally associated with the Battle of Ebenezer when the ark was lost and Israel was brought low by the Philistines (I Sam. 4). The enemy must have followed up their victory over the Hebrews on the battlefield by razing their chief city. Centuries later the prophet Jeremiah refers to this destruction (Jere. 7:12; 26:6, 9).

[57] *History*, p. 94.

[58] So Harrelson (*The City of Shechem*, p. 487).

[59] In an article in the *New York Times* (Nov. 13, 1960) G. E. Wright suggests this date as the result of excavations at Shechem in the summer of 1960. However, the report of this campaign in the *Bulletin of the American Schools of Oriental Research* (No. 161, Feb., 1961, 11-54) merely says that it occurred some time during the 12th century B.C.

[60] Reflected in Jacob's blessing of Ephraim and Manasseh (Gen. 48).

[61] Why Bethel in Ephraim was overlooked in this regard is a problem in itself. It is possible that Bethel did become the central sanctuary for a brief period after Shechem and before Shiloh, as might be deduced from Judg. 20:26-27 (cf. 20:18; 21:2). This is Noth's view (*History*, p. 94).

this probably represents a later post-exilic attempt to relate this northern priestly family to the line of Aaron. It is frequently argued that the family of Eli must have been Levitical because of the Egyptian names of his two sons, Hophni and Phinehas.[62] In all probability the family was Levitic in the broad sense, and quite possibly they were even blood descendants of the Levites of the Mosaic period. That it was Aaronic, however, is unlikely.[63] Whether this priesthood was appointed by all the tribes as a whole or merely represented the local Levitical priesthood of Shiloh who took care of the ark when Shiloh became the central sanctuary must remain an open question.[64]

I Samuel 1 speaks of a great annual festival at Shiloh to which Elkanah and his family pilgrimaged. Concerning this feast at Shiloh John Bright comments:

> Though we are not told, this was probably the autumn feast of Ingathering at the turn of the year. It is exceedingly probable, too, and very likely in connection with this annual feast, that there was a regular ceremony of covenant renewal—whether annually or every seven years (Deut. 31:9-13)—to which the tribesmen would come with their tribute to the God-King, to hear his gracious deeds recited and his law read, and then with blessings and curses to take anew their oath of allegiance to him.[65]

The ark would have been used in this covenant ceremony at Shiloh. With the ark presumably was the E covenant legend in one of its oral forms. It would have been read and re-enacted as the people of Israel each year repeated their covenant vows to their covenant God. In general the ceremony would have been celebrated in much the same way as previously had been done at Shechem.

Thus the house of Eli was involved with the covenant festival of the amphictyony. One of its members presumably served as covenant mediator, as Joshua had done at Shechem. This association of the house of Eli with the amphictyonic covenant ceremony and the "kingdom of priests" covenant theology reflected in its official cult legend will be

[62] So Albright, Stone Age, pp. 193, 215.
[63] The Aaronic priesthood came originally from the Hebrews in southern Palestine and centered at Hebron before the time of David. See Chap. Five.
[64] See Noth, History, p. 98.
[65] History, p. 149. Noth evidently takes the same position (History, pp. 97-98).

important to keep in mind when we consider David. Abiathar, the priest from Nob who served with David, was descended from the house of Eli.[66] Abiathar seems to have been David's primary contact with old northern amphictyonic traditions and theology throughout his long and successful career.

I Samuel 1–3 associates Samuel also with the cult at Shiloh. In chapters 1–2 at Shiloh Hannah receives the promise that she will have a son, and later, in accordance with her vow, she brings the young Samuel back to this shrine to minister before Yahweh. And chapter 3 contains an account of the call of Samuel before the ark at Shiloh.[67] If these chapters do preserve an authentic historical memory, as seems likely, Samuel would have had a knowledge of the basic cultic and theological traditions of the Israelite amphictyony. As a regular participant in the annual covenant ceremony at Shiloh during part of his early life, he would have been acquainted with some form of the E covenant legend and undoubtedly was deeply influenced by the kind of covenant theology it reflected.[68] This would seem to be the basic reason for his ambivalent attitude toward the kingship when it emerged in the latter part of his life.

An event occurred during Samuel's youth which made the kingship almost inevitable if the Israelites were to maintain their integrity as a people and retain their distinctive covenant faith. That event was their decisive defeat by the Philistines in the battle of Ebenezer in 1050 B.C. (I Sam. 4). The Philistines had come to Palestine within less than a century after the conquest under Joshua. In the Samson narratives (Judg. 14–16) they first appear on the Old Testament scene.[69] These legendary stories seem to reflect the authentic memory of a series of border incidents between the Philistines and the Hebrews in the southwestern part of Palestine.[70] The Philistines were evidently a

[66] It would seem from I Sam. 14:3; 22:9, 20; 23:6 that Abiathar was the son of Ahijah (Ahimelech) who was the son of Ahitub who was the son of Phinehas who was the son of Eli. See Albright, *Archaeology and the Religion of Israel*, p. 202.

[67] I have sought to interpret the significance of I Sam. 3 in my article "The Prophetic Call of Samuel."

[68] Muilenburg thinks that in I Sam. 12 Samuel actually functions as covenant mediator ("The Form and Structure of the Covenantal Formulations").

[69] The references to them in the book of Genesis are evidently anachronistic.

[70] It was also probably Philistine pressure that forced the Danites to move north from the territory they originally occupied in Palestine.

fragment of the sea people and originally inhabitants of the coast of Asia Minor and the Aegean Islands. In the thirteenth century they began to move southward and attempted to invade Egypt. In successive invasion efforts they were defeated by Marniptah (1224-16 B.C.) and Ramses III (1175-44). So they turned to Palestine and by the second half of the twelfth century were firmly established in its southwestern section. Their five main cities were Gaza, Ashkelon, Ashdod, Ekron, and Gath, each of which was governed by a king. By the middle of the eleventh century they were well enough organized to attempt to conquer the whole of Palestine. This attempt is recounted in I Samuel. It was a deadly serious threat to the Hebrew people.

I Sam. 4-6 is concerned with the fate of the ark of the covenant in the first hot war between the Philistines and the Israelites. The decisive battle took place at Ebenezer. The Philistines gathered their forces at Aphek; the Hebrews were at Ebenezer. In an initial skirmish the Israelites were defeated. But then they sent for the ark, upon which Yahweh of hosts was believed to be invisibly enthroned. It would see them through this conflict victoriously! This was the ark of Yahweh! But it did not! The Hebrews were utterly routed in the battle. Their armies were completely disintegrated. Their cult center, Shiloh, was destroyed, as the Old Testament implies and archaeological excavations have confirmed. Worst of all, their most sacred shrine, the ark, was captured by their enemies. This was a disastrous defeat for the Hebrew people and their loosely organized twelve-tribe amphictyony. It was one of the lowest periods in the entire history of Israel.

Since the ark was taken by the Philistines at this time, it was obviously separated from the E covenant legend. Up to this point the E legend had evidently been preserved and transmitted orally by circles in charge of the ark. When the ark went with the Philistines, the E covenant legend would have remained in the minds and hearts of certain Hebrew religious figures who had been at Shiloh. Since the entire Elohist epic was a product of northern Israel, one can assume that when David later brought the ark to Jerusalem (II Sam. 6), the E covenant legend did not go with it. It remained in the North and later emerged in connection with the cultic activities of Jeroboam I after the division of the Davidic kingdom. Its kind of covenant theology was of decisive importance at that time.

At the time of the battle of Ebenezer, however, its "kingdom of priests" theology and the loosely organized twelve-tribe amphictyony undergirded by it were thoroughly discredited. They were completely inadequate in the face of the Philistine ascendancy. The Hebrews needed a much stronger form of government. They had to have a king!

Chapter Five

The Emergence of
the Kingship in Israel

I SAMUEL 7–12 [1] TELLS HOW ISRAEL GOT A KING.[2] THIS WAS AN EPOCHAL
event in the history of the Hebrews. It was a radically new departure.
Most of Israel's neighbors had long had kings. But Israel had not had
a king before—at least not an earthly king. They were the covenant
people of Yahweh and *Yahweh was their king*. "Rule over us, you and
your grandson also; for you have delivered us out of the hand of
Midian," they said to Gideon after his brilliant victory over the enemy.
But Gideon said to them: "I will not rule over you, and my son will not
rule over you; Yahweh will rule over you" (Judg. 8:22-23). Yahweh
was their ruler; he was their leader; he was their king. To be sure, the
twelve-tribe amphictyony was a religio-political organization which

[1] I and II Samuel have preserved many traditions that are of great historical value
concerning Saul and David. Although there are areas of obscurity and uncertainty, it
is generally recognized that the historian is on fairly firm ground when dealing with
this period. For discussions of the literary sources in I and II Samuel see the standard
commentaries, and also Noth, *Überlieferungsgeschichtliche Studien* I, pp. 61-72 and L.
Rost, *Die Überlieferung von der Thronnachfolge Davids*, BWANT, III, 6 (1926).

[2] The classical work on the emergence of the kingship in Israel is Albrecht Alt's
"Die Staatenbildung der Israeliten in Palästina," *Kleine Schriften*, II, 1-65.

allowed for the possibility of a certain kind of political leadership among the Hebrew tribes. It was charismatic leadership, however. The Book of Judges preserves the memory of the exploits of a number of these charismatic leaders during the amphictyonic period—Othniel (Judg. 3:7-11), Ehud (3:12-30), Shamgar (3:31), Deborah and Barak (chs. 4–5), Gideon (chs. 6–8), Jephthah (chs. 11–12), Samson (chs. 13–16). Their authority was by no means unconditional, though, and was evidently limited to the crisis which called them to leadership. The amphictyony did not provide for a national leader who was to be the center of political and religious authority *for his whole life,* and whose power was to be transferred to his son and his son's son and the son of his son's son. But as a result of the Philistine crisis this was exactly what the Hebrews got. Such a kingship was fully established at Jerusalem with David, and the first definite step in this direction was taken when Saul became king.

After the defeat of the Israelites at Ebenezer, the Philistines were able to establish their authority with fair effectiveness over most of Palestine west of the Jordan river. In the central mountain range they installed garrisons to keep the Hebrews subservient (I Sam. 10:5; 13: 3-4, 23). By means of a monopoly on iron they attempted to prevent the conquered covenant people from making arms to use in a rebellion (I Sam. 13:19-22). This was the situation which obtained for some thirty years.[3]

This weakened condition of the Hebrews left them vulnerable to attack from the east by old nomadic enemies. Eventually the Ammonites, who previously had been repelled by Jephthah (Judg. 11–12), attacked Jabesh-gilead (I Sam. 11). This was a city east of the Jordan and evidently outside Philistine domination. In connection with the crisis caused by this attack Saul emerged.

Saul, Israel's First King

Saul was the first king of the Hebrew nation—if he can actually be called a king. He really did not know how to be a king. Nor did he ever have an adequate theological foundation for his kingship. At

---

[3] From *ca.* 1050 B.C., the time of the destruction of Shiloh, to *ca.* 1020 B.C., the date of the emergence of Saul. See Bright, *History,* p. 466.

least, he was the first national leader who bore the title. Saul was a tall man, shy, sensitive, more frequently controlled by his passions than his mind. There was a basic instability about him, but at the same time the Old Testament traditions suggest a kind of grandeur in the man. The son of Kish of the tribe of Benjamin, Saul was a native of Gibeah, a town located three miles north of Jerusalem. It was probably not fortuitous that the first king of Israel came from Benjamin. Benjamin, as W. F. Albright points out, was the most central tribe and at the same time one of the weakest in the Israelite confederacy. "In a confederacy where tribal jealousy ran high, it was of great importance that the new king should not excite particularistic friction from the start."[4]

There are three traditions concerning Saul's selection as king.[5] I Sam. 10:17-27 is probably the latest account.[6] In this story Samuel calls all the people of Israel to Mizpah and conducts a lot to select a king. This tradition belongs with I Samuel 8 and 12, where it is stressed that the kingship, even though permitted by Yahweh, was nevertheless a kind of apostasy. Although late, it undoubtedly preserves the authentic memory of a theological opposition to the kingship when it emerged. It is not improbable that this source reflects some real reservation in Samuel's own mind concerning this new departure in Israel's life.

I Sam. 9:1–10:16 is a dramatic and popular account of Saul's selection by Samuel to be king.[7] It is the story of the young farmer who sets out to find his father's asses, but instead finds a kingdom. Saul is led by his servant to an obscure seer, Samuel, for information concerning the lost animals. Samuel seizes the opportunity to anoint Saul privately as "prince" over the people Israel. In this story Samuel expresses no reservations concerning the kingship; on the contrary, it is in accordance with the revealed will of Yahweh who has selected

[4] Albright, *From the Stone Age to Christianity*, p. 222.
[5] Each may originally have been associated with a different cult center. See Hans Wilhelm Hertzberg, *Die Samuelbücher. Das Alte Testament Deutsch* (Göttingen: Vandenhoeck & Ruprecht, 1956), pp. 59, 65, 68.
[6] It is usually assigned to the "Samuel Source" in I Samuel. It may originally have been associated with the cult site of Mizpah.
[7] It is to be assigned to the "Saul Source" in I Samuel. It may originally have been associated with the cult site of Ramah.

Saul as prince over Israel in order to save them from the Philistines.

The third account is found in I Samuel 11,[8] and it is probably the most authentic historically.[9] This is the story of the attack on the city of Jabesh-gilead in Transjordan by the Ammonites. When Nahash, king of Ammon, laid seige to Jabesh-gilead, its residents appealed for help to their fellow Israelites across the Jordan. Their call was answered by Saul. As had happened to Gideon, Jephthah, and Barak before him, the spirit of Yahweh rushed mightily upon Saul (I Sam. 11:6). He was a charismatic leader on this occasion. He belonged to the old amphictyonic order. He cut a yoke of oxen to pieces and sent throughout all the territory of Israel with the message: "Whoever does not come out after Saul and Samuel, so shall it be done to his oxen" (vs. 7). The Israelites blazed forth under his leadership to Jabesh-gilead, where they attacked and cut to pieces the Ammonite armies. They were victorious and Saul had led them. A new leader had appeared among the Hebrews. Here was the man who could lead the nation against the Philistines. He had the spirit of the Lord. Here was the man who should be king. "So all the people went to Gilgal, and there they made Saul king before Yahweh in Gilgal" (I Sam. 11:15). Gilgal was presumably chosen because it was outside Philistine domination, and also because it was an old and important cult site of the tribe of Benjamin.

The Hebrews now had a king and this king organized for war against the Philistines. To say that Saul "organized" is perhaps putting it too optimistically. Saul never had much of an organization. He was a charismatic man, not an organization man. In this respect Saul belonged much more to the old order than to the new. Even at the height of his power as king he had no military conscription, no taxes, no harem. He selected his own home, Gibeah, as his capital, and excavations on the site have revealed that it was characterized by a rustic simplicity.[10] He erected a fortress there, but he had no palace. Nor was there a royal chapel at Gibeah. Nob seems to have been the chief cult site after he became king (I Sam. 21–22). We hear nothing of court officials like those that later obtained at Jerusalem. I Sam. 20:25 sug-

[8] It too is usually assigned to the "Saul Source." It may originally have been associated with the cult site of Gilgal.

[9] Noth, *History*, p. 168.

[10] See Wright's description (*Biblical Archaeology*, p. 122).

gests the simplicity of Saul's royal council.[11] It consisted of his son Jonathan, his cousin Abner, who was the captain of the tribal volunteers, and his personal armor-bearer David.

In his wars with the Philistines, Saul had some initial success. These early victorious encounters of the Hebrews under Saul with the Philistines are recounted in I Samuel 13–14. Of course, the nature of these early conflicts must be understood. They were in the Palestinian hills, not in the plains against the chariotry of the Philistines. What was involved was the expulsion of the Philistine garrisons from Israelite territory by superior tactics. We cannot be certain concerning the exact course of these battles, but John Bright suggests [12] that there was first an encounter in which a Philistine post was taken (I Sam. 13:3). After reprisals on the part of the Philistines (I Sam. 13:17-18), there was a battle at the pass of Michmash, in which Jonathan played the decisive role (I Sam. 14). As a result of this encounter, the Philistines were driven out of the hills. These initial successes, however, were not victories over the assembled might of the Philistines or even a considerable portion of it. An encounter of the Israelites under Saul with the total military might of the Philistines was to come later at Mt. Gilboa—disastrously so (I Sam. 31).

As Israel's first king, Saul had many problems. All of them contributed in one way or another to Israel's crushing defeat by the Philistines at Gilboa and Saul's own tragic end. His first problem was himself. He was possessed by a deep-seated emotional instability. He was a highly excitable person, as his association with the ecstatic prophetic guilds indicates (I Sam. 10:10-11; 19:18-24). He was subject to periods of extreme elation and extreme depression. This was evidently one of the reasons David was first associated with him (I Sam. 16:14-23). The music of David's lyre was able to soothe Saul. Saul was also subject to periods of extreme suspicion, even of those who were closest to him, members of his own tribe and family (I Sam. 22:6-8). Had the Philistine threat been merely temporary, Saul's emotional instability might have been no great problem. But continued responsibility in a

[11] Cf. Noth, *History*, pp. 174-75.
[12] *History*, p. 168.

time of sustained national crisis was more than a man like this could endure.

An even greater problem for Saul was theological in nature. This problem resulted from the fact that the official covenant theology of the twelve-tribe amphictyony simply had no place for a kingship. Saul's theological problem was personified in Samuel. After the fall of Shiloh, Samuel had evidently returned to his home in Ramah where he seems to have been involved in the administration of covenant law (I Sam. 7:17).[13] It can be assumed that the memories of the annual covenant renewal ceremony at Shiloh in his youth remained alive in.Samuel's heart. The covenant theology reflected in the E cult legend would have exercised a continuing influence upon his thinking. Yahweh's covenant was with *all the people* and not with any authoritarian dynasty—priestly or royal. Equally vivid in Samuel's memory, however, would have been the destruction of Shiloh by the Philistines. As he passed from youth to maturity the continued Philistine occupation of Israelite territory would have kept this memory alive with burning intensity. It is not impossible that Samuel gradually came to see the absolute necessity of some kind of a kingship for the Hebrews if they were to throw off the galling yoke of the Philistines. But how could a kingship be reconciled with his "kingdom of priests" covenant theology? This was evidently the dilemma with which Samuel was faced.

It is perhaps not fortuitous that the traditions do not make Samuel's attitude toward the kingship completely clear. He may never have been completely clear in his own mind about it. It does seem fairly clear that the primary basis of Saul's original selection as king was his charismatic activity in connection with the Ammonite war.[14] This testified to the fact that he had been called and endowed by Yahweh. It is also evident that Saul officially became king only after *all the people* had gathered together at Gilgal and acclaimed him king (I Sam. 11:15). Less certain, however, is Samuel's precise role in the developments. That he did have a part is attested by all three accounts of Saul's

[13] See Martin Noth, "Amt und Berufung im Alten Testament," *Bonner Akademische Reden*, 19 (Bonn: Peter Hanstein Verlag, 1958), p. 21.

[14] Alt, "Die Staatenbildung," pp. 17 ff., 22-23; *idem*, "Das Königtum in den Reichen Israel und Juda" (*Kleine Schriften* II), pp. 118-19; Bright, *History*, p. 167; Noth, *History*, pp. 167 ff.

designation as king. In the tradition that is probably most authentic (I Sam. 11) Samuel's role is least significant, and it is possible that he did not appear in the original version at all.[15] Although its present form is "very anecdotal," [16] perhaps I Sam. 9:1–10:26 preserves the most reliable memory of Samuel's part in Saul's selection as king. In its present form it tells of Samuel's private anointing of Saul to be "prince" (nagid) over Israel, but an earlier version may simply have had an account of Samuel's inspiring Saul "to make his first public appearance in the name of the God of Israel," [17] the sole purpose of which was the relief of Jabesh-gilead. But it was precisely because of his success in this war with the Ammonites (which had been inspired by Samuel) that the assembly at Gilgal took place to make Saul king. If Samuel actually convened the assembly at Gilgal, as I Sam. 11:12-14 says,[18] it would have been with a divided mind. He must have had deep reservations about placing permanent political power over the covenant people of Yahweh in the hands of one man.[19] The gravity of the Philistine threat alone made it expedient to take this unprecedented step.

The sole purpose of Saul's kingship would have been to wage war against the Philistines.[20] The presence of a permanent threat to Israel's existence as a people necessitated a permanent national office. What was primarily involved in Saul's kingship evidently was the continuing authority to call up the Israelite volunteer armies.[21] Thus his authority extended over all the Hebrew tribes. Just how long it was understood

[15] Many commentators suggest that vss. 12-14 are secondary, as well as the name "Samuel" in vs. 7. So George B. Caird, "The First and Second Books of Samuel," *The Interpreter's Bible* (Nashville: Abingdon Press, 1953), II, 939-40; cf. Hertzberg, *op. cit.*, pp. 67, 71.

[16] This expression is Noth's (*History*, p. 169).

[17] *Ibid.*

[18] Noth takes the position that Samuel actually did convene the assembly: "As 'man of God,' which would in itself command respect, and now for the first time really as the spokesman of God who had called and inspired Saul to his act of liberation, an authority in Israel, even though bearing no office, Samuel may in fact have played an active part in the events that now took place" (*History*, p. 170).

[19] In this respect, the tradition in I Sam. 10:17-27 (cf. chs. 8 and 12) of the assembly convened by Samuel at Mizpah to select a king would be authentic.

[20] On the nature of Saul's kingship see above all Alt, "Die Staatenbildung," pp. 23 ff. (cf. *idem*, "Das Königtum," pp. 119 ff.).

[21] Alt, "Das Königtum," p. 119.

that Saul's kingship should continue is uncertain. It was undoubtedly intended that Saul should remain king for the duration of the Philistine threat. That his kingship should continue for the duration of his life regardless of any military threat is less sure, although not unlikely. It is quite apparent, however, that Saul's kingship was never conceived dynastically.[22] Jonathan seems never to have expected to succeed his father, and after Saul's death, his son Esh-baal reigned at Mahanaim only because of the support of the strong man Abner (II Sam. 2:8 ff.). Saul's kingship, then, was basically charismatic and democratic. He was made king by all the people because of his charismatic gifts.[23]

It is quite evident that in Samuel's mind Saul's authority was strictly limited to the political sphere and was explicitly excluded from the religious. This may have been a more general understanding too, since the cult center during Saul's reign was located at Nob (I Sam. 21-22) and thus was separated from the political capital at Gibeah.[24] In any event, Samuel's eventual break with Saul clearly involved the question of the king's sacred and secular functions. There are two traditions concerning this break. In one (I Sam. 13:8-15) Saul offers a sacrifice for which Samuel condemns him. In the other (I Sam. 15) Saul breaks the amphictyonic law relating to the *cherem* [25] in connection with a war against the Amalekites. In both traditions Saul is rejected as king by Samuel. Comments Bright: "The probability is that Samuel, having hoped to keep the new order subservient to the old, suspected Saul of grasping at religious as well as at political authority." [26] For one who had a "kingdom of priests" covenant theology this was too much. Although there is no evidence that Samuel ever led a movement to displace Saul as king before his death, his action must have cost the

[22] This is stressed by Alt, "Die Staatenbildung," pp. 29 ff.).

[23] Alt suggests that a covenant was made between Saul and the people when they made him king at Gilgal, even though it is not explicitly mentioned in I Sam. 11 ("Die Staatenbildung," p. 23).

[24] It is undoubtedly significant that after the division of the Davidic kingdom, the cult center in northern Israel was always separate from the political capital, in stark contrast to the situation at Jerusalem.

[25] The *cherem* law decreed that in a holy war all spoil belonged to Yahweh and must be destroyed. On I Sam. 15 see especially Anderson, *Understanding the Old Testament*, pp. 128-29.

[26] *History*, p. 171.

king many supporters and diminished his authority among the tribes. The mere fact that the man of God had turned against him, however, must have been even more devastating for Saul than the loss of tribal support. As a result of Samuel's rejection of him, he became increasingly uncertain of himself and suspicious of others. "Now the Spirit of Yahweh departed from Saul, and an evil spirit from Yahweh tormented him" (I Sam. 16:14). His suspicions were particularly directed against David, his young armor-bearer.

David was yet another of Saul's problems. A Judean of Bethlehem (I Sam. 16:1-3), David was evidently first associated with Saul as his personal musician and armor-bearer (I Sam. 16:14-23). With his radiant personality and outstanding military ability (I Sam. 17), he soon was being praised in a song which was not calculated to soothe the troubled spirit of the king:

> Saul has slain his thousands,
> And David his ten thousands. I Sam. 18:7

The fact that David gained the friendship of Saul's son Jonathan and the hand of his daughter Michal served not to reconcile but only further to estrange the two. Saul's jealousy of David increased to the point of virtual insanity and finally David was forced to flee for his life.

From this point Saul disintegrated rapidly. His mad suspicions were directed against his closest followers and even Jonathan (I Sam. 22:7-8; 20:20-34). When he heard that the priests of Nob had given aid to David as he fled the royal court, he had them brutally murdered (I Sam. 22:9-19). As Bright remarks: "This was clearly not the work of a rational mind." [27]

The flight of the Judean David, of course, resulted in a division in the ranks of the Hebrews. Even at full strength, the chances of Saul's armies in an all out war against the Philistines were minimal. With a schism their fate was sealed. Saul and his kingship were doomed.

When David fled from the insane Saul, he went to southern Palestine. This was decisive for the whole subsequent history of Israel. In southern Palestine was the old six-tribe amphictyony, the official covenant

[27] *Ibid.*, p. 172.

theology of which was dynastic in character. This was precisely the kind of covenant theology that was indispensable if a dynastic kingship was to be incorporated fully into Yahwism.

The Six-Tribe Amphictyony at Hebron

Martin Noth seems to have been the first to recognize the existence of the old six-tribe amphictyony at Hebron.[28] In a summarizing statement he has written:

Calebite Hebron formed not merely the natural centre of the south Palestinian mountains but also possessed in its immediate vicinity the famous tree sanctuary of Mamre (the modern haram rāmet el-khalīl) which was probably at the same time the religious centre for all the south Palestinian tribes which appear to have been united around this centre in a confederation of six tribes forming a separate group within and alongside the great Israelite confederation of the twelve tribes. These six tribes (Judah, Caleb, Othniel, Cain, Jerahmeel, Simeon) led a life of their own, which, though it did not isolate them from the greater whole, did give them a special position.[29]

The name "Hebron" in Hebrew means "association" or "league" and thus was appropriate for the cult center of an amphictyony. Not a great deal is known about ancient Hebron. The Old Testament reveals precious little information concerning this old cult site. Nor have major archaeological excavations ever been conducted there which might illuminate its history during Old Testament times.[30] The city is some nineteen miles south of Jerusalem. Before it was called Hebron, the name of the city is said to have been Kirjath-arba (Gen. 23:2; Josh. 14:15; 15:18, 54, etc.), which in Hebrew means "fourfold city." Num. 12:22 says that it was built seven years before Zoan in Egypt. This would mean that it already existed in the Bronze Age.[31] A particularly sacred site in the vicinity of Hebron was that on which the "oaks of

[28] Noth, *Das System der zwölf Stämme Israels*, pp. 107-8.
[29] *History*, pp. 181-82.
[30] For what little has been done see Evaristus Mader, *Mambre. Die Ergebnisse der Ausgrabungen im heiligen Bezirk râmet el-halîl in Südpalästina. 1926-28* (Freiburg i. Br.: Wewel, 1957).
[31] See Noth, *History*, p. 33.

Mamre" were found (Gen. 13:18; 18:1 *et al.*). It has been identified with the present *ramet el-halil,* some two miles from Hebron.

The patriarchal traditions associate Hebron particularly with Abraham. According to the Jahwist,[32] the shrine at Hebron was founded by him (Gen. 13:18). It also seems probable that J's tradition of God's covenant with Abraham in Gen. 15:7-21 is to be located at Hebron, since it is the last site mentioned by J before this incident (Gen. 13:18). J's story of Yahweh's promise that Abraham will have a son is specifically placed there (Gen. 18:1). Since the traditions in Genesis 15 and 18 are associated with Hebron, and neither Genesis 16 nor 18 suggests a journey for Abraham, it is probably correct to assume that P's tradition of Yahweh's covenant with Abraham should be associated with this site (Gen. 17). Further, P specifically states that Sarah, Abraham's wife, died at Hebron and was buried there after Abraham had purchased the cave of Machpelah from Ephron the Hittite (Gen. 23). Here also Abraham, Isaac, Rebekah, Jacob, and Leah are all said to have been buried (Gen. 49:30-31; 50:13).

Hebron appears again in the time of the conquest. The spies go to Hebron during their scouting expedition (Num. 13:22). Later Joshua captures and destroys the city (Josh. 10:36-39; 11:21-23), after which it is said to have come into the possession of Caleb (Judg. 1:20; Josh. 14:12; 15:13-15). There is almost complete silence concerning Hebron from the period of the conquest until the time of David. It is referred to then as one of the cities to which David sent a portion of the spoils after his victory over the Amalekites (I Sam. 30:31). After Saul's death, David goes to Hebron where he is anointed king of Judah (II Sam. 2:1-3). He reigns there seven and one-half years (II Sam. 2:11) and six of his sons are born at this town (II Sam. 3:2-5). Upon the death of Esh-baal, the tribes of Israel come to David at Hebron, where he makes a covenant with them and they anoint him king over all Israel (II Sam. 5:1-5). After David moves to Jerusalem, Hebron is mentioned infrequently. It is at this city, however, that Absalom begins his revolt against David (II Sam. 15:7-10). And the Chronicler reports that it was

[32] S. R. Driver, *The Book of Genesis. The Westminster Commentaries* (London: Methuen & Co., 1926), p. 154. The following section follows Driver's source division.

fortified by Rehoboam (II Chron. 11:5, 10). This is the last reference to it until after the exile (Neh. 11:25).

If Noth is correct that there was a six-tribe amphictyony centering at Hebron in the premonarchical period, it would have been comprised of those tribes that moved directly north from Kadesh to occupy southern Palestine at the time of the thirteenth century conquest under Joshua.[33] Judah and Simeon evidently had belonged to the early six-tribe Leah amphictyony at Shechem [34] and were already familiar with such a phenomenon. With these two tribes, then, were joined Caleb, Othniel, Jerahmeel and Cain (Kenites) to form the new amphictyony. The name of this southern amphictyony seems to have been "house of Judah" in contradistinction to the name of its leading tribe "Judah." [35] Of these six tribes, Judah and Simeon evidently also belonged to the twelve-tribe amphictyony which centered at Shechem and later at Shiloh. But the smaller confederation in the South continued its life and conducted its worship of Yahweh in accordance with its own interests and understanding during this general period from the last half of the thirteenth century until the last of the eleventh when David emerged. The larger amphictyony was loosely enough organized and sufficiently tolerant to permit the distinctive southern interpretation of Yahwism.

The presence of the Kenites in the six-tribe amphictyony was evidently of some importance in the maintenance of the particular understanding of Yahwism which obtained in the South. Since the Kenites were in all probability the original worshipers of Yahweh and Moses learned this divine name from Jethro, his Kenite father-in-law,[36] it would be expected that Kenite institutions and theological emphases would have been especially prevalent in the southern confederation. Foremost among these evidently was the institution of a priestly dynasty.[37] Exod. 18:12 (cf. Exod. 24:1-2, 9-11) seems to preserve the memory of this institution among the Hebrews at

[33] See Chap. Four, pp. 107-8. Jerahmeel presumably joined the group soon after the conquest, although it is not specifically mentioned until I Sam. 27:10.
[34] Chap. Three, pp. 78 ff.
[35] Noth, *History*, p. 182.
[36] Chap. One, pp. 25-26.
[37] See Chap. Three, pp. 85-90.

Kadesh, and Numbers 11, 12, and 16 may reflect controversies in which it was the bone of contention. To be sure, the old Kenite idea of a priestly dynasty assumed a special form among the Hebrews. It was related to the Mosaic covenant. In the southern amphictyony, however, Yahweh's covenant was not understood to be with all the people, but rather with the priestly dynasty, and only through the dynasty with the people. This is clearly expressed in the J covenant legend, which presumably was an extremely important tradition of the southern amphictyony.

1. The covenant was first with Moses: "And Yahweh said to Moses, 'Write these words; in accordance with these words I have made a covenant with you and with Israel'" (Exod. 34:27). Through Moses, of course, it was also with the people.

2. Moses was the first covenant mediator of a dynastic succession: "And Yahweh said to Moses, 'Lo, I am coming to you in a thick cloud, that the people may hear when I speak with you, and may also believe you for ever'" (Exod. 19:9a).

3. This succession was traced from Moses to Aaron to Aaron's sons, Nadab and Abihu, all of whom participate in the covenant meal (Exod. 24:1-2, 9-11).

In the South, then, during the period from the conquest until the emergence of David, covenant theology centered in the Aaron-Nadab-Abihu priestly dynasty.[38] It was believed that Yahweh's covenant was with this dynasty "for ever" (19:9a). The result in the South was a concentration of religious, and possibly to some extent political, authority in this one priestly dynasty. Some kind of a hierocracy evidently existed in the southern amphictyony.

Of course, during this period the official theology of the twelve-tribe amphictyony was quite different, as has been stressed in the previous chapter. Although southern circles must have been unhappy about the situation, they were in no position to change it. Moreover, during this period they enjoyed the security provided by the charismatic northern leaders who drove off enemies that threatened the

[38] It is interesting that Johannes Hempel suggested that the Aaronids were perhaps from Hebron, because of the city list in Josh. 21:9-19 and P's interest in Hebron (Gen. 23:1 ff.; 25:7 ff.; 49:29 ff.; 50:13). *Die althebräische Literatur und ihr hellenistisch-jüdisches Nachleben* (Berlin: A. K. Verlags, 1930), pp. 152-53.

Hebrews' occupation of Palestine. It was expedient for Judah and Simeon to retain their ties to the larger amphictyony. At the same time, however, the southern attitude was clearly expressed by such traditions as the one found in Num. 11:16-17, 24-25. Like Exod. 24:1-2, 9-11, this tradition places the seventy elders in a position of subordination to a higher priestly authority. Its primary concern would seem to be the assertion that "valid" spirit must come from Moses and the dynasty connected with him, i.e., that of Aaron-Nadab-Abihu. The story was probably directed against the North during the period of the Judges. The northern experiences of the spirit, it was held, were invalid. But the time would come, southern circles undoubtedly hoped, when things would be different. All authority would actually *be* where it really belonged. Until that day arrived, the tendency in the South was to be somewhat aloof from the North.

The most important cult shrine of the amphictyony at Hebron evidently was the tent of meeting.[39] It had been brought to Hebron by these southern tribes when they moved north from Kadesh at the time of the conquest under Joshua. It must have played a significant cultic role at Hebron. In the Mosaic period the primary function of the tent seems to have been that of serving as a shrine where oracles were imparted.[40] But at Hebron it seems also to have been used in connection with a covenant ceremony of which the J covenant legend in an early form was the liturgy.[41]

The Covenant Ceremony at Hebron

In this connection a proposal by Hans-Joachim Kraus concerning an ancient tent festival in southern Palestine is significant.[42] Kraus has suggested that Lev. 23:39-44 preserves the memory of an early autumnal festival in Israel observed annually in the seventh month. Originally "tents" rather than "booths" or "tabernacles" were used in the ceremony, and the tent of meeting was of central importance in its observance. The tradition concerning the tent of meeting in

---

[39] Chap. Two, pp. 67-68; cf. von Rad, *Studies in Deuteronomy*, p. 43 and Kuschke, "Die Lagervorstellung der priesterlichen Erzählung," p. 95.

[40] Chap. Two, pp. 65-66.

[41] Chap. Two, pp. 68-70.

[42] Kraus, *Gottesdienst in Israel*, pp. 23-27.

Exod. 33:7-11, as well as P's description of Israel's encampment in the wilderness (Num. 1–3, etc.), provide supporting evidence for this thesis.[43] However, this premonarchical festival was probably not celebrated at Beersheba, as suggested by Kraus,[44] but at Hebron, where the tent of meeting was located. Nor was it observed by the whole twelve-tribe amphictyony,[45] but by the southern six-tribe amphictyony, of which Hebron was the central cult site. Finally, the main theme of the festival was not the "realization of the wilderness period," as proposed by Kraus;[46] it was a covenant observance in which the J covenant tradition, attached to the tent of meeting, was used as the festival legend.

Perhaps it is not entirely fortuitous, then, that traditions in the books of Genesis and II Samuel make Hebron a covenant site. According to both the Jahwist (Gen. 15:7-21) and P (Gen. 17), it was *at Hebron* that God made the covenant with Abraham. In II Sam. 5:1-5 we are told that the elders of Israel came to David *at Hebron* where he "made a covenant with them before Yahweh," after which they anointed him king over Israel. Hebron must have been widely recognized as a covenant site, and the primary reason was because of the covenant ceremony observed there by the six-tribe amphictyony.

Caution must be exercised in coming to conclusions concerning the covenant festival of the six-tribe amphictyony at Hebron. That it was an annual ceremony, as was the case in the North, seems probable. Kraus' research in regard to the old southern "tent festival" would seem to indicate this. If it was an annual autumnal festival, it would have been observed in a different month from the one celebrated in the North, in order to avoid conflict. The southern festival probably took place in the seventh month (Lev. 23:39-43; I Kings 8:2), because the eighth month was used in the North (I Kings 12:32).[47] The tribes of Judah and Simeon were presumably represented at both ceremonies.

[43] Kraus makes extensive use of Kuschke (*op. cit.*).
[44] Kraus, *op. cit.*, p. 34.
[45] *Ibid.*, p. 29.
[46] *Ibid.*, p. 33.
[47] In selecting the eighth month for his festival Jeroboam was evidently returning to an old tradition of the twelve-tribe amphictyony.

The tent of meeting would have been used in the covenant festival. In this connection it was a "tent of meeting" in the full sense of the Hebrew expression.[48] It was a "tent of meeting" because it was the central cult shrine where the members of the amphictyony "met" for the annual ceremony. That they lived in tents during the festival seems highly probable, as is suggested by Exod. 33:7-11 (cf. Num. 1-3; Lev. 23:39-43). It was also the "tent of [the] meeting" between Yahweh and "Moses," i.e., the priest officiating at the ceremony.

Most of the details concerning the ceremony and its course must come from an analysis of the J covenant tradition, the festival liturgy, which was evidently read and re-enacted in the ceremony.

1. One element would have been a cultic theophany in which Yahweh's presence was vividly perceived. In the J covenant legend there are actually two theophanies. The first is the general theophany for all the people which attests to them the validity of the office of covenant mediator (Exod. 19:9a, 11b-13, 18). The second is the special theophany to the covenant mediator himself (Exod. 34:1-4; 33:18-23; 34:5).

A number of theophanic expressions are used in the J covenant tradition.[49] In Exod. 19:9a Yahweh tells Moses that he is coming in a (1) "thick cloud." According to 19:18 his coming is (2) "in fire" as (3) "smoke" (twice) encompasses the mountain. In the special theophany to Moses, the covenant mediator requests to see Yahweh's (4) "glory" (33:18). Yahweh agrees to let his glory pass by while Moses stands in the cleft of the rock (33:22). When the theophany occurs, it is said that Yahweh descends in "the cloud" (34:5), which suggests the very close connection between Yahweh's person and his glory.

This theophanic language is somewhat further removed from natural phenomena than that of E. The Elohist's covenant legend seems to reflect a thunderstorm, with its thunders, lightnings, and thick cloud (Exod. 19:16, 19; 20:18, 21). In J the "cloud" could be related to a thunderstorm and Yahweh's coming to Moses faintly suggests a passing windstorm. On the other hand, however, 19:18

[48] Chap. Two, p. 64.
[49] Cf. Chap. Two, pp. 48-49, 66.

leads one to think more of a volcano, with smoke, fire, and the mountain quaking. Although natural imagery does suggest itself in the J legend, on the whole it is rather faint. Yahweh comes down in "fire" (19:18); he is in the "cloud" (19:9a; 34:5); he lets his "glory" pass by (33:22). This language is stylized; it has a pronounced theological, even cultic character. There would seem to be little question that the cult has strongly affected the present text.

Just how such a theophany was depicted in the cult at Hebron is difficult to determine. It seems likely that in the North the "trumpet" was blown in connection with the ark and indicated the voice of Yahweh as he was present to his people in the cult. It would seem fairly certain that in the South the cult theophany occurred in connection with the tent of meeting. The similarity between the theophany of the J covenant legend and those connected with the tent of meeting in the early tent traditions would indicate that.[50] One would suspect that fire and smoke in some way were employed in connection with the tent to indicate the cultic descent of the "glory" of Yahweh. Not only in the J tradition are fire and the "glory" of Yahweh closely related (Exod. 19:18; 33:18, 22), but also in the Priestly Writing (Exod. 24:17; Num. 16:18, 35; Lev. 9:23 ff., et al.). Smoke would have been the natural accompaniment of the cultic fire (Lev. 16:2, 12-13; cf. Isa. 6:1 ff.).[51] The "clouds" of smoke would have enveloped the "glorious" fire which suggested Yahweh's cultic presence. More than this it would be imprudent to say concerning the cult theophany on the basis of the limited traditions which the Old Testament has preserved in this regard. However the cultic theophany at the tent of meeting may have been depicted in detail, the important point was that *Yahweh's shining presence came down and "met" with the covenant mediator during the covenant ceremony.*

That the primary cult theophany occurred only for the priestly official distinguishes the southern ceremony sharply from that in the North, where the one theophany was for all the people and where

[50] See Chap. Two, p. 66.
[51] On this point see Eichrodt, *Theologie des Alten Testaments.* Teil 2 (Leipzig: J. C. Hinrich'schen Buchhandlung, 1935), 9; Edmund Jacob, *Theology of the Old Testament* (New York: Harper & Brothers, 1958), p. 80; and especially Beyerlin, *Herkunft und Geschichte der ältesten Sinaitraditionen,* pp. 154-55, 183-84.

Yahweh's presence enthroned upon the ark was as available to a layman as to a priest. In the South the people undoubtedly knew when the theophanic moment had come and followed the event from afar, as Exod. 33:8-10 suggests. But the people themselves were not immediately involved in the theophany. If what was happening, however, was not happening immediately *to* them, it was happening *for* them. Indeed the whole meaning of their life as a covenant people was believed to be involved in this cultic coming of their God. For Yahweh's "glory" was being manifested to a member of that priestly dynasty with which he had made a special covenant and which was viewed as the center of their existence as his covenant people. Thus through the covenant mediator Yahweh was in a real sense coming into their life in the cult. This was a crucial cultic moment and it must have corresponded in significance to the proclamation of Yahweh's name in the northern cult.[52]

[52] The affinities between the theophany in the J covenant legend and in the Priestly Writing are striking and significant. One salient characteristic of the theophany in J is the picture of Yahweh encompassed by the cloud. "Fire" (19:18) and the "glory" (33:18, 22) seem to be closely linked to Yahweh's presence, while the "smoke" (19:18) or "cloud" (19:9a; 34:5) form a kind of covering for him. The tradition suggests that the "glory," Yahweh's earthly form, is of such a nature that it cannot be immediately perceived by the ordinary mortal, but must be encompassed by a protective covering. This idea is almost precisely the same as that which is found in P. There too Yahweh manifests his "glory" in the "cloud" (Exod. 16:10; 29:43; Num. 14:10; 16:19; 17:7; 20:6). Another characteristic of the theophany in the J legend is the "descent" of Yahweh to the mountain (19:11b, 18, 20; 34:5; cf. 19:9a). Yahweh dwells above in heaven (24:9-11), and when he manifests his presence to his people in a theophany he must "come down" to them. The Priestly Writing has preserved a picture which is very similar. According to P, in the wilderness the "glory" of Yahweh from time to time would "appear in the cloud" to the people for specific purposes (Exod. 16:10; 29:34; Num. 14:10; 16:19; 17:7; 20:6). These points of affinity suggest that the "Kabod-Moed" theology detected by von Rad in P (*Studies in Deuteronomy,* pp. 37-44) had its root in this southern covenant ceremony, just as the "Name" theology stemmed from the northern covenant ceremony (Chap. Four, p. 113, n. 34). What constitutes the "Kabod-Moed" theology, according to von Rad, is, first, the descent of the glory of Yahweh upon the tent, and second, the phenomenon of the cloud which accompanies it (*op. cit.,* p. 39). This is almost precisely a description of the theophany in J. Von Rad himself believes that this "Kabod-Moed" theology of P (which is also found in a similar form in Ezekiel) has ancient roots. He connects it specifically with the old accounts of the tent of meeting (*Ibid.,* p. 42). He suggests that the tent originally belonged to the South as the sanctuary of the old six-tribe amphictyony at Hebron, and thus the "Kabod-Moed" theology was "an old tradition observed in South Israel which appears resuscitated in Ezekiel and P" (*Ibid.,* p. 43). The present writer is in complete agreement with von Rad, but would be even more specific. "Kabod-Moed" theology had

2. Another important element of the ceremony was the announcement of Yahweh's name and nature. This part of the festival was evidently somewhat less significant than it was in the northern cult. For the South the manifestation of the *visible* "glory" of Yahweh was more fundamental than the *audible* announcement of Yahweh's name. Nor in the Hebron ceremony was the name of Yahweh proclaimed to the people, as was the case in the North. In the J legend, it is the covenant mediator alone who hears the name and nature of God announced (Exod. 34:6).

It is interesting that there is no specific reference to the event of the exodus in this legend, unlike the E covenant tradition (Exod. 19:4; 20:2). In the northern cult the event of the exodus was viewed not only as the foundation of the original covenant but also its remembrance was the basis of each renewal of the covenant. The J tradition, on the other hand, merely contains the general statement concerning Yahweh's mercy, graciousness, steadfast love, and faithfulness (Exod. 34:6-7). It might be argued that the omission of any reference to the exodus event indicates that it was unknown in southern circles. This seems hardly possible, since elsewhere in the J legend the event appears in connection with the Passover (Exod. 34:18). The more probable explanation is to be found in the nature of the covenant theology reflected in the J tradition. Dominating this tradition is the Aaron-Nadab-Abihu priestly dynasty. Yahweh had made a covenant with this dynasty; its office was to continue "for ever;" and it was the very center of the life of the covenant people. Of crucial importance, therefore, was the preservation of this priestly institution. The institution was viewed as more important than the event which originally created a covenant people for Yahweh.[53] Consequently the exodus received no stress in this ceremony.

3. A third element in the southern covenant ceremony was Yahweh's

its original root in the covenant ceremony of the six-tribe confederation at Hebron when Yahweh manifested his presence in a glorious theophany to the priestly covenant mediator.

[53] This line of thought was suggested to me by Jacob's treatment of the Hebrew monarchy, which structurally was very similar to the priesthood: "The adoption of the monarchy ran the risk of making the covenant into an institution whose stability could be guaranteed only by the presence of the sovereign. The purely institutional side of the covenant threatened to become more important than the event iself." *Op. cit.*, p. 214.

law. The code of law in the J covenant legend (Exod. 34:10-26) has frequently been referred to as the "ritual decalogue." However, a comparison of this "ritual decalogue" with the "ethical decalogue" of Exodus 20 in order to discover which is earlier, as frequently has been done, would not prove particularly fruitful in interpreting its significance. H. H. Rowley is more helpful in illuminating the significance of the code when he relates it to the southern Hebrew tribes.[54] He thinks of it as originally a Kenite code of laws which was taken over by the Hebrews in the South and gradually adapted to their life and culture. Although some of these laws may well have been Kenite in origin, Rowley's attempt to dissociate this code entirely from Mosaic Yahwism is questionable. The laws requiring exclusive (Exod. 34:14) and aniconic (34:17) worship of Yahweh are Mosaic, if any laws in the Old Testament derive from him. In this respect, therefore, Walther Eichrodt's position is much more accurate when he refers to Exod. 34:10 ff. as a local expression of the Mosaic law which was formulated in one of Israel's larger sanctuaries.[55] This code must be understood in connection with its liturgical usage at a cult center, and specifically the southern city of Hebron, the chief sanctuary of the six-tribe amphictyony.

The general cultic character of this code has long been recognized. The fact that it consists exclusively of apodictic law, the type which was uniquely fitted for recitation in a covenant ceremony, has seldom been taken seriously, even by Albrecht Alt, who was the pioneer in the study of apodictic law.[56] It is true that not all of them are found in the pristine apodictic form as Alt defined it, i.e., both categorical and negative. Several of them are expressed positively. Only *six* of the laws found there are negative in form.[57] Perhaps, however, it is not unimportant that there are only six pure apodictic laws in this collection. Since the twelve curses of Deuteronomy 27 correspond to the twelve tribes of the Shechem amphictyony, it is quite possible

[54] *From Joseph to Joshua*, p. 157.
[55] Eichrodt, *Theology*, I, 85, n. 1.
[56] His consideration of Exod. 34:10 ff. is exhausted in part of a footnote ("Die Ursprünge des israelitischen Rechts," p. 317, n. 1).
[57] Chap. Two, p. 49.

that these six laws originally were meant to correspond to the six tribes of the Hebron amphictyony.[58]

When Alt, even though in a deprecatory manner, says that the development of Exod. 34:10-26 has been more influenced by regulations concerning the cultic obligations of laity formulated by priests than by the apodictic elements of the decalogue in Exodus 20,[59] he is very close to the facts. The southern priesthood undoubtedly influenced the collection and formulation of the original code of six laws which was intended to impress upon all the people their special cultic obligations. By observing these laws, which were presented to them in the covenant ceremony, the people expressed their loyalty to Yahweh and to the priestly dynasty with which Yahweh had made a covenant and under whose authority they stood.

It would be quite erroneous, of course, to conclude that the southern tribes did not feel themselves bound to obey Yahweh's ethical law as expressed in such northern collections as Deuteronomy 27 and Exodus 20. The southern tribes, Judah and Simeon, were members of the twelve-tribe amphictyony, and there is little question that they, along with the other tribes in the South, fully recognized their responsibility to keep Yahweh's ethical will as expressed in his law. At the same time, however, the southern group was interested in preserving a special, and to them *basic,* emphasis within Yahwism. This they did in part by formulating and using in their covenant ceremony a special collection of cultic law.

4. A fourth element of this Hebron liturgy would have been an oath of the people. There would seem to be little question that the fundamental tendency in the South was to subordinate the laity to the priestly dynasty. The J covenant legend makes this abundantly

[58] If this is the case, the larger collection of laws in Exod. 34:10-26 probably reached its present form when the J covenant tradition was combined with the E legend to make it appear that the former was an account of the restoration of the covenant after it had been broken by the sin of Israel reflected in Exod. 32. By means of expansion and addition the "redactor" attempted to form a decalogue (cf. 34:28) which would correspond in form to the basic code of the broken covenant. True to the spirit of the code, he used only apodictic law in the work of redaction. His success was limited, but perhaps what he intended was a decalogue like this: (1) vss. 11-16; (2) vs. 17; (3) vs. 18; (4) vss. 19-20; (5) vs. 21; (6) vss. 22-24; (7) vs. 25*a*; (8) vs. 25*b*; (9) vs. 26*a*; (10) vs. 26*b*.

[59] Alt, *op. cit.,* p. 317, n. 1.

clear. The people are sternly warned against approaching or touching the holy mountain (Exod. 19:12-13; cf. 33:8-11). They have no voice in the appointment of the covenant mediator (19:9a). Nor do they participate in the meal that seals the covenant; only their representatives, the seventy elders, are permitted to do so (24:1-2, 9-11). Their participation in the ceremony is limited throughout, in striking contrast to the full participation of the people in the E covenant legend.

Nevertheless the people do have a part in the covenant liturgy reflected in the J tradition. Yahweh's covenant is with them too, even though only through the covenant mediator: "And Yahweh said to Moses, 'Write these words; in accordance with these words I have made a covenant with you *and with Israel*'" (34:27). Their obligation as a covenant people is expressed in the cultic law which is set before their elders (19:7). And they take the formal oath of obedience to Yahweh's will as expressed in his law: "And all the people answered and said, 'All that Yahweh has spoken we will do'" (19:8). This was not an unimportant moment in the southern covenant ritual, even though for the most part the role of the people was that of spectator rather than active participant.

5. A final major element of this covenant ceremony was the covenant meal. This was the act that sealed the covenant. In the J covenant legend there is no reference to the twelve tribes, as is true of the E account of the sealing of the covenant (Exod. 24:4). Nor do all the people participate in this part of the ceremony, as in the E ritual (Exod. 24:7-8). Only Moses, Aaron, Nadab, and Abihu, and the seventy elders go up the mountain to behold God, and eat and drink the covenant meal (Exod. 24:1-2, 9-11). The seventy elders represent the people, but their position is clearly a subordinate one.[60] The most important participants are Moses, Aaron, Nadab, and Abihu, i.e., the southern priestly dynasty that claimed its succession from Moses through Aaron. By participation in the covenant meal the status of the dynasty was affirmed and secured.[61]

[60] As is also the case in Num. 11:16-17, 24-25.

[61] It is interesting in this connection to observe that in P's account of the ordination of the Aaronic priesthood a sacred meal plays an important role (Lev. 8:22-32), along with the manifestation of Yahweh's "glory" at the tent of meeting (Lev. 9:6, 23). It is quite possible that Leviticus has preserved the memory of very early cultic traditions.

This analysis of the covenant ceremony in the South, of course, must be viewed as tentative. A fuller understanding must await further research, especially in the Priestly Writing which quite probably has preserved many old southern Israelite traditions. In any event, this covenant ceremony was observed regularly at Hebron by the southern six-tribe amphictyony from the time of Joshua to that of David. And the J covenant legend comprised its basic liturgy.

David in Southern Palestine

When David fled from Saul, therefore, and went to southern Palestine, he was going to an area where the kind of covenant theology reflected in the J covenant legend was dominant. The nature of this official southern covenant theology must be stressed. It was a *dynastic, unconditional, perpetual* covenant theology. Yahweh's covenant was viewed as being fundamentally with the priestly dynasty and only through the dynasty with the people; and this covenant had been established "for ever" (Exod. 19:9a). The covenant in the E tradition, on the other hand, is with *all the people* and is *conditional,* as is clearly indicated by Exod. 19:3-6. These two legends reflect two different kinds of covenant theology. The "kingdom of priests," conditional covenant theology of E is of great importance for the Old Testament. The entire book of Deuteronomy, for example, mirrors this understanding of the covenant. But the dynastic, unconditional, perpetual covenant theology is also important in the Old Testament. It appears, of course, here in the J covenant tradition, but not here alone.

Essentially the same theology is found in the Priestly Writing, where Yahweh promises a perpetual covenant to Phinehas, the grandson of Aaron through Eleazar, because of his defense of the faith:

10 And Yahweh said to Moses, 11 "Phinehas, the son of Eleazar, son of Aaron the priest, has turned back my wrath from the people of Israel, in that he was jealous with my jealousy among them, so that I did not consume the people of Israel in my jealousy. 12 Therefore say, 'Behold, I give to him my *covenant of peace;* 13 and it shall be to him, and to his

descendants after him, the *covenant of a perpetual priesthood*,[62] because he was jealous for his God, and made atonement for the people of Israel.' " Num. 25:10-13; cf. Num. 18:19

A very similar understanding of covenant is also to be found in both the J (Gen. 15:7-21) and the P (Gen. 17) traditions of the covenant Yahweh makes with Abraham at Hebron. In both narratives God's covenant is with one man and his seed; and no conditions are placed upon the recipient, i.e., it is unconditional. On this latter point George Mendenhall has commented:

Both in the narrative of Gen. 15 and 17, and in the later references to this covenant, it is clearly stated or implied that it is Yahweh himself who swears to certain promises to be carried out in the future. It is not often enough seen that no obligations are imposed upon Abraham. Circumcision is not originally an obligation, but a *sign* of the covenant, like the rainbow in Gen. 9. It serves to identify the recipient(s) of the covenant, as well as to give a concrete indication that a covenant exists. It is for the protection of the promisee, perhaps, like the mark on Cain in Gen. 4.[63]

It is the same kind of covenant—dynastic, unconditional, perpetual —that Yahweh is said to have made with David. It is expressed succinctly in II Sam. 23:2-5:

> 2 The Spirit of Yahweh speaks by me,
>   his word is upon my tongue.
> 3 The God of Israel has spoken,
>   the Rock of Israel has said to me:
> When one rules justly over men
>   ruling in the fear of God,
> 4 he dawns on them like the morning light,
>   like the sun shining forth upon a cloudless morning,
>   like rain that makes grass to sprout from the earth.
> 5 Yea, does not my house stand so with God?
>   For he has made with me an *everlasting covenant*,[64]
>   ordered in all things and secure.

---

[62] A literal translation might be: "covenant of a priesthood forever ['*olam*]." The same Hebrew word appears in Exod. 19:9a.

[63] *Law and Covenant in Israel and the Ancient Near East*, p. 36.

> For will he not cause to prosper
> all my help and desire?

It was not simply fortuitous that the kind of covenant theology dominant in southern Palestine—the region of David's birth and of his early career after his flight from Saul—became the official theology of the land later when he was at Jerusalem.

After David was forced to leave Gibeah, he first went to Nob, where the priests descended from the house of Eli resided (I Sam. 21:1-9). There he secured provisions for his further flight. As a result of his stay at Nob, the priests there were slain by the angry Saul (I Sam. 22:1-23). David next made his way to Adullam, where he began to gather a group of men about him:

And every one who was in debt, and every one who was discontented, gathered to him; and he became captain over them. And there were with him about four hundred men. I Sam. 22:2

These four hundred men represented the beginning of his mercenary army. This army was not like Saul's army, which was comprised of volunteers from the various tribes; this was a professional army loyal to David personally. David's professional army, which had its beginning here at Adullam, was extremely important throughout his whole subsequent career.

From Adullam David went a little farther south to Keilah (I Sam. 23:1-13). It was here that Abiathar joined him. A descendant of Eli through Phinehas and Ahitub (I Sam. 14:3: 22:11, 21 ff.), Abiathar evidently represented David's main contact with northern covenant theology through the entirety of his successful career as king. And it was an ominous day for the unity of the Davidic kingdom when Solomon later exiled Abiathar (I Kings 2:26-27).

Finally, David went even farther south, to the rugged wilderness of Judea southeast of Hebron. There he lived the life of an outlaw, in and around En-gedi, Ziph, Carmel, and Maon (I Sam. 23-26). He

---

[44] A literal translation would be: "a covenant forever ['olam]." The same Hebrew word appears in Exod. 19:9a.

lived off the land, as the extortion story in I Samuel 25 makes clear. During this period he was frequently pursued by Saul, and on one or two occasions is said to have spared the king's life (I Sam. 24; 26). Eventually David found it expedient to become a vassal of Achish of Gath, who turned over the city of Ziklag to him (I Sam. 27). Since Achish was something of a dolt, David was able to carry on raids against traditional nomadic enemies of the Hebrews while convincing Achish that he was making expeditions against the Hebrews themselves.

If there was a six-tribe amphictyony centering at Hebron during this time, David's relations with its members were quite close. With five of its six tribes he seems to have had direct contact.

1. He himself was a native of Bethlehem of the tribe of *Judah* (I Sam. 16:1, 18; 17:12, *et al.*).

2. He married Abigail, the wife of Nabal, who was a *Calebite* (I Sam. 25:3).

3. Ahinoam, whom he also took as a wife during this period (I Sam. 25:43), was evidently a *Kenite*.[65]

4. Ziklag, the city David received from Achish (I Sam. 27:6) and out of which he carried on his raiding expeditions, was located in *Simeonite* territory (Josh. 19:5; I Chron. 4:30).

5. I Sam. 30:29 states that David sent spoil to "the cities of the *Jerahmeelites*" after one of his raids.

It is also interesting in this regard that *Hebron,* presumably the cult center of the six-tribe amphictyony, is specifically mentioned as a place to which David sent spoil (I Sam. 30:31).

If there was an annual covenant ceremony at Hebron in which the J covenant legend was used, David would undoubtedly have been aware both of the festival and the covenant theology reflected in its liturgy. He would have known about the priestly dynasty at Hebron with which Yahweh was believed to have made his covenant, thus ensuring the perpetual continuation of the dynasty. *He would also have understood that there is a basic similarity between a priestly dynasty and a royal dynasty.*

The outlaw phase of David's career came to an end with the death

[65] Noth, *History,* p. 180.

of Saul at Mt. Gilboa (I Sam. 31). The Philistines gathered their forces at Aphek for this final battle against Saul, a battle in which David fortunately did not have to participate (I Sam. 29). Then the battle took place and it ended in complete disaster for the Hebrews.

> Now the Philistines fought against Israel; and the men of Israel fled before the Philistines, and fell slain on Mount Gilboa. I Sam. 31:1

Saul died too!

When the news of Saul's death reached David, he was ready. From this point he moved rapidly to become Saul's full successor, and even more! His first step in this direction was to become king over the "house of Judah" at Hebron.[66] This event evidently took place with the consent and perhaps the encouragement of the Philistines.[67] Unfortunately the Old Testament has preserved little information concerning this important incident. It is succinctly recorded in II Sam. 2:1-4:

> 1 After this David inquired of Yahweh, "Shall I go up into any of the cities of Judah?" And Yahweh said to him, "Go up." David said, "To which shall I go up?" And he said, "To Hebron." 2 So David went up there, and his two wives also, Ahinoam of Jezreel, and Abigail the widow of Nabal of Carmel. 3 And David brought up his men who were with him, every one with his household; and they dwelt in the towns of Hebron. 4 And the men of Judah came, and there they anointed David king over the house of Judah.

There is obviously insufficient material here to enable one to reach many conclusions concerning this event, but certain things would seem to be clear. The event took place, of course, at Hebron, the central cult site of the six-tribe amphictyony. The initiative in moving to Hebron came alone from David, after having ascertained Yahweh's will in the cult. When David went up, he took with him the band of mercenaries which he had been gathering about him for some time. It was only then that the men of Judah came and anointed David

[66] David's dates as king are 1000-961 B.C.
[67] See Noth, *History*, p. 183.

king over the "house of Judah," i.e., the six-tribe amphictyony. It is possible that dissatisfaction with the Aaronic hierocracy at Hebron was one factor involved in this move on the part of the men of Judah. Another, undoubtedly, was the popularity David enjoyed in the South as the result of his many gifts to the various tribes (I Sam. 30:26-31). But decisive was the military power at David's disposal in the form of his professional army.[68] Even if they had been strongly opposed to the move, there was probably little alternative for the southern tribes. So Noth's comment on the event is, if anything, an understatement: "We are not given any details regarding the process by which David was elected king over the 'house of Judah' but we shall not be far wrong if we assume that David himself played a part in persuading the southern tribes to make this move." [69]

David remained in Hebron as king over Judah for seven and a half years (II Sam. 2:11). As a worshiper of Yahweh, he would have been a participant in the cult activities there. He would have come to know thoroughly the nature of the Hebron cult as well as its dominant theological concerns and emphases. If Nathan was a "south Israelite," as von Rad says,[70] David may have first come into contact with him during this period; for it seems quite likely that Nathan stands in some relation to the "tent" tradition at Hebron.[71]

After the death of Esh-baal, Saul's son (II Sam. 4), David became king of Israel, i.e., the northern tribes, too. This event was preceded by a series of moves on David's part to ingratiate himself with the people of the North (II Sam. 1-4). When it took place, it took place *only* after a covenant had been made between David and the elders of Israel:

1 Then all the tribes of Israel came to David at Hebron, and said, "Behold, we are your bone and flesh. 2 In times past, when Saul was king over us, it was you that led out and brought in Israel; and Yahweh said to you, 'You shall be shepherd of my people Israel, and you shall be prince

---

[68] Alt stresses the importance of David's mercenaries in his rise to power ("Die Staatenbildung," pp. 41 ff.).

[69] Noth, *History*, p. 182.

[70] Von Rad, *Studies in Deuteronomy*, p. 43; cf. Kraus, *Gottesdienst*, p. 70.

[71] Von Rad, *op. cit.*, p. 43.

over Israel.' " 3 So all the elders of Israel came to the king at Hebron; and King David made a covenant with them at Hebron before Yahweh, and they anointed David king over Israel. II Sam. 5:1-3.

We are not informed concerning the content of this covenant, but one can be certain that it contained definite stipulations which limited the sovereignty of David's kingship in the North.

As king over both North and South, David began to consolidate his kingdom. His first major problem was the Philistines. As long as he had been a local dynast, ruling only over the southern Hebrew tribes, the Philistines had been quite tolerant of David. But now he had become a real threat, so they moved against him. Strangely we have few details concerning David's decisive battles against the Philistines, which Noth terms "the fundamental and most lasting successes of a life that was rich in success." [72] The memory of these conflicts is preserved in II Sam. 5:17-25. There were evidently two main battles, both of which were fought in the vicinity of Jerusalem. The second ended in complete victory for the Hebrews under David.[73] The Philistines were forced to withdraw to their own borders and seem never again to have posed a serious threat to the Israelites.

Now David had full freedom to develop a state in accordance with his own interests and desires. This he did, however, only after he had secured himself in a new capital. His new capital was Jerusalem, which became the center of a great empire and an entirely new way of life for the Hebrew people.

[72] Noth, *History*, p. 189.
[73] For more details on these battles see Bright, *History*, pp. 177-78 and Noth, *History*, pp. 187-89.

Chapter Six

The Kingship
at Jerusalem

THE SELECTION OF JERUSALEM TO BE HIS CAPITAL WAS ONE OF DAVID'S
many brilliant moves.[1] Inhabited by a people called Jebusites, it was
already an important city before the time of the conquest under Joshua.[2]
Until David arose, however, the Hebrews had been unable to conquer
it. Thus it remained a Canaanite enclave in their territory. It was located
on a mountain some 2,550 feet above sea level in the central Palestinian
hills. Since it lay on the boundary between the northern Hebrew tribes
and those in the South, it belonged to neither group. This no doubt was
an important factor in David's choice of it as his capital. Had he
selected Hebron, he would have alienated the North. If his selection
had fallen on some northern city, such as Shechem, the southern tribes
would have been disaffected. But Jerusalem was in neutral territory and
made a happy compromise choice.

[1] On the city of Jerusalem see especially J. Simons, *Jerusalem in the Old Testament*
(Leiden: E. J. Brill, 1952 and L. H. Vincent, *Jérusalem de l'Ancien Testament* (Paris:
Librairie Lecoffre, I, 1954, II-III, 1956). A good brief treatment is to be found in
Wright and Filson, *The Westminster Historical Atlas to the Bible*, pp. 105-9.
[2] It figures prominently, for example, in the Tel el Amarna tablets of the fourteenth
century B.C.

Before he made Jerusalem his capital, of course, David had to capture it (II Sam. 5:6-10; cf. I Chron. 11:4-9). It was such a strong fortress that its Jebusite inhabitants boasted that even the "blind and the lame" could defend it (vs. 6). Not even the "hale and the hearty" were able to ward off David's attack, however, and it fell into his hands. Just how David accomplished this feat is not clear, since the Hebrew text is quite corrupt.[3] It is possible that Joab led a daring group of warriors up through the city's water shaft and surprised its defenders (vs. 6). They then could have opened a gate and allowed the main body of David's army to storm the city. Whatever the details of Jerusalem's capture, it is certain that David's own mercenary army was responsible (vs. 6). The Israelite tribal levies did not figure in the conquest. David did not displace the native Jebusite population when he took control of the city, but allowed them to carry on their life there as before. He moved his own household and mercenaries into the new capital. Although the Jebusites still comprised the vast majority of its population, there was no question as to who the new ruler of the city was. It received a new name: "the city of David" (II Sam. 5:9). Jerusalem became David's personal possession and he was its king.[4]

David's Kingship at Jerusalem

Under David Jerusalem became the center of a great empire.[5] The international situation, of course, was quite propitious for the building of an empire in David's time. None of the larger nations was in a position to prevent it. Egypt had been relatively impotent since the twelfth-century invasion by the Philistines and other sea peoples. The twenty-first Egyptian dynasty that ruled during the age of David was weak and disunited. In Asia Minor the Hittite empire had come to an end in the latter half of the thirteenth century, and no other nation had emerged to replace it. Nor was there a people in Mesopotamia sufficiently strong to prevent the establishment of a mighty Davidic empire. It had been centuries since Babylonia had ceased to exist as a

---

[3] See Caird, "The First and Second Books of Samuel," *Interpreter's Bible*, II, 1070-71; cf. Bright, *History*, p. 179.

[4] See Alt, "Die Staatenbildung," pp. 45-46.

[5] On the Davidic empire see especially Alt, "Das Grossreich Davids," *Kleine Schriften*, II, 66-75.

world power, and it would be centuries before she would again arise as such. At the beginning of the tenth century Assyria experienced a brief resurgence of strength, but then quickly suffered a relapse. Not until the ninth century was this nation again to become a threat to world peace. Thus a quiescent international situation greeted David as he came to Jerusalem and made his desire to build an empire a definite possibility.

Before he embarked on foreign wars of conquest, David first completed the conquest of Canaan. There were still a number of Canaanite city-states in Palestine, especially on the coastal plain, in the plain of Jezreel and in Galilee, which had never been conquered by the Hebrews (Judg. 1:27-36). Control of these was taken over by David, probably for the most part by peaceful means.[6] Whereas they previously had been subject to the Philistines, these city-states now recognized the authority of Jerusalem and were incorporated into the Davidic state.

When he had secured himself completely within the borders of Palestine, David moved out to engage in aggressive war against neighboring peoples. These wars of aggression differed radically from Saul's defensive wars and so marked a real break with Israel's past.[7] Four conquests of states on David's borders are recorded in the Old Testament, although we cannot be certain concerning their correct chronological order. To the south he overwhelmed Edom in a campaign of which the decisive battle occurred in the Valley of Salt (II Sam. 8:13-14; I Kings 11:15-18). After a bloody slaughter of the male population, David organized Edom as a province over which he placed governors. To the southeast Moab was conquered and was also treated with cold-blooded brutality (II Sam. 8:2). Two thirds of the soldiers of the nation were put to death. Moab became a vassal state and was forced to pay tribute to Jerusalem.

To the east David attacked Ammon. This campaign is recorded in considerable detail in a narrative which includes the incident of David's affair with Bathsheba (II Sam. 10–12). The war started when a delega-

[6] On this move by David see especially Alt, "Die Staatenbildung," pp. 50 ff. and *idem*, "Das Grossreich," pp. 68-69.

[7] See Alt's treatment of this new departure and the possible reasons for it ("Die Staatenbildung," pp. 54-56 and "Das Grossreich," pp. 69-70).

tion sent by David to Ammon on the occasion of a change of monarchy was insulted. After two attempts by Arameans to help their Ammonite neighbors proved unsuccessful, the latter were roundly defeated by David's armies under the leadership of Joab. Rabbah, the Ammonite capital, fell after a long seige and the royal crown of the nation was placed on David's head (II Sam. 12:30). Thus David became king of Ammon. Soon after this, David turned to settle the score with the Arameans to the northeast (II Sam. 8:3-8). His energies were directed primarily against Hadadezer, king of Zobah, who had intervened in the Ammonite war and was evidently the most powerful ruler among the various Aramean tribes. He defeated Hadadezer, and then also conquered the city of Damascus, which became the residence of the governors David appointed to administer his Aramean domains. This campaign brought a great deal of booty to David and it also resulted in lavish tribute from Toi, king of Hamath, which lay far to the north on the Orontes River (II Sam. 8:9-10).

To the northwest David evidently secured himself by peaceful means. There is no record of a conflict with any of the Phoenician cities on the coastal plain. Toward the latter part of his reign [8] David is said to have made a treaty with Hiram of Tyre, which was the foremost of the cities of Phoenicia (II Sam. 5:11-12).

Once his conquests were completed, David was ruler over a very sizeable empire. It extended from the Mediterranean Sea in the west to the desert in the east. To the south it touched the Gulf of Aqaba and on its northern boundary it reached almost as far as Kadesh on the Orontes. He was king of Israel, Judah, Jerusalem, and Ammon. He ruled over the provinces of Damascus and Edom, which were administered by governors he appointed. He was also sovereign over the vassal monarch of Moab, and possibly over Hadadezer of Zobah.[9] The administration of such a vast and complex empire naturally necessitated organization.[10] Fortunately one of David's many gifts was that he knew how to organize. He was not a charismatic man; he was an

---

[8] Bright, *History*, p. 183, n. 43.

[9] Noth, *History*, p. 197.

[10] There is evidence that much of the pattern for David's organization at Jerusalem was ultimately Egyptian in origin. See R. de Vaux, "Titres et fonctionnaires égyptiens à la cour de David et de Salomon," *Revue Biblique*, XLVIII (1939), 394-405.

organization man. In this regard his personality differed from Saul's as day does from night. The center of the Davidic state, of course, was at Jerusalem. To its organization, first of all, belonged David's army. The army was divided into two branches. The Israelite militia was under Joab, a kinsman of David (II Sam. 8:16; 20:23). This consisted of tribal volunteers and as an institution was rooted in the amphictyonic period of Israel's life. The troop of foreign mercenaries was under Benaiah (II Sam. 8:18; 20:23). This second branch was responsible to David personally and had no competing tribal loyalties. It was a comparatively new institution in Israel, having begun only at Adullam when David was fleeing from Saul (I Sam. 22:1-2). In addition to the top military officers, there was a "recorder," or royal herald, Jehoshaphat (II Sam. 8:16; 20:24) and a "secretary," or secretary of state, Sheva [11] (II Sam. 20:25). There was also an officer in charge of forced labor, Adoram (II Sam. 20:24). And finally, there were two official priests, Zadok and Abiathar (II Sam. 8:17; 20:25). At the top of all this organization, however, was David! He not only reigned, he actively *ruled* his empire.

But what had all this to do with Yahweh of Sinai? That was the question which presented itself at Jerusalem. And it was a question which received a definite answer. Although the answer did not satisfy all the people of ancient Israel, it satisfied at least some of them. The result was a new theology that centered at Jerusalem in addition to the new empire that centered there.

The two most important chapters in this connection are II Samuel 6 and 7.

1. According to II Samuel 6, the ark of the covenant, the central object of the old twelve-tribe amphictyony, was brought to Jerusalem and placed in the tent of meeting, the central cult object of the old six-tribe amphictyony.

2. II Samuel 7 contains the oracle of Nathan that promises that David's "house," i.e., dynasty, and his kingship will be made sure "for ever" before Yahweh.

---

[11] In II Sam. 8:17 the name appears as Seraiah. It probably was an Egyptian name originally, Shavsha (I Chron. 18:16) or Shisha (I Kings 4:3). See Bright, *History*, p. 184, n. 47.

Besides David, the three most important people in this connection were Abiathar, Zadok, and Nathan.

1. Abiathar was of the house of Eli, which had been in charge of the ark at Shiloh before that city fell and the ark was lost to the Philistines. Thus Abiathar was familiar with northern theology and institutions.

2. Nathan was evidently a "south Israelite," perhaps from Hebron, the site of the tent of meeting.[12] Thus Nathan would have been familiar with southern theology and institutions. He was not a priest, however.

3. Zadok was probably a member of the old Jebusite priesthood of Jerusalem when David conquered it.[13] He would thus have been a priest of "El Elyon" (Gen. 14:18, 19, 20, 22; II Sam. 22:14; Ps. 18:14, et al.). When Yahwism became the new religion at Jerusalem after it had been conquered by David, Zadok was evidently willing to accommodate himself to the situation.

A conjecture as to what may have happened in the time of David is as follows.

1. At Abiathar's suggestion, the ark of the covenant was brought to Jerusalem.[14] The ark was the symbol of the old twelve-tribe amphictyony. It stood for the unity of the whole people Israel, and its presence in Jerusalem was absolutely necessary for a united kingdom.[15] The northern *symbol* was brought to Jerusalem, but the northern theology in the form of the E covenant legend—democratic, charismatic, prophetic—stayed in the North. It was eventually taken to Bethel, as we shall see.

2. Probably at Nathan's suggestion, and certainly with his co-operation, the tent of meeting was brought from Hebron to Jerusalem. In

---

[12] Chap. Five, p. 154.

[13] As H. H. Rowley has contended ("Zadok and Nehustan," *Journal of Biblical Literature*, LVIII [1939], 113-142 and "Melchizedek and Zadok," *Festschrift Alfred Bertholet* [Tübingen: J. C. B. Mohr, 1950], pp. 461-72).

[14] I Kings 2:26 explicitly relates the ark to Abiathar.

[15] On the significance of this act for Jerusalem see especially Martin Noth, "Jerusalem und die israelitische Tradition," *Gesammelte Studien zum Alten Testament* (München: Chr. Kaiser, 1957), pp. 172-87; cf. *idem, History*, p. 191.

THE PEOPLE OF THE COVENANT

Jerusalem the ark was placed within "the tent" (II Sam. 6:17).[16] This was a highly symbolic action, for the J covenant tradition had been attached to the tent of meeting, just as the E tradition had been attached to the ark. This suggested what was happening theologically. Just as the ark was being covered by the tent, so the covenant theology of the North was superseded by that of the South.[17] At this time the general theological position in regard to the covenant represented by the J legend became official in Jerusalem.

3. Of course, this theology was not brought to Jerusalem without change. At Hebron covenant theology centered in the Aaron-Nadab-Abihu dynasty. This priestly dynasty had been viewed as the continuing center of the life of the covenant people. When the tent of meeting was brought to Jerusalem with the dynastic covenant theology associated with it, the Hebron priesthood remained at Hebron.[18] It was Nathan who came with the tent. Nathan was a religious figure, but he was not a priest. At Jerusalem he was a court prophet. Zadok, who was a priest, was evidently willing to adjust to the new situation. Abiathar was also a priest, but his theological convictions probably caused him to have certain reservations about what was being done.

In any event, the Davidic innovation consisted of the *transfer of the center of covenant theology from a priestly dynasty to a royal dynasty.* This change was realized through an oracle of Nathan to David (II Sam. 7),[19] the central thesis of which is found in verse 16:

And your house and your kingdom shall be made sure for ever ['ad 'olam] before me; your throne shall be established for ever ['ad 'olam].

[16] Note that Arnulf Kuschke takes the position that the ark was placed in the tent of meeting for the first time by David ("Die Lagervorstellung der priesterlichen Erzählung," p. 89).

[17] This is not to say that other theological traditions associated with the ark did not persist and influence the Jerusalem cult. For instance, the "dwelling" theology associated with the ark certainly did. See von Rad, "Zelt und Lade."

[18] It is not difficult to understand how Absalom was later able to begin his rebellion at Hebron (II Sam. 15:7-12). A powerful priesthood still resided there that David had succeeded in alienating. The later explanation in the Priestly Writing of the demise of the Nadab-Abihu branch of the Aaronic dynastic tree is found in Lev. 10.

[19] Rost (*Thronnachfolge Davids,* pp. 47 ff.) finds the original core of II Sam. 7 in vss. 1-7, 11b, 16, 18-21, 25-26 and dates it in the age of Solomon. In a recent article Martin Noth has argued for the essential unity of practically the whole of II Sam. 7 with a Davidic date ("David und Israel in II Samuel 7," *Mélanges bibliques rédigés en l'honneur de André Robert* [Paris: Bloud & Gay, 1957] pp. 122-30). I am persuaded by Noth.

Coming from the Davidic period also would be the "last words of David" in II Sam. 23:1-7, the basic theme of which is in vs. 5:

> Yea, does not my house stand so with God?
> For he has made with me an everlasting
>   covenant [berith 'olam],
> ordered in all things and secure.

Through the oracle of Nathan, therefore, the tradition concerning the eternal covenant of Yahweh with David and his dynasty emerged. Basically, it should be underlined, this was the same kind of covenant theology that had previously obtained at Hebron. There it had been maintained that Yahweh had made a covenant with the Aaronic priestly dynasty "for ever" (Exod. 19:9a).

This would seem to explain why the kingship won full acceptance in the South but never in the North.[20] The dynastic principle as such had existed in the form of a priestly dynasty in Kenite Yahwism even before Moses. Later in the southern six-tribe amphictyony, to which the Kenites belonged, the dynastic principle was combined with the covenant and found expression in the Aaronic dynasty. The substitution of a royal dynasty for a priestly dynasty as the center of covenant theology in the Davidic era was a definite innovation. No doubt there were many who bitterly resented, and perhaps resisted, this new departure. But at the same time a dynastic kingship was much more easily accommodated to southern theology than to the northern "kingdom of priests" covenant theology with its idea of charismatic leadership. Apart from practical problems, it was relatively simple from the theological standpoint to accommodate the kingship to southern covenant thinking.

From the time of David the king undoubtedly had a prominent role in the Jerusalem cult. The precise character of this role has been the subject of much dispute in Old Testament scholarship. Hans-Joachim

---

[20] See Alt's treatment of the nature of the kingship in the North and the South: "Das Königtum in den Reichen Israel und Juda." He shows clearly that the charismatic ideal obtained in the kingdom of Israel and the dynastic in Judah. Although he is very much aware of the problem, Alt finds no satisfactory explanation for the quick acceptance of the dynastic principle in the South. See especially p. 128.

Kraus, however, has made a very good case for an annual "Royal-Zion Festival" in Jerusalem.[21] The basic themes of this celebration were: (1) Yahweh's choice of Jerusalem to be his dwelling place, and (2) his choice of the Davidic dynasty to rule over his people. The first is the theme of II Samuel 6 and the second is the theme of II Samuel 7. Both occur in the blessing which Solomon delivers at the dedication of the temple on the occasion of the autumnal festival in Jerusalem:

I have chosen Jerusalem that my name might be there and I have chosen David to be over my people Israel. I Kings 8:16 [22]

It is probable, Kraus contends, that II Samuel 6 and 7 were originally cult legends which were used in this celebration. Presumably they were read and re-enacted as the festival was annually observed. There would have been a solemn processional led by the king in which the ark of the covenant, the throne of Yahweh, was brought up to Zion (II Sam. 6; cf. Ps. 132). This represented Yahweh's coming to Zion to take up his royal abode once again. Then the cult prophet would have proclaimed the oracle of the everlasting reign of the Davidic dynasty (II Sam. 7).[23] I Kings 8, in which both themes are prominent, would presumably preserve the memory of the observance of this Royal-Zion Festival on the occasion of the dedication of the Solomonic temple. If there was such a celebration, many psalms would have had their origin in it. This would be the case of royal psalms of the Psalter (132; 78:65-72; 24b; 2; 72; 89, et al.),[24] as well as the Zion psalms (84; 87; 122, et al.)[25]

In keeping with the uniqueness of Israel's faith, therefore, this celebration had a pronounced historical character. It centered in two actual events of the tenth century B.C.: the bringing of the ark to

---

[21] Kraus, *Die Königsherrschaft Gottes im Alten Testament* (Tübingen: J. C. B. Mohr, 1951), pp. 27-99.

[22] Following the reading of LXX[B] and II Chron. 6:6; cf. Kraus, *op. cit.*, p. 43.

[23] I would question Kraus's suggestion that a renewal of the Sinaitic covenant also figured in this celebration at Jerusalem from the time of the early monarchy (*Ibid.*, pp. 45-47). It was evidently a part of the festival in the time of Josiah (II Kings 23:1-3), but there is little evidence that this was the case before the fall of the northern kingdom and the northern traditions were brought to Jerusalem.

[24] *Ibid.*, pp. 51-78.

[25] *Ibid.*, pp. 78-81.

Jerusalem and Nathan's oracle concerning the Davidic dynasty. There is little doubt, of course, that many other features were subsequently incorporated into this festival. A number of them were evidently borrowed from other cultures, especially Egypt and Mesopotamia.[26] Such themes as Yahweh's kingship, his enthronement, and his creative activity were probably prominent in the annual Jerusalem rites. They are reflected in many psalms which can be associated with the cult at Jerusalem. That the reigning king of the house of David was ever officially considered divine, as was true in other cultures of the ancient Orient, is quite unlikely. As the anointed of Yahweh, he was a sacral person; indeed he was the adopted son of God (II Sam. 7:14; Ps. 2:7). But the dynasty to which he belonged had a definite beginning at a particular point in history when it was so willed by Yahweh, who was King of the king.[27] This fact was remembered annually in the cult.

The latter part of David's reign was filled with difficulty. This difficulty for the most part was connected with his throne. The paramount question was who would be David's successor.[28] It should be kept in mind that there were three primary centers of power involved in the events: (1) Jerusalem, the seat of the new political and theological order established by David; (2) Judah, i.e., the southern tribes which formerly had formed the six-tribe amphictyony at Hebron; (3) Israel, i.e., the northern tribes, among whom were many who still took seriously the "kingdom of priests" covenant theology.

The oracle of Nathan (II Sam. 7) seems to have determined decisive-

[26] On Egyptian influence on the Jerusalem kingship and cult see especially von Rad, "Das judäische Königsritual," *Gesammelte Studien zum Alten Testament,* pp. 205-213; and *idem, Theologie,* I, 48-49 and the literature cited therein. On Mesopotamian influence see especially the classical work on the subject: Sigmund Mowinckel, *Psalmenstudien* II. *Das Thronbesteigungsfest Jahwäs und der Ursprung der Eschatologie* (Kristiana: Dybwad, 1932). His position is summarized in English in his book, *He That Cometh* (Nashville: Abingdon Press, 1956), Chapter 3. Subsequent writings on the subject are too numerous to mention. See the works referred to by Bright, *History,* p. 205, n. 96.

[27] On this point see especially Noth, "Gott, König, Volk im Alten Testament," *Gesammelte Studien zum Alten Testament,* pp. 188-229.

[28] The events of this period are particularly well documented. They are told in the "Court History" source, viz., II Sam. 7; 9-20; I Kings 1-2. See the standard commentaries on Samuel, and also Rost, *Thronnachfolge Davids.*

165

ly that one of David's sons would succeed him. Now the only question
was which son. David, who was so decisive in most areas of his life,
was strangely indecisive in this one. He possessed the power to desig-
nate his successor, but he delayed until almost his dying moment and
thus contributed greatly to the series of tragedies that struck his household. Amnon was David's first-born (II Sam. 3:2) and seems to
have been viewed by many as the logical successor of his father. But
Amnon was slain by Absalom (II Sam. 13–14); so Absalom entered
the picture as the likeliest candidate.[29] He was not certain of his status
in the eyes of his father, however, so he determined to settle the
question in his own way. He led a rebellion against David (II Sam.
15–19). The revolt began at Hebron (II Sam. 15:10), the city of his
birth (II Sam. 3:3) and also the former home of the priestly dynastic
theology of the covenant. It evidently was still the residence of many
who continued to nourish deep grievances against David. The fact
that the Aaronic dynasty had been replaced by the Davidic dynasty as
the center of covenant theology must have been bitterly resented at
Hebron. Joining in the revolt, for entirely different reasons, were men
of the northern tribes (II Sam. 15:13). One reason for their participation may well have been their unhappiness at continually being forced
to participate in David's wars of conquest.[30] But their understanding
of the nature of the covenant must have made them dissatisfied with
the Davidic kingship as an institution. So their participation in the war
would have resulted less from any love for Absalom than from their
hatred of David. Even though David was forced to leave Jerusalem
for a period during its course, the rebellion eventually failed, and
Absalom was killed. The loyalty of David's mercenaries was clearly
one important factor in the failure of the revolt (II Sam. 15:14-29), as
was Hushai's deceitful advice to Absalom in Jerusalem (II Sam. 17).
But lack of any real unity between the two main sources of Absalom's
support—the men of Judah and the men of Israel—must also have
contributed greatly to it. Hostility between the two groups was sim-
mering at the conclusion of the affair (II Sam. 19:41-43). Even before

---

[29] He was the third-born of David (II Sam. 3:3). What happened to Chileab, the
second of David's sons (II Sam. 3:3), we are not told.

[30] As Alt suggests ("Die Staatenbildung," p. 56).

David returned to his capital, this hostility erupted into another rebellion (II Sam. 20). This one was led by Sheba and had the support only of the North. With the help of the southern tribes, however, David was able to quell this revolt too.

The question of the throne succession was still not settled. Now Absalom was dead. The next son was Adonijah (II Sam. 3:4). Adonijah viewed himself as the logical successor, as did a number in the Jerusalem court. As the result of a palace intrigue, however, the son who was to sit on the throne of David was not Adonijah, but Solomon.

Solomon's Kingship at Jerusalem

I Kings 1–2 tells of the power struggle that eventuated in the crowning of Solomon, David's son by Bathsheba, as king. David was old and impotent. It was clear to all that his days were numbered, so the conspiracies began. The alignments behind the two chief contenders for the kingship are precisely what might have been expected.

Behind Adonijah stood:

1. Joab, the military leader who was the commander of the Israelite levies, the old twelve-tribe amphictyonic institution. Unfortunately for this side few if any of these troops seem to have been in Jerusalem.

2. Abiathar, the priest whose family came originally from the cult center of Shiloh and who seems to have represented the northern theological viewpoint in the court.

Behind Solomon stood:

1. Bathsheba, his mother and David's favorite wife, to whom David may or may not have promised that her son would succeed him. What was important was that the senile king seems to have been convinced that he made the promise.

2. Benaiah, in charge of the Cherethites and Pelethites, the royal mercenary army. This royal guard was an innovation of David and did not belong to the older amphictyonic order. It was very much in evidence during the intrigues and no doubt played a decisive role in the outcome.

3. Zadok, a southern religious figure, probably a priest of the pre-

Davidic Jerusalem cult. From the time of Solomon he was the head of the official priestly family at Jerusalem.

4. Nathan, another southern religious figure. He was probably from Hebron, the home of the J covenant tradition and dynastic covenant theology. He, of course, was responsible for the oracle which established the house of David "for ever" (II Sam. 7).

The group that represented the new order with its royal dynastic covenant theology emerged victorious in this conflict. Solomon received David's blessing and was anointed king at "the tent" (I Kings 1:39).[31] It is probably no accident that there is no record of a covenant made by Solomon with the northern tribes when be became king. David's covenant with the elders of Israel when he was made their king undoubtedly involved definite limitations of his sovereignty over them (II Sam. 5:3).[32] The lack of any such covenant between Solomon and the North was ominous for the future of the Davidic kingdom.

After the death of David, Solomon moved to establish himself firmly in the throne. Among his first deeds was the brutal execution of Adonijah, who had evidently made some new attempt to claim the crown (I Kings 2:13-25). Next he deposed Abiathar and exiled him to Anathoth (I Kings 2:26-27). In accordance with David's death-bed instructions (I Kings 2:5-7), he had Joab killed (I Kings 2:28-35). Finally, Shimei, a former enemy of David (II Sam. 16:5-14), was dispatched (I Kings 2:36-46).

It was perhaps the exile of Abiathar that was more fateful for the future of the united kingdom than any other action on Solomon's part. Abiathar had been David's continuing contact with northern covenant theology through his long reign. He had joined David at Keilah when David was fleeing from Saul (I Sam. 23:6) and remained with him thereafter. Now the Jerusalem court no longer had this contact. It must have contributed directly to the division of the kingdom.

In general it can be said that the Solomonic kingdom was sustained

[31] The dates of Solomon's reign are 961-922 B.C. Besides the final two chapters of the "court history" (I Kings 1-2), the main source of our knowledge of Solomon is "the book of the acts of Solomon." It is referred to in I Kings 11:41 and seems to be the basic document used by the Deuteronomic author of I Kings 3-11. See the standard commentaries on the problem.

[32] See Chap. Five, pp. 154-55.

primarily by the momentum that David had created. In *foreign policy* Solomon seems to have instituted little that was new; rather he sought to continue the policies of David as best he could. He had trouble, though, with some of his satellites. I Kings 11:14-22, 25 tells of a revolt of Edom led by Hadad, a prince who had sought refuge in Egypt while David was still king. The revolt occurred soon after Hadad learned that David and Joab were dead, so it must have been relatively early in Solomon's reign. Hadad was not able to control all of Edom, it would seem; otherwise Solomon could not have continued to make use of the port at Ezion-geber on the Gulf of Aqaba throughout his reign.[33] Solomon also had difficulty to the north in Syria. According to I Kings 11:23-25 a certain Rezon son of Eliada seized Damascus and made himself king there. This may not have involved the loss of all of Aram, but it was a serious blow to the Solomonic empire.

Not long after his accession, though, Solomon received a new ally in Egypt. This is indicated by the fact that he took an Egyptian princess into his harem (I Kings 3:1). We are not certain which Pharaoh gave his daughter to Solomon, but it is generally believed to have been one of the last of the feeble Twenty-first Dynasty. That Solomon constructed a house especially for this princess suggests the significance he attached to this alliance (I Kings 7:8).

As was true of David, Solomon had quite close relations with Hiram, king of Tyre in Phoenicia (I Kings 5:1-12). Hiram was king of the city that dominated the whole Phoenician coast from Mt. Carmel northward during this period. There were excellent ports on this coast, and this natural advantage enabled the Phoenicians to become the great maritime nation of the age. It was consequently a great asset for the Hebrews to be allied with such a people. The Phoenicians also controlled the forests of Lebanon. This too was important for Solomon, since Hiram supplied timber for the extensive building projects of the Hebrew king.

In connection with foreign policy Solomon's activities in regard to national defense should be mentioned.[34] During his reign a number of Palestinian cities were fortified, including Jerusalem, the capital, Hazor,

[33] See Noth, *History*, pp. 205-6.
[34] See Bright, *History*, p. 192.

in Galilee, Megiddo, in the important pass of Jezreel, Gezer, Beth-horon, and Baalah, guarding the western approaches from the plain, and Tamar, south of the Dead Sea (I Kings 9:15-19). Moreover, for the first time in Israel's history horses and chariots were introduced into the military system. According to I Kings 10:26 and II Chron. 9:25 Solomon had four thousand stalls for horses, fourteen hundred chariots and twelve thousand horsemen.[35] None of these armaments, however, was ever used in battle. Solomon's age was an age of peace. He was not a military leader and fought no wars.

With no major wars on the international scene, Solomon was able to concentrate on *domestic development*. His has been called a "Golden Age"; and it was, of a sort. There was great economic prosperity. Israel experienced a real economic boom under Solomon. Agricultural productivity increased. Since the old Philistine monopoly of iron had been broken, the iron-tipped plow came into general use.[36] This meant that the soil could be cultivated much more easily and there was consequently a rapid increase in its yield. Business in general was good. The relation of Israel to the surrounding nations was such that trade was encouraged and flourished. Many must have become rich during the period. Solomon himself engaged in various commercial enterprises. He started trade on the Red Sea by establishing a port at Ezion-geber (I Kings 9:26-28; 10:11-12, 22). According to I Kings 10:22 Solomon dealt in gold, silver, ivory, peacocks, and apes. In addition to the Red Sea trade, he seems to have carried on caravan trade with Arabia (I Kings 10:1-10). Although it is not referred to in the Old Testament itself, Solomon also seems to have had a thriving copper industry. Archaeological excavations have uncovered a copper refinery at Ezion-geber which is dated in the Solomonic age.[37] Finally, it seems that he dealt extensively in international commerce involving horses and chariots (I Kings 10:28-29).[38]

There was also cultural development in the age of Solomon. The

[35] Excavations in Palestine have illumined greatly this area of Solomon's activity. See G. E. Wright's description of Megiddo with its horse stables (*Bibilical Archaeology*, pp. 130-32).

[36] Bright, *History*, p. 196.

[37] See Nelson Glueck, *The Other Side of the Jordan* (New Haven: American Schools of Oriental Research, 1940), pp. 50-113.

[38] See Bright's comments (*History*, pp. 195-96).

impetus for this development unquestionably came from the dynamic and creative Davidic era, but the peace of the time of Solomon allowed it to flower. One of the most significant activities of the period was in the area of literature. As in other cultures of antiquity, this literary activity would have centered in the cult. In the Solomonic age this meant the temple. I Kings 4:29-34 associates Solomon with wisdom literature, and this is undoubtedly an authentic tradition.[39] Wisdom was a significant phenomenon of various cultures in this age, especially in Egypt. So in this respect, Israel would have been participating in an international cultural movement. It is accordingly not at all improbable that parts of the book of Proverbs go back originally to the Solomonic period.

Prose was produced too. The court history of David (II Sam. 7; 9-20; I Kings 1-2) comes from this age. Also the stories of Samuel and Saul were collected and written down. Above all, the Jahwist epic of the Pentateuch was composed in the time of Solomon.[40] The various traditions that were used in this epic probably were first collected in the time of David. These would have included the traditions of the exodus, the wilderness wandering, the conquest, mythological stories, and the patriarchal legends, including the Abraham sagas from Hebron. Not the least of these traditions would have been the *J covenant legend*. Of course, with the emphasis on David and his seed in the Jerusalem cult, the J legend would not have been used liturgically there. Containing the tradition of Yahweh's eternal covenant with the Aaron-Nadab-Abihu dynasty, it was probably something of an embarrassment to the Davidic house. In any event, if these traditions were collected during the time of David, they were probably written down as an epic during the early part of Solomon's reign. And the entire epic to some extent reflected the older Hebron theology by stressing the continuity of Yahweh's covenant people from the time of Abraham.[41]

[39] See especially Alt, "Die Weisheit Salomos," *Kleine Schriften*, II, 90-99.

[40] An excellent treatment of the Jahwist epic is to be found in Anderson, *Understanding the Old Testament*, pp. 154-82; see also von Rad, *Genesis* (Philadelphia: The Westminster Press, 1961), pp. 13-30.

[41] Note the Jahwist's great concern for the "seed" of the patriarchs in the book of Gen.: 12:7; 13:15, 16; 16:10; 22:17, 18; 24:7; 26:3, 4, 24; 28:13, 14; 32:13. There is nothing like this emphasis in E. On the contrary, E faces the real possibility of the *discontinuity* of the people for God's sake (Gen. 22:1-14).

There was also great building activity during the reign of Solomon. Reference has already been made to the fortifications he constructed at various key sites throughout the country. It was particularly at Jerusalem, however, that Solomon built. He enlarged the city of David to the north and constructed a number of buildings there. A list of some of them is found in I Kings 7:1-8: (1) the House of the Forest of Lebanon; (2) the Hall of Pillars; (3) the Hall of the Throne; (4) his own house; (5) to which was attached the house of the Pharaoh's daughter.

To later ages, of course, it was the temple which was the most important of all Solomon's building projects (I Kings 5-8). Its site was the elevated, rocky threshing floor of Araunah, the Jebusite, which David had previously acquired (II Sam. 24:18, 24-25). It had probably been a sacred site from time immemorial.[42] The temple was essentially a Canaanite structure.[43] In architecture, furnishings and cult symbolism it followed the temple patterns current in Palestine, Phoenicia, and Syria. We are actually told that its architect came from Tyre in Phoenicia (I Kings 7:13-14), and its builders as well as material came from the same source (I Kings 5:18). As John Bright points out,[44] the temple served a dual purpose. It was, first, a dynastic shrine, or royal chapel. Second, it was intended as the national shrine of the Israelite people.

Since its structure and much of its symbolism was Canaanite, the temple must have been viewed with horror by many Israelites whose faith was rooted in the nomadic Mosaic age and faith. However, the temple was not completely discontinuous with Israel's past. It would seem that the temple represented the final stage of a cultic development which began with the ark of the covenant and the tent of meeting in the time of Moses. Although both of these shrines presumably originated in the Mosaic age, they were located in different parts of Palestine subsequent to the events at Kadesh. The ark was at Shechem and Shiloh as the chief cult object of the twelve-tribe amphictyony. The

[42] Noth, *History*, p. 208.

[43] See G. E. Wright's description and treatment of the Jerusalem temple (*Biblical Archaeology*, pp. 136-145); cf. Alt, "Verbreitung und Herkunft des Syrischen Tempeltypus," *Kleine Schriften*, II, 100-115.

[44] Bright, *History*, p. 197.

172

tent was at Hebron as the main shrine of the southern six-tribe amphictyony. David seems to have been the one who first brought the two together (II Sam. 6:17). The tent of David's time would have been a more elaborate structure than the older desert shrine, since for the first time it served to house the ark. If the suggestion of F. M. Cross is correct that the tabernacle in the Priestly Code (Exod. 25-31; 35-40) for the most part is a description of the Davidic tent,[45] the shrine at this point would have been enlarged and divided into two sections. The first part was the "holy place" (*hekal*); the second was the "holy of holies" (*debir*) and contained the ark. The next and final step in this cultic development would have been the construction of the temple by Solomon. The last that is heard of the two nomadic shrines, the ark and the tent,[46] is in I Kings 8, which recounts the dedication of Solomon's temple (vss. 1-4). The ark was placed in the holy of holies of the temple. What happened to the tent we are not told; but it was no longer considered important, since the temple had superceded it.[47]

There is no question that for all its splendor the "Golden Age" of Solomon resulted in a great burden for many people. For one thing, it involved a tremendous economic burden. Solomon's ever-expanding government involved ever-increasing expenses. His building projects must have been very costly. Not only their initial cost, but their upkeep required much money. Indeed the whole governmental structure, with its officials not only in Jerusalem but throughout the kingdom, would have been tremendously expensive. These expenses had to be met. Efforts in this direction were made in several ways. It is unlikely that all the profits of Solomon's commercial enterprises went into his own personal treasury. Some of them undoubtedly went to meet govern-

[45] "The Tabernacle," p. 63.

[46] Apart from Jeremiah's reference to the ark (Jer. 3:16).

[47] It was evidently in this period that a new word was appropriated to express Yahweh's relation to the temple. The verb *yarad* ("come down") had expressed his relation to the tent (Chap. Two, p. 66). The verb *yashab* ("to dwell, to be enthroned") had expressed his relation to the ark (Chap. Two, p. 58). Now the verb *shakan* ("to tent, to tabernacle") was used (I Kings 8:12). This seems to have been an attempt to combine theologically both ideas of God's immanence and transcendence. From the verb *shakan* was derived the noun *mishkan* ("tabernacle") which is a peculiar expression of P. On the word *mishkan* see particularly Cross, *op. cit.*, pp. 65-68.

mental expenses. Also there were tolls that he exacted from merchants passing through his territories (I Kings 10:15). These would have made a tidy sum.

The primary source of governmental income, to be sure, would have been taxation. Taxes both in the form of money and goods were levied. To facilitate the collecting of taxes Solomon divided the country into twelve districts (I Kings 4:7-19).[48] Each had a governor responsible to the king; and two of the governors were married to Solomon's daughters. For the most part these districts disregarded the old tribal boundaries of the amphictyony, a fact which must have been like salt in northern wounds.[49] Solomon's definite policy seems to have been to weaken tribal loyalties as much as possible in order to consolidate power more firmly in the crown. Taxation of money and goods did not prove adequate to meet the growing expenses of the Solomonic state, so another form of taxation was instituted—of labor. This was the hated corvée, forced labor of subjects. It must have been galling on the independent Israelite spirits, and certainly contributed greatly to Solomon's unpopularity. In I Kings 9:20-22 it is stated that only Canaanites were impressed into these labor gangs. I Kings 5:13 and 11:28 state otherwise, however, and there is little doubt that Israelites too were forced to participate.

This increasing economic burden borne by the people was paralleled by increasing luxury and ostentation in the Jerusalem court. According to I Kings 4:22-23 one day's food supply for Solomon's household consisted of thirty measures of fine flour, sixty measures of meal, ten fat oxen, twenty pasture-fed cattle, a hundred sheep, besides harts, gazelles, robucks, and fatted fowl! And his family consisted of seven hundred wives and three hundred concubines (I Kings 11:3), besides children, of course.

So the rich grew richer and the poor grew poorer. Under Yahweh, the righteous God of Sinai, such conditions could not continue to exist! This was undoubtedly the conviction of many. An explosion was imminent.

[48] See Alt, "Israels Gaue unter Salomo," *Kleine Schriften*, II, 76-89.

[49] The place of Judah in the organization of districts is not clear. See the discussions in Bright (*History*, pp. 200-201) and Noth (*History*, p. 212, n. 2).

Not only was there an economic burden on the people; there was also a *theological burden* which they were forced to bear—particularly by the people of the North. The oracle of Nathan had given a theological foundation to the throne of David:

Yahweh declares to you that Yahweh will make you a house. . . . And your house and your kingdom shall be made sure *for ever* before me; your throne shall be established *for ever*. II Sam. 7:11*b*, 16

This oracle must have been taken with increasing seriousness in the time of Solomon. As it was rehearsed annually in the cult it served to enhance more and more the significance and prestige of the Jerusalem kingship. The unconditional divine approval of this human institution implied by the oracle was undoubtedly resented deeply by many worshipers of Yahweh. David had evidently achieved some sort of a *modus vivendi* with northern theological circles, however tenuous it may have been. Abiathar was probably the key figure in this regard. The expulsion of Abiathar by Solomon, though, must have opened the way in Jerusalem for a complete theological justification of an ever-increasing concentration of authority in the hands of the king. There was no longer anyone in the court circles to represent the northern theological viewpoint and thus modify to some extent excessive claims for the person of the king. Psalms 132 and 89 perhaps illustrate the difference in theological emphasis between the time of David and that of Solomon. Although the former affirms the oath of Yahweh in respect to the continuation of the Davidic dynasty, it stresses the obligation that his sons have of obedience to the divine will and suggests that the relationship is contingent:

> *If* your sons keep my covenant
>   and my testimonies which I shall teach them,
> their sons also for ever
>   shall sit upon your throne. vs. 12

This psalm may reveal the influence of northern covenant theology and might indicate some kind of a Davidic "compromise." Psalm 89, on the other hand, contains no suggestion of a contingent relation of Yahweh to the house of David:

> 29 I will establish his line for ever
>   and his throne as the days of the heavens.
> 30 If his children forsake my law
>   and do not walk according to my ordinances,
> 31 if they violate my statutes
>   and do not keep my commandments,
> 32 then I will punish their transgression
>   with the rod
>   and their iniquity with scourges;
> 33 but I will not remove from him my steadfast
>   love,
>   or be false to my faithfulness.
> 34 I will not violate my covenant,
>   or alter the word that went forth
>   from my lips.[50]

It reflects the kind of unconditional royal covenant theology that must have been increasingly emphasized in the court of Solomon.

Late in Solomon's reign [51] the burdens borne by the northerners became so great that an explosion almost occurred (I Kings 11:26-31, 40). A prophet of Shiloh, Ahijah, met a certain Jeroboam, as the latter was leaving the city of Jerusalem. Jeroboam, of Ephraim, was an official in the Solomonic government. The prophet took his new garment and tore it into twelve pieces. Ten he gave to Jeroboam with the words: "Take for yourself ten pieces; for thus says Yahweh, the God of Israel, 'Behold, I am about to tear the kingdom from the hand of Solomon, and will give you ten tribes" (vs. 31). As a result of this encounter Jeroboam is said to have "lifted up his hand against the king" (vs. 26). The revolt was abortive, however, and Jeroboam was forced to flee to Egypt for refuge. But northern coals continued to glow, and after the death of Solomon they broke forth into furious flame.

[50] Hebrew: vss. 30-35.
[51] After 935 B.C., according to Bright (*History*, p. 208, n. 105).

The Break with the Jerusalem Kingship

Following the death of Solomon in 922 B.C. Rehoboam, his son, went to Shechem for a momentous conclave (I Kings 12:1-20). He seems to have had no difficulty in gaining acceptance as king by the South. His relation to the North was much less certain. For this reason it was necessary for him to go to Shechem, the site where the twelve-tribe amphictyony had been established and which continued to be its center until it was replaced by Shiloh. Shechem was a northern symbol and it probably galled Rehoboam to be forced to go there. When he arrived he was met by "all Israel" (vs. 1). It is unlikely that Jeroboam was at this assembly, at least when it began.[52] This was a matter which the people themselves were to decide. Before they would accept Rehoboam as their king, he would have to accede to their demand: "Your father made our yoke heavy. Now therefore lighten the hard service of your father and his heavy yoke upon us, and we will serve you" (vs. 4). The "yoke" referred to certainly included the corvée imposed by Solomon, but by implication these words meant something more. The Israelites at Shechem wanted a lightening of the *theological* yoke that had been placed upon their necks. This was a demand for Rehoboam to recognize that his sovereignty would have definite limitations in the North. His authority was not to be absolute. Rehoboam's older advisors counselled him to accept the terms; but his younger men urged the contrary. It was the advice of the latter that he heeded when he said: "My father made your yoke heavy, but I will add to your yoke; my father chastised you with whips, but I will chastise you with scorpions" (vs. 14). Immediately the cry of rebellion went up:

> What portion have we in David?
> We have no inheritance in the son of Jesse.
> To your tents, O Israel!
> Look now to your own house, David.
>
> I Kings 12:16

[52] This is implied by vs. 20. His name in vss. 3 and 12 would have been added later. See James Montgomery, *A Critical and Exegetical Commentary on the Books of Kings, International Critical Commentaries* (Edinburgh: T. & T. Clark, 1951), pp. 248 ff. and Norman Snaith, "The First and Second Books of Kings," *The Interpreter's Bible* (Nashville: Abingdon Press, 1954), III, 113.

So Israel departed to their tents, and all efforts by Rehoboam to put down the rebellion were futile.[53]

It was at this point that Jeroboam reappeared on the scene. He was a native of Zeredah in Ephraim (I Kings 11:26-27) and thus a northerner. He seems first to have come to prominence as a "servant of Solomon" in the construction of fortifications at Jerusalem (I Kings 11:26-27). Later he was placed in charge of forced labor in his native territory, "the house of Joseph" (I Kings 11:28). His unsuccessful revolt against Solomon had forced him to find refuge in Egypt (I Kings 11:40). Solomon's death, however, had made it possible to return to Palestine. Having already been designated a future king of Israel by Ahijah the prophet (I Kings 11:29-39),[54] now "all Israel" called him to their assembly and "made him king over all Israel" (I Kings 12:20). It should be noted that he did not take the office of his own power, but rather the *people* made him king.

Although he is not specifically mentioned in connection with these events at Shechem, the influence of Ahijah the Shilonite upon them may well have been decisive. It was Ahijah, of course, who had been instrumental in precipitating the revolt of Jeroboam against Solomon. It may not be sheer coincidence that Ahijah is called "the Shilonite." This probably does not merely mean that he happened to be a resident of Shiloh. In fact, this may not have been the case at all, since Shiloh seems to have been totally destroyed by the Philistines in the preceding century, and there is little evidence of subsequent reoccupation.[55] Rather this title evidently indicates that he was a descendant of the house of Eli, the amphictyonic priests of Shiloh.[56] These later Shilonites may have been those who preserved the E covenant legend after it had been separated from the ark and fostered the theology reflected

[53] It is likely that the invasion of Shishak aided the North in the rebellion (I Kings 14:25-28). See Bright, *History*, pp. 213-14.

[54] See Noth, *History*, p. 227.

[55] Chap. Four, p. 121, n. 56.

[56] Comments Norman Snaith: "The revolt (of Jeroboam) had the strong and vigorous support of the descendants of the house of Eli, who had been priests of the ark of Shiloh, and indeed from the earliest days (I Sam. 2:27-28)" (*op. cit.*, p. 109).

in it. It is impossible to determine where and how this liturgy was used between the fall of Shiloh in 1050 B.C. and the division of the kingdom in 922 B.C. It is quite possible that an annual covenant ceremony continued to be observed in some cult center during this period, however few may have participated in it.[57] In any event, Ahijah came from Shilonite circles and presumably was strongly under the influence of northern theology. Like others who accepted northern covenant theology, Ahijah evidently believed that Yahweh's covenant was with all the people, and not with any dynasty, priestly or royal, in behalf of the people. And in so far as theological conviction motivated his actions, this would have been the position of Jeroboam too.

After he became king of the northern kingdom, one of Jeroboam's first acts was to strengthen the defenses of Shechem, his temporary capital (I Kings 12:25).[58] The selection of Shechem was important because it had been the central cult site of the twelve-tribe amphictyony when it was first established. Shechem became the political capital in the time of Jeroboam, but not the religious center of the northern kingdom. Since the people of the North had learned the unhappy consequences of combining the kingship with the cult during the time of David and Solomon, Shechem was thereby unsuitable as the new religious center. Subsequent to this time political capital and cult center were always separate in the North. Jeroboam also fortified Penuel on the other side of the Jordan (I Kings 12:35).[59] The northern patriarch, Jacob, of course, was traditionally associated with both Shechem (Gen. 33:18-20; ch. 34; 35:1-4) and Penuel (Gen. 32:24-32).

Jeroboam also acted decisively in the realm of the *cult* (I Kings 12:26-33). It is generally recognized that in its present form this tradi-

---

[57] Gilgal would be one likely site. James Muilenburg has shown that Samuel functions as a covenant mediator in I Sam. 12, which has its setting there. See Muilenburg, "The Form and Structure of the Covenantal Formulations."

[58] See Walter Harrelson's comments on this action of Rehoboam (*The City of Shechem*, p. 503).

[59] Noth thinks that he left Shechem to take up residence at Penuel as the result of some temporary emergency (*History*, p. 231).

tion comes from the hand of a southern writer quite unfavorably disposed toward Jeroboam.[60] The later southern position was that the whole of Jeroboam's cultic activity was one gigantic case of idolatry: "And this thing became a sin" (vs. 30). However, this very statement suggests the possibility that Jeroboam's original activity was not a sin; rather it "became" a sin, which was a subsequent development. There are good reasons for agreeing with A. T. Olmstead:

> Jeroboam's revolt was no revolt against Yahweh's cult. If not instigated by the prophetic party, it met with their approval, and history proves that they were right. During the centuries which immediately followed, every fundamental advance in Hebrew religion originated in the north.[61]

What Jeroboam, who named one of his sons "Abijah" ("My father is Yahweh" I Kings 14:1), intended to do was to return to Mosaic Yahwism as it was understood in the North.

It was obvious from the first that the northern kingdom would have to be related officially to Israel's religious traditions if it was to endure. There was a strong pull toward Jerusalem for the people of the North, since the ark of the covenant was there. And there is certainly a real core of truth in the passage:

> 26 And Jeroboam said in his heart, "Now the kingdom will turn back to the house of David; 27 if this people go up to offer sacrifices in the house of Yahweh at Jerusalem, then the heart of this people will turn again to their lord, to Rehoboam king of Judah." I Kings 12:26-27

Jeroboam's first step in his religious reorganization was to establish two shrines, one at Dan in the northern part of his kingdom and the other at Bethel on the southern boundary. It was the latter, however, that was by far the more important of the two.

Bethel was located in Ephraim, just as was Shiloh, the former cult center of the twelve-tribe amphictyony. It stood on the main north-south ridge road of central Palestine, some eighteen miles south of Shiloh and twelve miles north of Jerusalem. An earlier name for the town is said to have been Luz (Gen. 28:19; 35:6, et al.). Bethel has been

[60] See, for example, Anderson, *Understanding the Old Testament*, pp. 193-95.
[61] *History of Palestine and Syria* (New York: Charles Scribner's Sons, 1931), p. 353.

identified with the modern site of *Beitin.*[62] The first appearance of the city in the Old Testament is in the Abraham traditions. According to the Jahwist,[63] after first having built an altar at Shechem, the patriarch "removed to the mountain on the east of Bethel, and pitched his tent, with Bethel on the west and Ai on the east, and there he built an altar to Yahweh and called on the name of Yahweh" (Gen. 12:8). He is said to have visited this sanctuary a second time after his return from Egypt (Gen. 13:3-4). The Old Testament traditions, however, especially connect Bethel with the northern patriarch Jacob. All three strands—J, E, and P—have preserved traditions which stress Jacob's relation to Bethel. In Gen. 28:10-22 there is a JE [64] account of Jacob at Bethel, while Gen. 35:9-13, 15 contains a P [65] tradition which places him at the same site. Both passages stress the cultic significance of Bethel. Just as J has preserved an Abraham narrative in which Shechem and Bethel are closely connected, so E [66] in Gen. 35:1-4 has a Jacob tradition in which the two cult sites are coupled. After the patriarchal traditions in Genesis, Bethel is mentioned only occasionally until the time of Jeroboam. Judg. 1:22-26 contains an account of the destruction of Bethel at the time of the conquest under Joshua.[67] And during the period of the Judges the ark is said to have been at Bethel at one time (Judg. 20:18, 26 ff.). A little later the city is connected with the name of Samuel (I Sam. 7:16; 10:3). It was Jeroboam, however, who was responsible for Bethel's greatest fame.

At the shrine at Bethel, as well as at Dan, Jeroboam is said to have

[62] Excavations were first conducted on this site in 1934 under the direction of W. F. Albright, and were recently resumed by James L. Kelso. A summary of the excavations can be found in the article by Kelso, "Bethel," *Biblical Archaeologist,* XIX (May, 1956), 36-43. The excavations have revealed that Bethel was first occupied around 2200 B.C. With the exception of a few brief periods following the devastation of war, the site seems to have been used continuously well into the Christian era. One of the most notable discoveries at the site was evidence of violent and complete destruction of the city during the second half of the thirteenth century B.C., presumably the work of the Hebrew invaders under Joshua.

[63] S. R. Driver, *The Book of Genesis,* p. 148.

[64] *Ibid.,* pp. 264-67.

[65] *Ibid.,* pp. 309-10.

[66] *Ibid.,* pp. 308-309.

[67] It is quite possible that the tradition in Josh. 7:1–8:29 orignally concerned Bethel rather than Ai. See Wright, *Biblical Archaeology,* p. 80.

erected a "golden calf" with the words: "You have gone up to Jerusalem long enough. Behold your gods, O Israel, who brought you out of the land of Egypt" (I Kings 12:28b). Unquestionably this text has undergone a deliberate distortion by a southern editor. Originally it was in the singular and probably was used only with the calf at Bethel: "Behold your *God,* O Israel, who brought you out of the land of Egypt." [68] That the calf at Bethel was not intended by Jeroboam to be an idol seems fairly certain. It was viewed as a pedestal for Yahweh. "Conceptually," writes W. F. Albright, "this practice was no more idolatrous than the equally symbolic representation of YHWH in the temple of Solomon as an invisible Presence enthroned on the cherubim." [69] Not only was the calf at Bethel no more idolatrous than the ark, but it must have been set up precisely as *the northern counterpart to the ark.* David had taken the ark to Jerusalem and Solomon had placed it in the temple. There was no possibility of recovering that shrine for the northern cult. The only alternative was to acquire a substitute. This was the "calf," or "bull," which probably had long been associated with the Bethel cult.[70] It is possible that during this time a tradition emerged which attempted to relate the calf to the Mosaic period.[71] If so, it has been preserved in Exod. 32:2-6. Originally the tradition was favorable to the calf and may have read:

2 Aaron said to them (the people), "Take off the rings of gold which are in the ears of your wives, your sons, and your daughters, and bring them to me." 3 So all the people took off the rings of gold which were in their ears, and brought them to Aaron. 4 And he received the gold at their hand, and fashioned it with a graving tool, and made a molten calf; and they said, *"This is your God, O Israel, who brought you up out of the land of Egypt!"* 5 When Aaron saw this, he built an altar before it; and Aaron made proclamation and said, "Tomorrow shall be a feast to Yahweh." 6 And they rose up early on the morrow, and offered burnt offerings and

[68] See Anderson (*op. cit.,* pp. 194-95) and Montgomery (*op. cit.,* p. 255), who suggest that in the original tradition there was only one calf and that at Bethel.

[69] Albright, *The Biblical Period,* p. 31.

[70] See Meek, *Hebrew Origins,* pp. 136 ff.

[71] The writer takes this position in his *Sinai Covenant Traditions,* pp. 118 ff.

brought peace offerings; and the people sat down to eat and drink, and rose up to play.

It was Aaron himself who was responsible for the calf, the tradition affirmed, and it was certainly not idolatrous.[72] When Jeroboam, therefore, erected the calf at Bethel and said to the people: "This is your God, O Israel, who brought you up out of the land of Egypt," his intention was "to connect the religion of the Northern Kingdom with the main stream of the Mosaic tradition, the chief theme of which was the Exodus from Egypt." [73]

In connection with the calf at Bethel, Jeroboam also established a feast: "And Jeroboam appointed a feast on the fifteenth day of the eighth month like the feast that was in Judah, and he offered sacrifices upon the altar" (I Kings 12:32). A feast in the eighth month would have been the autumnal festival. If the intention of Jeroboam, as Walter Harrelson puts it,[74] was "to renew Israel's devotion to the God of the covenant," it is reasonable to conclude that the central theme of this festival was related to Yahwism. It was in all probability a *covenant festival in which the E covenant legend was used.*

This is suggested by the fact that Ahijah of Shiloh was a key figure behind Jeroboam early in his career. The E covenant legend, as we have seen, was probably at Shiloh when that town was destroyed. The legend would have remained with Shilonites after the ark was captured by the Philistines. Since Shilonites were presumably behind the northern break with Jerusalem, it would have been natural for the E covenant legend to have been used in the cult at Bethel which became the main cult center of the North. If the E legend was used as the liturgy of a covenant ceremony in the autumnal festival at Shechem in the twelfth century and at Shiloh in the eleventh century, it was probably also used in the autumnal festival at Bethel in the tenth century.

[72] If this tradition did originally have a positive attitude toward the calf, then later when the calf at Bethel did become an idolatrous object under the influence of Canaanite religion, the tradition of the calf at Sinai was changed so that it too became idolatrous in the story. This would have been done by later traditionists under the influence of prophetic thinkers like Hosea (10:5; 13:1-3). Thus the originally favorable tradition concerning the golden calf at Sinai would have been changed into a polemic against it.

[73] Anderson, *op. cit.*, p. 195.

[74] Harrelson, *op. cit.*, pp. 503 ff.

The calf at Bethel would have served the same function as the ark had served at Shechem and Shiloh. It was a symbol of the invisible presence of the God of Sinai who had brought the children of Israel out of Egypt and in response to which act they had entered into his covenant.[75]

The present version of Jeroboam's cultic activity at Bethel specifically denies that the priesthood there was Levitical: "He also made houses on high places, and appointed priests from among all the people, who were not of the Levites" (I Kings 12:31). This charge in all probability results from the animus of "the hostile Deuteronomic editor," [76] and is without basis in fact. If Levites were in charge of the covenant ceremony at Shechem and Shiloh, there is no good reason to question that they were later active at Bethel.[77]

It is quite possible that the E covenant legend reached its final literary form as it was used in the cult at Bethel.[78] Up to this point the legend presumably had been in the process of oral development. That would have been the case when it was used at Shechem and Shiloh. In the time of Jeroboam, however, and in connection with his cultic reforms it probably reached approximately its present form.[79] Furthermore, it

[75] Walter Harrelson (op. cit., pp. 503 ff.) has plausibly proposed that the tradition of Jacob's pilgrimage from Shechem to Bethel in Gen. 35:1-3 is to be associated with the cultic activities of Jeroboam. Following Alt ("Die Wallfahrt von Sichem nach Bethel"), he believes that this passage reflects a cultic ritual in which both Shechem and Bethel were involved. It was connected with the covenant ceremony. The initial ceremonies of renunciation of foreign gods and cultic purification took place at Shechem. After that, there was a processional to Bethel where the covenant ceremony was completed. I would propose a slightly different interpretation. This tradition quite possibly is simply stating that the covenant ceremony first observed on Palestinian soil at Shechem (Josh. 24) by Israel was later transferred to Bethel. This interpretation, to be sure, would not necessarily exclude that of Harrelson.

[76] The expression is Albright's (Stone Age, p. 229).

[77] Harrelson too holds that there were Levites in the Bethel cult (op. cit., pp. 507-8); cf. Brinker, The Influence of Sanctuaries in Early Israel, p. 171.

[78] It has frequently been maintained, of course, that the entire E epic comes from Bethel. Robert Pfeiffer, for example, takes this position (Introduction to the Old Testament [New York: Harper & Brothers, 1941], p. 168). He thinks that E was written at Bethel in the middle of the eighth century.

[79] The question might further be raised as to whether the decalogue reached its form at this time too. It is generally recognized that the twelve laws in the form of curses in Deut. 27 correspond to the twelve tribes of the amphictyony organized at Shechem. Is it not possible, then, that the ten laws of the decalogue were selected from a larger body of apodictic law at this time for use in the covenant ceremony to correspond to

has been plausibly suggested [80] that Jeroboam's building of Shechem, Penuel, and Bethel was a definite attempt on his part to connect his kingship with the patriarchal tradition. These were the three places with which Jacob, the supreme patriarch of the North, had been most closely associated. Accompanying the renewal of the Jacob traditions was the literary collection of the Jacob saga. Writes Walter Harrelson:

When the decisive break between Israel and Judah-Benjamin has occurred, then is the time for the religious traditions of the two people to begin to reinforce the schism. It is highly probable that the so-called J traditions have already been collected, in some form or other, in the south. Thus it may be that the nucleus of the E traditions began to be collected around the figure of Jacob in the north, as Jeroboam sought to stress the legitimacy of the Bethel worship over against that of Jerusalem.[81]

One might go a step further and suggest that the entire E epic may have been written in this period. Just as the J epic was probably written a few decades earlier during the reign of Solomon, the E epic could well have been composed in Bethel at the end of the tenth century. Thus not only the Jacob sagas and the E covenant legend, but traditions of the exodus, the wilderness wanderings, the conquest, and others would have been gathered together for the purpose of creating a northern counterpart to the great southern epic. A tenth-century date is much earlier than the eighth-century date frequently assigned to E, but it is quite within the realm of possibility.

If Jeroboam did establish an annual covenant festival in which the E covenant legend was used, it is possible that the ceremony was observed in one way or another up until the time of the fall of the northern kingdom in 722 B.C.[82] We have no direct information concerning this festival from the period from 922 to 722, of course. In the eighth century both Amos and Hosea are specifically critical of the

---

the ten tribes of the newly organized northern kingdom? This is not to deny the possible Mosaic origin of any or all of these laws. The proposal is simply that ten basic laws, which had long been known, were now placed in this form for recitation in the covenant ceremony at Bethel.

[80] Harrelson, op. cit., pp. 505-6.

[81] Ibid., p. 506.

[82] In this case some oral form of the E legend would have continued in use as the festival liturgy even after the E epic had been written down.

corrupted cult at Bethel, but there is no reason to doubt that such a ceremony might have continued even then. This would not be the only time in history that the people of a religious community corrupted a cult which used a theologically superior liturgy. In fact, it is quite possible that Hosea was using the liturgy of Bethel (i.e., some version of the E covenant legend) to attack the corrupted cult at Bethel.[83] No doubt the Bethel cult experienced frequent periods of corruption. The presence of the calf at Bethel would have contributed to this tendency. As Albright observes, "the pagan associations of the young bull were likely to lead to paganizing theology and to encouragement of syncretism."[84] This certainly happened. It is not impossible, in fact, that Jeroboam himself was later guilty of some sort of defection from Yahwism, as the story of his son's illness in I Kings 14:1-18 indicates.

One clear indication that the theology reflected in the E covenant legend continued to exercise a strong influence in the North is the nature of the northern kingship. Albrecht Alt's studies in this regard have emphasized the fact that the northern monarchy was a very unstable institution.[85] In the South, of course, the kingship was undergirded by a dynastic theology, with the result that there was one continuous dynasty for over four hundred years. Northern theology, however, resisted the concentration of power in the king. The covenant of Yahweh was with *all* the people, and not with any one person or royal dynasty. Consequently the charismatic ideal of the period of the Judges obtained in the northern kingdom, with the result that there were kings from nine different families during the two hundred years of its existence. It was not unusual in the North for a new king to emerge as the result of the activity of some prophet like Ahijah or Elisha. This would have been completely in accordance with northern theology. Of course, the unstable government in the North was one of its greatest weaknesses and was one reason for its early demise. But with the theology that dominated northern religious circles, there was

[83] I hope to pursue this idea in a future study.
[84] Albright, *The Biblical Period*, p. 31.
[85] Alt, "Das Königtum in den Reichen Israels und Juda."

never any real possibility of the establishment of a single dynasty like that in the South.

On the other hand, a great strength of the North was the fact that the prophetic movement emerged and flourished there. Northern Yahwism was favorable to this creative movement. The ecstatic groups of prophets, who form a basic root of the later classical prophetic movement, first appear in the North shortly after the destruction of Shiloh. Tradition associates them with Samuel (I Sam. 10:5-6; 19:18-25), and it is not unlikely that he was responsible for their incorporation into the main stream of Mosaic Yahwism.[86] In the century after the division of the Davidic kingdom the prophets Micaiah, Elijah, and Elisha appeared. That their activity was in the North resulted not only from the fact that there was unrighteousness there—it was in the South too—but also because northern theology permitted and encouraged such charismatic activity for Yahweh. In the eighth century too Hosea was a northern prophet and Amos prophesied in the North. Isaiah of Jerusalem was the first true southern prophet,[87] but he appeared when the northern kingdom was in its death throes and its religious traditions were moving south. One great contribution of northern theology, therefore, was the prophetic movement.

---

[86] The writer has dealt in more detail with this thesis in his article, "The Prophetic Call of Samuel."

[87] Men such as Nathan and Gad in Jerusalem during the time of David, although called prophets, seem to have been court officials rather than classical prophets proclaiming Yahweh's word to the whole people Israel.

Epilogue

THE TWO WAYS OF VIEWING THE COVENANT AS REFLECTED IN THE J and E covenant legends seem to have been a source of tension in the life of the Hebrews from the wilderness period. At Kadesh, soon after the Mosaic covenant was sealed at Sinai, a controversy over this very question evidently emerged and was a major cause of the split between the two groups of Yahweh worshipers. From that time until the fall of the northern kingdom in 722 B.C. "dynastic" covenant theology and "kingdom of priests" covenant theology tended to separate southern Israel and northern Israel. Throughout this long period there were those who were passionately committed to one or the other of the two theologies.

Even though these two theological emphases did continually tend to divide the North and the South, there were those who felt that somehow the two theologies belonged together. Each was necessary for the fulness of the life of the covenant people. "Dynastic" covenant theology testified to the historical *continuity* of this people who took seriously the fact that Yahweh revealed himself in the events of history. "Kingdom of priests" covenant theology continually protested any attempt to control the working of Yahweh's spirit in history and thus testified to the ever-present possibility of creative *discontinuity* in the life of the covenant people. Perhaps Mosaic Yahwism itself resulted from the combination of creative charismatic substance with traditional priestly forms of the Kenites and thus bore witness to the fact that the elements

188

of continuity and discontinuity must both characterize the life of the covenant people. After the division of the people at Kadesh, the two theologies continued side by side in Palestine in a kind of uneasy alliance, one centering in the North and the other in the South. It would seem that David made a real attempt to reconcile the two, but with the scales definitely weighted in favor of "dynastic" theology. This attempt ended in failure when the kingdom divided. Solomon's policies contributed significantly to this failure. Not until after the fall of the northern kingdom does there seem to have been an attempt to bring the two theologies again into some kind of a viable union. This was evidently a chief goal of the Deuteronomic reformation of 621 B.C. under Josiah. His untimely death, however, made this experiment short-lived.

Perhaps the most interesting testimony to the belief that these two interpretations of the nature of the covenant belong together is to be found in the Pentateuch itself. The theologian who combined the J and E covenant legends must have been sensitive to the fact that both traditions had something important to say about the true nature of the covenant. And the literary technique employed to combine them too attests to some theological and historical sensitivity. All the material belonging to the E legend is found in Exodus 19–24. Although a few verses in chapters 19 and 24 belong to J, the main portion of the J legend occurs in Exodus 33–34. The incident of the golden calf in chapter 32 is the tradition that serves to unite them. Thus in the present arrangement of these early traditions the covenant is made (chs. 19–24: the E version), the incident of the golden calf occurs which breaks the covenant (ch. 32), then the covenant is renewed (chs. 33–34: the J version). That the E tradition appears first possibly suggests the correct belief of the one who combined them that it somewhat more accurately reflects the original event than the J legend. Perhaps this order also indicates his understanding that the E legend was preserved by theological circles who were possessed by the deep conviction that the sin of Israel could indeed result in a broken covenant; the covenant was contingent. The J version of the covenant, then, would have been used for the account of the restoration of the covenant, and

189

thus for the final covenant ceremony at Sinai, because it emanated from theological circles who believed that the covenant was "for ever."

The traditions in chapter 32 which have been used to combine the two legends likewise suggest the work of a mind sensitive to historical and theological reality. The golden calf is central in the present arrangement of the traditions in this chapter. The golden calf, of course, was used by Jeroboam I at Bethel in connection with his cultic activities. Although it was not originally intended as an idol, it did later become such. But even more important it became a symbol of the division between the North and the South, a division which was basically theological. Likewise the tradition of the appointment of the Levitical priests in 32:25-29 emerged in connection with a similar theological controversy among the Hebrews. This was the event at Kadesh when the dispute concerning the nature of religious authority among the covenant people resulted in division. The one who combined the J and E covenant legends probably began with a tradition which preserved the memory of some actual sin of the people at Sinai. But the main traditions which he used in this connection were ones which had emerged from the two important events in the past when the Hebrews divided over the question of the basic character of the covenant. And in combining them, this theological thinker was attesting to his belief that somehow the two belonged together. "Kingdom of priests" covenant theology and "dynastic" covenant theology were both necessary to express the fulness of the life of the covenant people.

Selected Bibliography

Albright, W. F. *Archaeology and the Religion of Israel.* Baltimore: The Johns Hopkins Press, 3rd ed., 1953.
——. *The Biblical Period.* Pittsburgh: The Biblical Colloquium, 1950. Reprint from *The Jews: Their History, Culture and Religion,* edited by Louis Finkelstein. New York: Harper and Brothers, 1949.
——. *From the Stone Age to Christianity.* Baltimore: The Johns Hopkins Press, 1946.
Alt, Albrecht. *Kleine Schriften zur Geschichte des Volkes Israel.* München: C. H. Beck'sche Verlagsbuchhandlung. Erster Band, Zweite, verbesserte Auflage, 1959. Zweiter Band, 1953. Dritter Band, 1959.
Anderson, Bernhard W. *Understanding the Old Testament.* Englewood Cliffs, N.J.: Prentice-Hall, 1957.
Beer, Georg. *Exodus. Handbuch zum Alten Testament.* Tübingen: J. C. B. Mohr (Paul Siebeck), 1939.
Beyerlin, Walter. *Herkunft und Geschichte der ältesten Sinaitraditionen.* Tübingen: J. C. B. Mohr (Paul Siebeck), 1961.
Bright, John. "The Book of Joshua." *The Interpreter's Bible.* Vol. II. Nashville: Abingdon Press, 1953.
——. *Early Israel in Recent History Writing.* London: SCM Press, 1956.
——. *A History of Israel.* Philadelphia: The Westminster Press, 1959.
Brinker, R. *The Influence of Sanctuaries in Early Israel.* Manchester: University Press, 1946.
Buber, Martin. *Moses.* Oxford: East & West Library, 1946.

Budde, Karl. *The Religion of Israel to the Exile*. New York: G. P. Putnam's Sons, 1899.

Burney, C. F. *Israel's Settlement in Canaan*. London: Oxford University Press, 1921.

Caird, George B. "The First and Second Books of Samuel." Vol. II. *The Interpreter's Bible*. Nashville: Abingdon Press, 1953.

Cross, F. M., Jr. "The Tabernacle," *The Biblical Archaeologist*, X (1947), 45-68.

Dibelius, Martin. *Die Lade Jahves*. Göttingen: Vandenhoeck & Ruprecht, 1906.

Driver, S. R. *An Introduction to the Literature of the Old Testament*. New York: Charles Scribner's Sons, rev. ed., 1913.

Eichrodt, Walther. *Theology of the Old Testament*. Vol. I. Philadelphia: The Westminster Press, 1961.

————. *Theologie des Alten Testaments*. Teil 2. Leipzig: J. C. Hinrich'schen Buchhandlung, 1935. Teil 3. Zweite Auflage. Berlin: Evangelische Verlagsanstalt, 1949.

Gray, George Buchanan. *A Critical and Exegetical Commentary on Numbers*. New York: Charles Scribner's Sons, 1920.

Grollenberg. L. H. *Atlas of the Bible*. New York: Thomas Nelson, 1956.

Harrelson, Walter. *The City of Shechem: Its History and Importance*. New York: Union Theological Seminary dissertation, 1953.

Kraus, Hans-Joachim. *Gottesdienst in Israel*. München: Chr. Kaiser Verlag, 1954.

————. *Die Königsherrschaft Gottes im Alten Testament*. Tübingen: J. C. B. Mohr (Paul Siebeck), 1951.

Kuschke, Arnulf. "Die Lagervorstellung der priesterlichen Erzählung," *Zeitschrift für die alttestamentliche Wissenschaft*, 63 (1951), 74-105.

McNeile, A. H. *The Book of Exodus. Westminster Commentaries*. New York: Edwin S. Gorham; London: Methuen & Co., 1908.

Meek, Theophile James. *Hebrew Origins*. New York: Harper & Brothers, rev. ed., 1950.

Mendenhall, George E. *Law and Covenant in Israel and the Ancient Near East*. Pittsburgh, Pennsylvania: The Biblical Colloquium, 1955. Reprint from *The Biblical Archaeologist*, Vol. XVII, No. 2 (May, 1954), 26-46 and No. 3 (September, 1954), 49-76.

Morgenstern, Julian. "The Ark, the Ephod, and the Tent," *Hebrew Union College Annual*, XVII (1942-43), 153-265; XVIII (1943-44), 1-52.

Muilenburg, James. "The Form and Structure of the Covenantal Formulations," *Vetus Testamentum*, 9 (1959), 347-65.

————. "The History of the Religion of Israel," *The Interpreter's Bible*, Vol I, pp. 209-305. Nashville: Abingdon Press, 1952.

Mowinckel, Sigmund. *Le Décalogue*. Paris: Libraire Félix Alcan, 1927.

————. *Psalmenstudien II. Das Thronbesteigungsfest Jahwäs und der Ursprung der Eschatologie*. Kristiana: Dybwad, 1932.

Newman, Murray. "The Prophetic Call of Samuel," *Israel's Prophetic Heritage. Essays in Honor of James Muilenburg*. New York: Harper & Brothers, 1962.

————. *The Sinai Covenant Traditions in the Cult of Israel*. New York: Union Theological Seminary dissertation, 1960.

Nielsen, Eduard. "The Burial of the Foreign Gods," *Studia Theologica,* VIII (1955), 103 ff.

———. *Shechem: A Tradition-Historical Investigation.* Copenhagen: G. E. C. Gad, 1955.

Noth, Martin. "Amt und Berufung im Alten Testament," *Bonner Akademische Reden,* 19. Bonn: Peter Hanstein, 1958.

———. *Das Buch Josua. Handbuch zum Alten Testament.* Tübingen: J. C. B. Mohr (Paul Siebeck). Zweite, verbesserte Auflage, 1953.

———. "David und Israel in II Samuel 7," *Mélanges bibliques rédigés en l'honneur de André Robert,* pp. 122-130. Paris: Bloud & Gay, 1957.

———. *Gesammelte Studien zum Alten Testament.* München: Chr. Kaiser Verlag, 1957.

———. *The History of Israel.* New York: Harper & Brothers and London: A & C. Black, 2nd ed., rev. Eng. tr., 1960.

———. *Das System der zwölf Stämme Israels.* Stuttgart: W. Kohlhammer, 1930.

———. *Überlieferungsgeschichte des Pentateuch.* Stuttgart: W. Kohlhammer, 1948.

———. *Überlieferungsgeschichtliche Studien* I. Halle (Saale): Max Niemeyer, 1943.

———. *Das zweite Buch Mose. Exodus. Das Alte Testament Deutsch.* Göttingen: Vandenhoeck & Ruprecht, 1959.

Pedersen, Johannes. *Israel.* London: Oxford University Press; Copenhagen: Povl Branner. Vols. I-II, 1926. Vols. III-IV, 1940.

Pfeiffer, Robert H. *Introduction to the Old Testament.* New York: Harper & Brothers, 1941.

Pritchard, James B., editor. *Ancient Near Eastern Texts.* Princeton, New Jersey: Princeton University Press, 1950.

Procksch, Otto. *Theologie des Alten Testaments.* Gütersloh: C. Bertelsmann, 1950.

von Rad, Gerhard. *Genesis.* Philadelphia: The Westminster Press, 1961.

———. *Gesammelte Studien zum Alten Testament.* München: Chr. Kaiser, 1958.

———. *Der Heilige Krieg im Alten Israel.* Göttingen: Vandenhoeck & Ruprecht, 3 Auflage, 1958.

———. *Studies in Deuteronomy.* Chicago: Henry Regnery Co., 1953.

———. *Theologie des Alten Testaments.* Band I. München: Chr. Kaiser, 1957.

Rowley, H. H. *From Joseph to Joshua.* London: Published for the British Academy by the Oxford University Press, 1948.

———. "Melchizedek and Zadok," *Festschrift Alfred Bertholet,* pp. 461-72. Tübingen: J. C. B. Mohr (Paul Siebeck), 1950.

Sellin, Ernst. *Geschichte des israelitisch-jüdischen Volkes.* Band I. Leipzig: Quelle & Meyer, 1924.

Snaith, Norman. "The First and Second Books of Kings." *The Interpreter's Bible.* Vol. III. Nashville: Abingdon Press, 1954.

Weiser, Artur. *Die Psalmen.* I-II. *Das Alte Testament Deutsch.* Göttingen: Vandenhoeck & Ruprecht, 1950.

Wright, G. Ernest. *Biblical Archaeology.* Philadelphia: The Westminster Press, 1957.

————. "The Book of Deuteronomy." *The Interpreter's Bible.* Vol. II. Nashville: Abingdon Press, 1953.

————. *The Old Testament Against Its Environment.* London: SCM Press, 1950.

———— and Filson, Floyd Vivian. *The Westminster Historical Atlas to the Bible.* Philadelphia: The Westminster Press, rev. ed., 1956.

Index of Scripture

INDEX OF SCRIPTURE

199

INDEX OF SCRIPTURE

201

Index of Persons
and Subjects

INDEX OF PERSONS AND SUBJECTS